WARRIOR
MOTHERS

*Stories to Awaken
the Flames of the Heart*

THAÏS MAZUR

Rising Star Press
Santa Cruz, California

Rising Star Press
Santa Cruz, California
www.RisingStarPress.com

Interior design, composition and copyediting by Joanne Shwed,
Backspace Ink (www.backspaceink.com)

Cover and interior color pages design by Chuck Spidell, IllusioDesign
(www.illusiodesign.com)

Library of Congress Cataloging-in-Publication Data

Mazur, Thaïs.
  Warrior mothers : stories to awaken the flames of the heart / Thaïs Mazur.
    p. cm.
  ISBN 0-933670-11-7 (trade pbk. : alk. paper)
    1. Social action--Case studies. 2. Women social reformers--Case studies.
3. Women environmentalists--Case studies. 4. Women pacifists--Case studies.
5. Women political activists--Case studies. I. Title.
  HN49.W6M37 2004
  303.48'4'0922--dc22   2004018024

For my daughter Tenaya:
May she always find the warrior within
and her heart continue to open along the path

Contents

An author and teacher shares a story she wrote about Hindu mythology's Great Goddess Durga who is said to have won the battle over evil and who vowed to return if the life of the planet was ever again in danger of being destroyed.

A fifth-generation fisherwoman takes on major corporations in her Texas home town and demands that they stop dumping toxic chemicals into the San Antonio Bay.

On a vacation in Hawaii, a professor falls in love with whales and becomes one of the foremost leaders in the fight to ban Low Frequency Active Sonar testing, which kills thousands of marine mammals worldwide.

CONTENTS

Martial Arts—A Tool for Life

> *A public health nurse uses the wisdom of Aikido and somatic coaching to help survivors of sexual abuse and teaches children how to use the power they have to stay safe.*

Acknowledgments

Many insights were gained while gathering stories and writing this book. Sometimes it was a passing conversation; other times it was in-depth conversations with women who shared their fears and hopes for the world. The gratitude I feel encompasses far more people and moments than I can name.

Foremost, I am deeply grateful to the women who generously shared their lives with me and gave me permission to write their stories. Their candidness and passionate telling of their lives and work fueled my energy to continue the book, even while juggling motherhood and many other artistic projects.

Friends who deserve special thanks are: David Russell, my constant companion and creative partner; John Mazur, my 80-year-old father and continued intellectual and spiritual advisor; Sarah Shockely, for her insights and intuitive wisdom; Robbert van Santen, my soul mate and guide; Loie Rosenkrantz, the first one to read the rough manuscript and give me an enthusiastic green light to finish the book; Laura Stachel, for her beautiful hands; the women from Women In Black who have served as a continuing inspiration; the women who have courageously stood beside me on my many artistic endeavors; my martial arts compadres who continue to practice the path of the warrior; and the women in my life and in the world who are working for a better future.

Thank you!

Publisher's Disclaimer

Warrior Mothers is a compilation of personal experiences. Where possible, references are cited; however, many statements are made arising from the passion these women feel about their chosen focus. We encourage anyone interested in further exploration of the topics discussed herein to take action by doing their own research and forming their own opinions. Many sources are included to assist you in these efforts.

The publisher does not warrant the accuracy or reliability of the content. The publisher will not accept liability for any injuries or damages caused to the reader or persons or entities named herein that may result from the reader's acting upon or using the content herein contained. The information presented strictly reflects the opinions, perceptions and knowledge of those who tell their stories.

We hope to awaken this flame in each reader: the desire to take action in a way meaningful and important to you.

Author's Note

Conversations with the women in this book took place over a period of weeks and sometimes months; gathering and writing these stories took a total of two years. Although many of the stories reference world events, many of those events have already changed. Some of the women were interviewed before the 2003 U.S. invasion of Iraq; others were interviewed afterwards.

In our rapidly changing world, it is difficult to capture each and every response to current events in the pages of any book. This book is not so much about the present situation as it is about being fueled to make changes—ignited to take action—right now … in your world.

Introduction

Stories have always held a powerful place in my life. I grew up with my parents' stories of relatives in Ukraine who survived the ravages of war; of my Scottish grandfather who trapped his way across Canada in the dead of winter; and of my pioneer grandmother, Frankie, who could outshoot any man. I was always fascinated by other people's stories and, at a young age, became a consummate interviewer of everyone I met. I was intrigued with the details, the passages, the road map of their lives. I guess you could say I was a map maker of sorts, recording the stories of each person's journey and stowing them away to help me navigate through my own life. I believe personal stories are the fabric of our world and our future.

This book arose out of my search for hope and for the "warrior mother" spirit. The concept of warrior mother was inspired by my own journey, recounted in the Prelude following this Introduction. I began by interviewing women in my immediate circle, which soon expanded to women across the country including artists, scientists, writers and therapists—all working in small and large ways to create a better future for our planet.

For this book, I used an interview process in which I asked each woman a series of open-ended questions: What life events shaped who you are today? What does "warrior mother" mean to you? What do we need to do in order to change the current state of the world? I wanted to know the details of their lives and their vision for healing the world. Remarkable resiliency and passion were expressed as each woman talked about her life and work.

I took the interviews and wrote first-person narratives. Some of the women chose to answer my questions through their own writing. Many of the women I called were immersed in their work during the interview process. Diane Wilson spoke to me from her cell phone while she was sitting on the steps of the nation's Capitol on a 30-day fast to protest the war in Iraq. Rhonda Anderson was on her way to educate single moms about lead poisoning in their neighborhood. Lourdes Portillo was in the middle of releasing her award-winning documentary film about the unsolved murders of over 800 young women in Juárez, Mexico.

The stories in this book encompass many lifestyles and situations of women who have committed simple and courageous acts. These stories show us that making a difference in the world doesn't take a rich, famous or highly educated person. Sometimes, out of simple and ordinary lives, events occur that spur us into action. LaDonna Redmond tells the story about her infant son who was faced with a life-threatening illness from the food he was eating. She decided to organize the first black farmers' market and is now organizing the first organic food cooperative in her Illinois community. Terri Swearingen heard about a toxic incinerator being built 400 yards from a West Virginia elementary school and became a full-time activist to shut it down. Marsha Green fell in love with whales on a vacation in Hawaii and is now spearheading the battle against Low Frequency Active Sonar testing, which has killed hundreds of marine mammals.

These women showed me that it doesn't take a super heroine to create change. Most took their first step unknowingly, guided by a calling they could not ignore. It either launched them onto a path of harmony with their life or created a major turning point full of challenges and unknowns. Like throwing a pebble into a still pond, a simple thought became an act rippling outward, gathering energy like a wave rolling across the ocean. Whether it involved their family, their community or the world, each woman was moved by a deep inner wisdom—an undeniable call—that transformed their lives and those around them ... a call awakening the flames of the heart.

Prelude

It was the night before winter solstice. I stood silently in a large room with a wood-planked floor. A brilliant light streamed in from all directions and the air quivered with a white radiance. My martial arts teacher stood in the center of the room and held out a red velvet sheath. I reached for the handle that emerged from the red cloth and pulled out a gleaming, broad sword. My teacher gracefully raised her two long fingers, in the mudra of compassion, and placed them on my third eye. "Remember."

I awoke from the dream and felt a surge of energy and clarity. I thought about the grace and power of the ancient broad sword form I had studied. After my baby was born, I had placed the sword in the corner of my home office where it stood like a bygone trophy. The dream rekindled the strength of the blade, cutting through the muck, going straight to the core. The message was clear: The coming year was going to reawaken the sword.

In the faint light of early morning, I reached out and put my hand on my brand new sleeping baby, feeling the rhythmic rise and fall of her chest. I gazed at my newborn and experienced a dramatic opening of my heart. Life … a miracle!

When I embarked on the path of motherhood, I felt a profound connection towards all people and all living things. With the events of September 11, 2001, holding my tiny daughter in my arms, I awakened to the vulnerability of life and felt an immense need to nurture and protect her from the darkness descending upon the world.

In the past year, my martial arts teacher and 20 other women who I knew have died of cancer. Each death heightened my awareness of the toxic state of our environment. I questioned the healthy future for my daughter. A feeling of despair fell over me, along with an urgent need to step forward and do whatever I could to help improve the future for all children and for this precious life on Earth. The stories that I had heard—about women in Bosnia crossing mountain passes in midwinter with their babies to escape enemy armies, the thousands of mothers around the world watching their children die of starvation and the mothers risking their lives to stand up to militias—became painfully real. My maternal instincts expanded to encompass the entire world; I was overcome with grief and rage about the injustices that threaten the most important thing of all: life.

I have taken a stand many times in my life. I have fought for the environment and for women's rights. I have marched against racism, poverty and sexism. I have worked in underground print shops and ran an underground newspaper. However, this feels different. I am a mother who is embracing the Earth with the same love that I have for my daughter. By weaving my triumphs and defeats into one solid net, wisdom and fire have awakened in my heart.

I find myself thinking about the heroines of our times and their courage inspires me: the Mothers of the Disappeared in Argentina who started an international, nonviolent peace movement by standing in silent vigil for their lost loved ones; and the mothers who crossed the border into Gaza in the Middle East and grabbed their soldier sons saying, "You will not fight in this unjust war!" and marched them back to Israel.

I have a new understanding of the women who take a stand against violence in their households and communities and who have no choice but to say, "No more!" Women who love deeply and openly; who weep and cry for the future of humanity and see the world for what it is.

For me, these women embody the warrior spirit I first encountered in my study of martial arts, where compassion and wisdom were the guiding principles. It makes sense that this spirit—coupled with the feminine-inspired values of nurturing, caring and support—is essential for raising the value of life, taking precedence over all other values such as materialism or domination.

Throughout history, we have witnessed this melding of warrior and nurturer in such inspired individuals as civil rights activist Rosa Parks, spiritual teacher Mother Teresa and physicist/ecologist Vandana Shiva. These luminaries have offered the world significant road maps for generations to come. There are many women today who are taking a stand against the seemingly impossible odds of adversarial corporate leviathans, rogue governments and the military industrial complex.

There are also women who have turned simple acts into potent tools for change. The image of women as protectors has been documented in many cultures as fierce, female deities rising up to defeat demons who threaten the world. The blending of this warrior spirit and the protector/nurturer creates an archetype that I have called the "warrior mother."

I began to think of ways that I could take action both as a woman and as a mother—a warrior mother. This led me on a search for paths of action and for women who were making important changes in their families, their communities and the world. I began interviewing women in my immediate circle and soon found women around the country who openly shared their own process and experience as an activist. From my research, I realized that this network of activists—a groundswell of women finding their voice and speaking out against that which is destroying the very foundation of life—is quickly growing as the threat of environmental catastrophes and impending wars increases daily.

Before I had my daughter, I was an energetic artist/activist who worked around the clock on different issues. When I was pregnant, I was certain that my days as a professional dancer, sculptor and writer were over. I was quietly resigned to the fact that I would be streamlining my life to raise my child. The first nine months after my daughter was born, I lived in total bliss under the veil of love hormones.

In 2000 when George W. Bush was selected president, something shifted. With the inauguration of Bush, I shuddered to think of the years of hard work to protect the environment and honor a woman's right to choose as well as other humanitarian efforts unravel before my eyes. I called the local Unitarian Universalist minister, Marianne, and said, "I am going to stand in silent vigil in solidarity with the international Women In Black movement. Come join me. Dress in black and meet me in front of the Town Hall."

Having just moved to a small town on the northern coast of California, this was a bold act. I put on a black dress and drove to the busy corner on Main Street. I was relieved to see Marianne already standing there, wearing a long black coat and holding a candle. We stood together for an hour while people raced by in their cars. The next month, there were five of us standing; within four months, there were 20 women and men, all wearing black and standing in the monthly silent vigil.

Then September 11th happened. Women with babies on their backs and in strollers joined our vigils. Soon after, the United States bombed Afghanistan and surrounding towns held their own monthly vigils. Now, in this small community, we stand every Friday for one hour, imagining peace and sending love out to the world ... a simple and powerful act.

The creative energy I have gained is not a mere river, as it once was, but a raging flood. The work I do now is a salutation to the life force that flows through a pregnant woman's womb. It is the tornado that launches women into animal wildness during labor. It is a tribute to all of the women who are working to protect and nurture the future so that we can live in a kinder, more ethical world. While the focus of this book is about and for women, this spirit also emerges in men: the spirit of the protective father to nurture their children and the Earth. It is through this nurturing and caring that we inherently connect with others, igniting the moral and spiritual core of our existence.

Historically, women have gathered and upheld the sanctity of life—a call to protect and nurture that which lives in our cellular memory. Thousands of years ago, in the inner sanctum of caves, women weren't just sitting around and nursing their young. They were into deep magic, creating the first agriculture, domesticating plants and animals, being midwives of birth and death. They were charting healing plants and using their hands to support life—not destroy it. Women wove the first net, basket and cloth to gather food and provide clothing.

The same thread that inspired women to weave the first net still flows in our consciousness. Although we live in a modern world, we are still the weavers of truth, courage and compassion, creating a net that holds our world in a strong and gentle way. When life calls out, we still rise like the "She Bear" to protect.

This reverence towards life has given women a special courage—a sacred courage that brings together the deep love of creation and the fierce instincts that all life must be honored. Women naturally want to make a place where children can gather and be healthy. They want children and grandchildren to live a life full of passion and choices. Women carry a unique social intelligence that has emerged from the feminine perspective and from their roles as creator and nurturer.

Women have the ability to host life and experience the monthly bleeding from our womb that richly attunes us to cycles of beginnings and endings. We feel our bellies move and quiver as a tiny human develops, getting ready for entry into the world. Women feel the immense pain and elation as a baby makes its way down the birth canal, twisting and pushing and straining with every contraction. Women create the most wholesome food known in the animal kingdom: breast milk. A doctor friend reminded me that the father provides half of the blueprint and the mother provides the other half as well as all of the building materials.

It makes sense that women are peace bearers. Women's nature is to maintain moral responsibility to others and transform opportunistic greed into sharing and cooperation. Women uphold a vision for a world where life is honored and protected rather than mutilated and destroyed. However, there is more than the biological experience of bearing a child. There is the essence of the Divine Mother, the Kali Yuga rising up and saying, "Enough is enough!" According to Hindu scripture, Kali Yuga (the Age of Kali) began 5,000 years ago. Near the middle of the 431st millennium AD, Kalki, the 10th and final avatar of Vishnu, is expected to appear at this time, riding a white horse and wielding a flaming sword to destroy greed, lies and unnecessary power and return the Earth to a state of paradise.

Many women around the globe are standing up for what they believe, deeply trusting what they know is right and showing their fury and fierceness in the face of opposition. These women are setting a precedent for all of us—heads of state, those raising families or any who share this precious planet on which we live.

Stricken by the bombardment of media and feelings of isolation, the troubles of the world seem insurmountable. Many find themselves immobilized, feeling ineffectual and powerless. When we try to imagine the amount of time and patience one needs to inspire change, we are struck by the magnitude of it. No ordinary human being would have the inclination to spend their lives working endlessly towards solving the problems of the world. There is no great money to be made, nothing to join and no guarantee that these actions will reach the intended goal.

Yet many of the women in this book were living ordinary lives—without money, fame or power—when they took their first step towards action. Each woman found herself personally affected by something that they could not neglect and their decision to act unleashed tremendous energy. When we begin with the first drop—like a fountain turning into a river—energy flows with unimaginable love and power, creating a dynamic blend of compassion with action. A spirit arises with an abundant source of energy that drives us towards righting the wrong.

Both men and women who are tired of the current state of the world and who are looking for a new approach will find that these stories show us what is possible. The health of the planet and the health of all life must balance out with the desire to drill for oil, make more money or create bigger and better corporations. This book is for people who are looking for a new vision for our world—a world that values human life and human dignity.

This book is not about philosophy. It is not about a new age. It is about this moment and the stark reality that we are killing the planet on which we live, poisoning our children and obliterating their birth right to live long and healthy lives. It is about clean air, real food and our right to know. It is about our collective remembrance of the deep feminine and the mother, in all of her forms, teaching us about love, compassion and integrity. It is about embracing the source of all creation and letting that be our guide; holding life, without question, in total reverence.

We currently live in one of the most challenging times in our planet's history with the rapid destruction of our environment, violence and terrorism on the rise around the world, diseases killing thousands of people and extermination of entire species of plants and animals. It is my hope that the stories in this book will inspire anyone who has a desire to make a difference but feels disempowered by the overwhelming state of the world.

Many people today are disillusioned and are looking for an alternative to the current dead-end paradigm, which is minimizing the quality of life, and ongoing desecration of the planet. The human values that make our world a livable place need to be honored. Under the shadow of corporate greed and war-mongering politicians, the price of human suffering and a poisoned world is causing our quality of life to deteriorate rapidly.

We need to collectively create a new paradigm and a new way in which we can shift the world so that it is healthy and supportive of all life. The key to this shift is the warrior mother spirit that can be unleashed in both men and women when they experience an undeniable call to rise up in the face of injustice.

I hope these stories awaken the calling within each of us and inspire us to take the first step towards making a difference. However awkwardly, gracefully or fiercely we begin the path, we will find that we are not alone. However small or large the action, we need only to reach out and find a thousand hands beckoning us. We will find a thousand hearts opening as we open our own heart. We will find the warrior mother arising in all of her glory and aliveness, leading us towards wholeness and hope for a better future.

CHINA GALLAND

The Story of Durga

China is the founder and director of the Images of Divinity Project and professor-in-residence at the Center for the Arts, Religion and Education at the Graduate Theological Union in Berkeley, California. A mother of three grown children, China is also the author of numerous books in-cluding Women in the Wilderness, The Bond Between Women: The Journey to Fierce Com-passion *and her critically acclaimed* Longing for Darkness: Tara and the Black Madonna. *She is a frequent speaker on women and spirituality and was also one of the pioneers of the women's wilderness movement.*

China offers the following story that she wrote about the Great Goddess Durga. In Hindu mythology, it is believed that when demons attacked the gods and conquered heaven, the ener-gies of the trinity of the Hindu gods coalesced to create Durga. She went to battle, armed with the weapons given to her by the other gods, and won the battle over evil. With blood dripping from her tongue and her eyes full of fire, she promised to return if the life of the planet was ever again in danger of being destroyed.

Many faiths and cultures have stories of female saints and goddesses whose protection of life is their foremost purpose. Perhaps no other story presents such a powerful metaphor for our time as the story of Durga. Her golden body blazing with the splendor of a thousand suns, seat-ed on her lion, Durga is one of the most extraordinary personifications of the warrior mother.

The world stood poised on the brink. Rivers dried up; plants refused to grow. People starved. There was war everywhere. Slaughter prevailed. Dancing stopped and singing was forgot-ten. The demons, known as "asuras," were loose in the world, raging unchecked across heaven and Earth, drunk with destruction. No one could stop them—not even the gods, who had been defeated one by one.

Humiliated, the gods withdrew to the heights of the Himalayas and took counsel amongst themselves, to no avail. Their dilemma was insoluble. They had lost all power against these demons and could only leave the world to its inevitable destruction. Then they remembered that this time had been foretold: a demon would come to destroy the world and only a wom-an could defeat it.

At this, the gods shot forth streams of fire that converged into a towering pillar of flames as high as the Himalayas. Out of this fire came the Great Goddess Durga, blazing with the light of a thousand suns, radiating her splendor throughout the universe. Riding a lion, wearing the crescent moon and smiling serenely, Durga had 10 hands and arms, powerful and ready, with weapons given to her by the gods themselves.

The Great Goddess Durga, the Warrior Queen—whose very name means "Fortress," "Unassailable" and "Beyond Reach"—rose up to fight a great demon, Mahisasura, and all his forces. She rode into battle with a roar that shook the Earth. The war between Durga and Mahisasura and his demons raged across heaven and Earth, day after day. Oceans boiled, the sky stretched thin and the mountains shook.

Every time Durga sighed, legions of female warriors sprang to her side. Demons were slain by the hundreds in the hail of weapons from the goddess and her forces. The battlefield was choked with bodies. The goddess consumed the demon army like a great fire devours a forest. When the battle was over, Durga had won.

Mahisasura, enraged by defeat, now took the form of the Buffalo Demon and began the battles anew. Each time Durga killed the Buffalo Demon, he would spring back to life in a more ferocious form. In what seemed to be the final struggle, Durga cut off the Buffalo Demon's head. Victory was in her hands. The gods praised and worshipped her and she retired to her throne in the Himalayas, riding her lion—but this was not the end.

This time, the lord of the demons himself, Sumbha, and his younger brother, Nisumbha, sought out Durga. They did not confront Durga in battle; they tried to seduce her and proposed that she marry Sumbha. Durga thanked them for the proposal, but reminded them of a vow she had taken to marry only the one who could defeat her in battle. Since Sumbha was clearly unable to defeat her, she had no choice but to refuse his hand.

Sumbha was infuriated. He and his brother commanded their forces to attack, but Durga reduced their troops to ashes with a mere glance. Sumbha sent in more demons and commanded them to drag Durga to him by her hair. Durga was enraged by his insolence. Her face grew as dark as a storm cloud, and the Goddess Kali sprang from her forehead—armed, black, enormous, terrifying and ready for battle.

Kali strode out onto the battlefield, laughing and filling the skies with her terrible cry. Bloodshed and death followed her every turn. She roared with pleasure as she devoured her foes. With each step, she trampled entire battalions. Chariots and riders, troops of elephants and soldiers were swept up and swallowed in her enormous, howling maw. Her long teeth gleamed and her sword slashed everything in her path. She laughed and reveled in the fury of demolishing the demon's foes.

Sumbha's army was put to fight and now only the demon Raktabija remained. He was a hideous demon. Every time a drop of Raktabija's blood fell to the ground, a thousand more demons would spring up for battle. Rather than attack directly to defeat him, Kali licked up the blood of his wounds until no more remained.

Raktabija was routed. Finally, even Nisumbha was killed, leaving Sumbha alone. Sumbha scoffed and railed at Durga, challenging her to prove herself and to fight him without the help of Kali and all her female warriors, but Durga could not be trapped. She accepted his challenge and, in an electrifying moment, absorbed Kali and all her female warriors back into herself. She rode alone on her lion into the battlefield. Serene and smiling, she challenged Sumbha to attack.

The struggle for the fate of the world began. Time stopped as the goddess and the demon embraced in their fight, turning and pitching and rolling across the sky. The cosmos groaned with the enormity of their encounter. At the last moment, Durga pierced Sumbha's heart with her dagger and he tumbled out of the heavens. The world was safe at last!

A great cry of victory rang throughout the world. All of the gods assembled to honor Durga and to crown her Queen of the Universe. Rivers returned to their courses; music, dance and song returned to the world. Plants grew, trees blossomed and joy could be found again.

The gods and all her followers begged her to stay and rule the world, but Durga would have none of it. She assured them that there was no need to fear. She would feed her devotees with her own body, but she would not stay and rule the world. She put aside all adulation, put away the vast display of her powers and withdrew from the world at the height of her victory with a promise: "Do not worry. If the world is ever in danger of being destroyed again, I will return."

CONTACT

http://www.imagesofdivinity.org

BIBLIOGRAPHY

Galland, China. *The Bond Between Women: The Journey to Fierce Compassion.* New York: Berkeley Publishing Group, Riverhead Books, 1998.

____. *Longing for Darkness: Tara and the Black Madonna.* New York: Penguin Putnam Inc., 1990.

____. *Women in the Wilderness.* New York: Harpercollins, 1980.

DIANE WILSON

Taking a Stand Against Chemical Polluters

"Don't just just sit on your hands in silence and believe in something. Put it into action!"

Due to her efforts to launch zero discharge as a movement within the U.S. and abroad, Diane has won numerous awards from both the environmental and fishing communities. She is currently involved in research to test Vietnamese and Hispanic fishermen for endocrine disruptors, heavy metals and polychlorinated biphenyls, commonly known as PCBs.

Diane has been interviewed on Amy Goodman's Democracy Now! *and has been photographed with UnReasonable Women for the Earth/CODEPINK's Medea Benjamin while protesting at a press event held by Secretary of the U.S. Department of Defense Donald Rumsfeld at the Armed Services Committee, paving the way for war on Iraq—a photograph that found its way to the front page of many of the nation's daily newspapers. Diane was the first recipient of CODEPINK'S Human Rights Award in June 2004.*

I was born in 1948 in Sea Drift, Texas—a tiny Calhoun County fishing village of 1,000 people located on the San Antonio Bay on the Texas gulf coast. My great-grandfather, my grandpa, my daddy and all of my brothers were fishermen and, at eight years old, I was working for my father as a deck hand. When I was growing up, speaking was painful for me. As a result, I made the perfect deck hand since no one wants a chatty person on a boat.

In my mind, the San Antonio Bay was personified as a wise feminine force—a grandmother. I could almost hear her talking to me: "Why, hello Diane. It's so good to see you again!" The old woman was everywhere—in the water, on the shoreline and in the salt air.

Every morning she greeted me, and I felt her warm welcoming as daddy and I headed out on our boat for a day of fishing.

I was the first fisherwoman in my family and, when I was 24 years old, I bought my own fishing boat; when I was 27, I got married and bought a safer, 42-foot shrimp boat named *See Bee*. Soon after, I began having children—four daughters and one son, who is autistic.

Besides fishing, the chemical industry was growing in our town. In 1950, Union Carbide was the first chemical plant on the San Antonio Bay; in 1954, Alcoa Aluminum set up a plant. I never paid much attention to the plants and, like most people in Sea Drift, I knew that the plants provided jobs. Soon, Dow Chemical, Carbon Graphite, British Petroleum, Dupont, Formosa Plastics and two of their downstream plants lined the rivers and the bay. These chemical plants kept low profiles and we never heard much about them.

That all changed in 1989. I had a dream that I was at a crossroads and something monumental was going to happen. Surrounding me were black pipes coming out of a chemical plant. I woke up and knew that there was something significant about that dream, but at the time I wasn't sure what it was.

About two weeks after I had the dream, a local fisherman started talking to me. He had lumps the size of tennis balls all over his arms and he told me that he had been diagnosed with three different kinds of cancer. He handed me an article written by the *Associated Press*, publicizing the first Toxic Release Inventory (a result of Congress passing the Community's Right to Know bill). The article reported Calhoun County as the #1 county in the nation for toxic releases to the land. With a population of 15,000, Calhoun was reported to harbor over 50 percent of all the toxic land waste in Texas.[1]

As I read the article, I felt a terrible sense of despair. I called a meeting to talk about this fisherman's cancer and the article. I knew there had to be some kind of correlation between the two and the public needed to know what was going on. I phoned the local community center to reserve an evening for the meeting and disclosed the meeting's agenda.

A few days later, the president of the local bank, the plant manager and the county commissioners showed up at the fish house where I worked and told me not to have the meeting. They tried to make private deals with me, offering to pay me money if I would cancel the meeting. Superintendents of security talked to me; senators contacted me and offered monetary kickbacks if I stopped questioning the industrial plants on the bay. Despite all of the warnings, I held the meeting.

A dozen people from the next town attended including businessmen, the mayor and members from the chamber of commerce. When I presented the Toxic Release Inventory facts and expressed my concerns about the possibilities of rising rates of cancer in our county, they told me, "You're crazy and you're a hysterical woman."

Days later, I found out that Formosa Plastics was going to build a massive chemical plant in Calhoun County: the biggest expansion in Texas history and the biggest in the U.S. in 10 years. Formosa was to be granted all of their permits, even though they had been kicked out of Taiwan for being a large-scale polluter.[2]

When I found out about Formosa Plastics' history, I decided to hire an environmental attorney who sometimes worked pro bono out of Houston. I knew I had to learn everything I could about chemical waste so I would be in a position to make my case. After a year, I met with the attorney. He told me that, as a citizen, I could question Formosa's permits by asking for a hearing if I thought I was going to be impacted by this plant.

I applied for a public hearing and was suddenly under attack. My fishing boat was sabotaged twice—once sinking underneath me—and I almost drowned in the middle of the bay. A helicopter landed in my front yard and someone in it shot and killed my dog and then shot at my mother-in-law. The cops didn't want to do anything and said that, if I ever got locked up, they would send me to the looney bin. All I was trying to do was to make sure that Formosa would put out zero discharge of toxins and recycle their waste!

The *truth* kept me going. Over the years, I've witnessed life in the bay dying. I've seen silver heads popping out of the water as hundreds of fish, poisoned by chemicals, gasped for air; one of the largest dolphin die-offs ever recorded in the history of the Mammal Stranding Network[3]; hundreds of dead pelicans and shrimp; bizarre green and brown tides that we never had before; and a red tide like a velvet cloth covering the entire bay. The chemical plants have discharge pipes that dump toxins directly into the bay and into the estuaries, which are nurseries where shrimp embryos, crabs and fish grow.

In addition, the San Antonio Bay has one of the largest underwater Superfund sites for mercury dumping in the U.S., which sits directly in the middle of the bay, right where the fishermen catch shrimp. It was put there by Alcoa Aluminum, who dumped mercury directly into the bay during a time when the danger of mercury was widely known. Reports of mercury contamination in Minamata, Japan, surfaced where children were born with severe deformities. Ironically, Alcoa bought the process from Japan after Minamata and its workers complained that the processing was out of control. Alcoa increased their production efforts and increased the amount of mercury that had to be "disposed."[4]

On the bay, mercury first showed up in the eggs of sea birds and then in fish, crabs and shrimp. Fishermen had relatives who worked for Alcoa and talked about the drums of mercury being buried in the bay, blobs of mercury floating on the water and mercury dissipating into the air and being inhaled by workers.

Fishermen are sometimes their own worst enemies. They won't organize because they can't agree on anything and don't know how to do anything else but fish. When they don't get a good catch, they intensify their efforts by getting a bigger engine, a bigger net or a bigger wheel, or they compete with each other to elevate their catch. Because of this, an additional burden is placed on the life of the bay to survive, which has a snowball effect. Any chance of the bay recovering from toxic pollution, chemical discharge and overfishing becomes impossible.

Many fishermen kept their mouths shut because of the fear of losing their fishing market. Because Sea Drift is such a small community, a lot of people work at the plants and no one wants to put another person's job at risk. Most of the chemical plants threatened to fire the workers if they got involved in any way with what I was doing.

The chemical plants had taken over the infrastructure of our tiny fishing village and bought the silence of an entire community, including the sheriff's department, the police department, the teacher's union, the mayor, the senator, the justice of the peace and council members. The eight major chemical plants dumping toxins into our rivers and bays were obliterating marine life. The fisheries and the bays were in crisis and the fishing industry was going further and further down.

I knew I had to do something that would catch the media and people's attention, so I decided to go on a hunger strike. It was one way that they (the chemical plants) could not control me. I was frightened but I decided that I *had* to do it. In the long run, it made the difference in getting the chemical plants to change their discharge of toxic chemicals.

My first hunger strike was over Formosa Plastics. I sat on a shrimp boat in the middle of the bay and reporters wrote an article about me. Weeks later, I decided to sink my own 42-foot shrimp boat on top of an illegal discharge in the bay to make a dramatic statement about how we were losing our livelihood due to careless chemical polluting. Three boatloads of U.S. Coast Guard officers surrounded me to keep me from sinking my boat. Nevertheless, I still got the attention of the chemical plants and the community.

My second hunger strike was for 30 days, sitting in the back of my pickup truck in front of the Union Carbide (now Dow Chemical) plant and protesting in solidarity with the Bhopal survivors in India because of our mutual connection with Union Carbide. Union Carbide had caused the world's worst industrial disaster when toxic gas escaped in Bhopal and killed over 20,000 people living in surrounding shanty towns.[5] Union Carbide had discharged over 5 million gallons a day of toxins into the bay since I was born.[6] Union Carbide had over 50 sites of benzene contamination (linked with leukemia) within the area that had a huge accident in 1991, injuring 32 workers and killing one.[7] I wanted Dow to accept responsibility for its subsidiary Union Carbide's victims in Bhopal and its responsibility to the people of Sea Drift.

Every morning, I sat in the back of my truck and passed out fliers to the workers, who talked to me about the plant on their lunch hour. I learned "the inside scoop" about Dow Chemical from the employees. Eleven days into the hunger strike, I entered the plant and climbed 70 feet up a tower in the ethylene unit, shackled myself to it and displayed a banner that read, "Dow is responsible for Bhopal!"

I experienced an amazing change during my hunger strikes. I am a big woman and have always had to fight weight. Typically, I cannot stay on a diet for even two days but, if I have a cause, I can do it for 30 days! Ghandi called this "soul power." When I was doing the hunger strike in solidarity with Bhopal, I received many e-mails from the people of India, sending their blessings and compassion through prayer circles.

My life as a fisherwoman has taught me that there are no seas with lines and divisions. Similarly, if there is a border that separates me as an American from the anguish and sorrow of my sisters and brothers in Bhopal and their fight for justice, then that is a false and lying line. All the great religions teach that we are one: one woman's pain is a pain to all; an injustice to one is an injustice to all.

In my small community, I received a tremendous amount of flak from politicians, my family, my husband and my friends. My years spent as a loner forced me to be inner directed—I learned to think about what I liked and didn't like and what I believed in. I instinctively know when something is a huge miscarriage of justice.

Becoming an activist has had its price. My mother cries whenever I walk into her house. "Diane, you're just trying to upset me by doing what you do!" My husband would not take care of the children or come pick me up when I was at meetings; he would sometimes lock the doors so I couldn't come home after a meeting, but I had to keep going.

Injustice infuriates me. I am a mother and a citizen of this planet and I don't know any mother who would stop protecting her child or family member. The bay is my grandmother and she is familiar with me and I with her. I can still see her face, I can feel her warmth and, at times, I can hear her voice. How can I possibly stop trying to put an end to the chemical dumping that is killing her?

Due to my efforts, there are now zero-discharge agreements from Formosa Plastics and Alcoa and zero-discharge resolutions passed by both the Calhoun County Commissioners Court and Sea Drift City Council. The Oil Chemical and Atomic Workers Union also passed a national resolution for zero discharge. There is still more work to be done and the town has now joined me in my efforts. I think they've realized that if a fisherwoman with a high school education can get compliance from a petrochemical plant, anyone can.

I now understand indigenous people who talk about being deeply connected to nature. When you are connected in this way, it is not something you have to *prove*. It is something that you *know*. You become the Earth and there will never again be any separation.

I believe the reason why the Earth is in such a period of destruction is that we are living under masculine rule, especially in western society, which reflects aggression, violence and separateness. We have totally removed ourselves from the trees, the ocean and each other. That is why the U.S. military can drop bombs in Iraq because Iraqis are not people. They are separate. They are "the other."

When I was 35 years old, I had a recurring dream about an old, weathered beach house that was strong. The inner rooms were adorned with shining wood, beveled glass, mirrors with reflecting light and beautiful antique furniture. The drawers were full of jewels. I asked my friend about it and she said, "Why, that's you!" It had never dawned on me that I was valuable. It was a real turning point in my life. Women were not valued during my childhood and, if a woman spoke, she was immediately considered dumb. As women begin to believe in themselves more, there will be change.

I was asked to speak at the 2001 Bioneers Conference (a network of visionary innovators who are working with nature to heal nature). At the end of my speech, I said, "A reasonable woman adapts to the world, an unreasonable woman makes the world adapt to her. So I encourage you all to be unreasonable!" Hundreds of women cried as they came up to me. Women went outside and called friends on their cell phones: "Start a project. I don't care what it is … just *start* it!"

Later in the day, I told Nina Simons, cofounder of Bioneers, that I had a vision of unreasonable women changing the world. I truly believe that you have to be unreasonable because, if you are polite and nice, you are going to get the status quo. That is what our country's leaders want: people to write nice letters to their congressmen, who put the letters in the trash can while everything remains the same.

Nina found the funds for 34 women—probably the most radical women in the U.S.— to have a retreat. After days of talking and visioning, we created a new movement named "UnReasonable Women for the Earth," which is gaining momentum around the country.

One of my favorite Ghandi principles is the idea of commitment. Anyone can do what he did if they have the same willingness to commit. Commitment is not about just giving $5 to the Sierra Club. Change is going to happen only if you take *real action*. It can happen with one person, with two people or with a group of people. People have to be counted; they have to stand up. Hopefully, I am showing my children that you have to take a stand for what you believe in. Don't just sit on your hands in silence and believe in something. Put it into action!

CONTACT

wilsonalamobay@aol.com

SUGGESTED LINKS

http://www.bhopal.net (The International Campaign for Justice in Bhopal)

http://www.bioneers.org (Bioneers)

http://www.unreasonablewomen.org (UnReasonable Women for the Earth)

FOOTNOTES START ON PAGE 198.

MARSHA GREEN

Fighting Intense Underwater Noise Pollution

"Once we understand what motivates our destructive actions, we can begin the internal work of changing ourselves."

Marsha has a Ph.D. in psychology and is a professor at Albright College in Pennsylvania. She teaches courses in animal behavior, ecological psychology, behavioral neuroscience and women's studies. In 1994, she founded the Ocean Mammal Institute (OMI), a nonprofit organization doing ecologically sensitive research on marine mammals. The OMI offers field research internships and educates people about marine environmental issues.

Since 1986, Marsha has researched the impact of humans, including noise from boat engines, on humpback whales and spinner dolphins in Hawaii. She also studies whale social communication. She has testified twice for the State of Hawaii on the impact of thrill craft on humpback whales and her research was instrumental in banning their operation during whale season.

In 1998, Marsha attempted to get a court order to stop the Navy's testing of Low Frequency Active Sonar (LFAS or LFA sonar) on endangered humpback whales in Hawaii. She lectures in the U.S. and in Europe on the impact of human-produced ocean noise on marine life and serves as scientific advisor to the European Coalition for Silent Oceans (ECSO). She has taken petitions to the Parliament of the European Union (EU) and the North Atlantic Treaty Organization (NATO) calling for the formation of a multinational task force to develop international agreements regulating noise levels in the world's oceans. She is currently a member of the Federal Advisory Committee on Acoustic Impacts on Marine Mammals, which will recommend ocean noise management actions to Congress.

Being in the company of whales has taught me many things. Separated by thousands of miles of ocean, humpback whales in the North Pacific all sing the same song, even though the song changes over time. It is the most complex song on Earth and science has not been able to explain how whales accomplish this. Being in the company of whales has shown me that it is possible to be both strong and powerful and graceful and nurturing, a balancing act for our times.

My first meeting with whales occurred in 1985 on a 25-foot Zodiac during a spring-break Hawaiian vacation. I saw humpback whales fighting with each other and I knew immediately that I had to study these amazing creatures! My specialization in psychology is animal behavior. When I got back to shore, I started making the necessary arrangements to return to Hawaii the next year. I began by observing whales from a shore-based site and recording all their behavior. I also started taking my students to Hawaii during our January interim term to observe whales and began looking for a research project that could involve my students.

In 1989, I began studying the impact of boats on whales. In my first vessel impact study, data showed that when boats got within one-half mile of a pod of whales, their behavior would change—sometimes significantly. I thought that, most likely, engine noise was affecting the whales because they are acoustic animals. Whales use hearing to find mates and food and to navigate. I wanted to study the effects of specific levels of engine noise on whales' behavior, so I applied for a research permit from the National Marine Fisheries Service (NMFS). Over time, my data showed that when whales are exposed to 120 decibels (dB) of engine noise, they swim away two to three times faster than they swim away from quieter boats. (All decibel levels are referenced to the intensity of a signal with a sound pressure level of 1 micro Pascal, water standard.) Other studies also reported that whales start to avoid sounds at about 120 dB and that number became the generally accepted standard for whale avoidance behavior among marine mammal scientists.[1]

While doing this research, I learned that the Scripps Institute of Oceanography was going to operate a loud, underwater sound project called ATOC (Acoustic Thermometry of Ocean Climate)—sponsored by the Defense Department's Defense Advanced Research Projects Agency—to see if global warming was actually occurring. The speed at which sound travels in water depends on the water temperature. Scripps planned to send a very loud, low-frequency sound over long distances (from California to Hawaii, for example) and measure how long it took to get from one place to the other. They would then determine the temperature of the water by the speed the sound traveled and see whether ocean temperatures were rising.

Some people questioned whether ATOC was a serious attempt at understanding global warming.[2] Others were concerned about how marine mammals would be affected by this loud, low-frequency sound because ATOC has a source level of about 195 dB (much louder than most normal ocean sounds and over 10 million times more intense than the 120 dB sounds that whales avoid; the decibel scale is logarithmic, so a sound of 130 dB is 10 times as intense as one of 120 dB).

Since there was a lot of objection to ATOC, Scripps agreed to give its Marine Mammal Research Program (MMRP) more emphasis before starting the main ATOC activities (i.e., initially, the sound source would be in the hands of marine mammal scientists who were studying the effects of ATOC on marine mammals). However, Scripps started broadcasting the sound source off California without the marine mammal researchers' knowledge.[3] When three humpback whales were found dead in the vicinity of the sound source, the response of the ATOC program manager—before any investigation was undertaken—was that there was zero possibility that the whales were killed by ATOC. The California Coastal Commission then voted to ask the NMFS to investigate ATOC's MMRP.

This event increased my concern about the effects of ATOC on marine life. I went to Honolulu where the State Department of Land and Natural Resources was holding a hearing to decide whether Scripps would be allowed to put a transmitter in the ocean to deploy ATOC off Kauai. I presented my research on the effects of engine noise on whales, which showed how the whales clearly avoid sounds of 120 dB and above. After I presented my research and expressed my concern about the effects of ATOC on whales, the first question they asked was, "Where do you get your funding?"

At the time, I had no idea why they would ask me that question. My assistant came up to me later and said, "Well, I guess we're going to have trouble doing the research now." I didn't know what she was talking about until I got a phone call several weeks later from the marine mammal scientist with whom I was working to measure the effects of various levels of engine noise on the whales.

"Marsha, you're not going to believe what happened," he said. "All of the research data and equipment that we use for recording the engine sounds, including our tapes of boat engine noise, were stolen from my laboratory." That was my introduction to the politics of ocean noise pollution.

According to the National Research Council Ocean Studies Board Review Panel, the ultimate results of ATOC's MMRP were inconclusive.[4] Dr. Paul Anderson (a member of ATOC's MMRP Advisory Board) said, "Very few of the possible impacts of ATOC have been addressed by MMRP in the field ... shore-based observations were largely ineffective ... boat-based observations produced very little information ... ATOC/MMRP performance suggests a lack of serious dedication to protecting marine organisms ... [the] MMRP has not met its objective."[5]

Because of the strong opposition to ATOC, there is now only one transmitter remaining that operates off Kauai. Perhaps because ATOC got such bad press, they have changed the name of the project to North Pacific Acoustic Laboratory (NPAL). ATOC's Environmental Impact Statement (EIS) estimated that physical harm to marine mammals may begin at exposure levels above 150 to 160 dB[6]; NATO also sets 160 dB as the threshold for injury.[7] Without any empirical data, NPAL increased the supposed safe exposure level for marine mammals to 180 dB—20 dB higher than ATOC's EIS.[8] NPAL is funded by the Office of Naval Research.

The ATOC controversy happened in the 1990s; during that time we learned that, between August 1988 and July 1994, the Navy had secretly tested a high-intensity active sonar technology called LFAS (or LFA sonar) at least 22 times with no environmental assessment prepared and without applying for the required exemption under the Marine Mammal Protection Act.[9] LFAS is designed to detect and track quiet submarines. The source level is about 240 dB, which is about one trillion times more intense than the 120-dB sounds that whales avoid. One scientist, analyzing hydrophone (underwater microphone) data from around the Pacific,[10] could hear the LFAS signal deployed from one source off California over the entire

North Pacific Ocean ... now *that* is noise pollution! When the Navy eventually had to write an EIS for LFAS, they raised the estimated threshold for injury, like NPAL, to 180 dB, which is one million times more intense than the sounds whales avoid. They also had no empirical data to indicate that this was a safe intensity.[11]

During an LFAS field trial in 1993, an experienced military diver was forced to surface after 45 seconds of exposure to the LFAS signal at about 150 dB or less. He sensed a strong vibration in his body and felt numb for two hours afterward.[12] A PADI divemaster, who was in the water during another of those secret tests, reported during a California Coastal Commission hearing that his lungs vibrated distinctly and he felt somewhat disoriented with each sound pulse. He later learned that the deploying vessel was about 150 miles away from him.[13] The likelihood of panicked behavior in unalerted recreational divers exposed to LFAS has been recognized as a serious concern by Navy doctors.[14]

The Natural Resources Defense Council (NRDC) found out about this secret testing and discussed it with the Navy in 1996. The Navy agreed to prepare an EIS and delay full deployment of LFA sonar until all legal requirements were met. To address the uncertainties about the impact of LFA sonar on baleen whales, the Navy decided to fund a scientific research program (SRP) and incorporate the results into the EIS. They then hired marine mammal scientists to do the research. Unfortunately, the testing mainly addressed effects on only four species of whales.[15] We learned later that LFAS can also injure, kill and displace fish, and there are concerns about sea turtles, squid and other species as well.[16] We know nothing about the effects on plankton, which, of course, fuel the marine food chain.

In the first two phases of the SRP, they tested for two months off California and found that blue and fin whales decreased their vocalizations by 30 to 50 percent when a low-level LFAS sound was on and that in-shore gray whales visibly avoided the sound during migration.[17] The third phase of testing on humpback whales in Hawaii showed that singing humpback whales increased the length of their songs by 29 percent when the LFAS sound was on.[18] It is important to note that all three phases of the SRP used sound source levels considerably quieter than what would have been used under full operational conditions.

These were all short-term studies (one month each), so they could not measure the actual effect of LFAS on the critical issues of finding mates and long-term reproductive success. In spite of these behavioral changes, the Navy concluded that the LFAS sound did not have a biologically significant impact on whales or other marine life.[19] However, the Marine Mammal Commission (a federal agency charged with protecting marine mammals) stated in their 1997 report to Congress that LFAS could potentially cause death from lung hemorrhage or other tissue trauma; temporary or permanent hearing loss; disruption of feeding, breeding, nursing and acoustic communication; and psychological and physiological stress, making animals more vulnerable to disease.[20] Given that the whales tested in all three phases of the study showed behavioral and/or distributional changes upon exposure to low levels of LFAS, it was highly probable they would show more dramatic responses to the full-scale sound source.

When I learned in January 1998 that the Navy was going to test LFAS on humpback whales off the Big Island of Hawaii in March 1998, I was very concerned because I thought they were going to test it at the actual deployment level of 240 dB, which I feared could be deadly. Additionally, the testing would occur just outside of the newly established U.S. Hawaiian Islands Humpback Whale National Marine Sanctuary during the breeding and calving season.

When I first learned about the testing in Hawaii, my entire body reacted—not just my mind. My body seemed to be moving on its own when I picked up the phone and called a lawyer with Earthjustice Legal Defense in Honolulu. I had already worked with them on the issue of parasail boats displacing whales from near-shore resting areas in Hawaii.

"Do you realize the Navy is going to test LFAS on humpbacks?" I asked the lawyer.

"Yes."

"What can we do to stop it?"

"We could try to get the court to issue a temporary restraining order," the lawyer suggested.

"What do we need to do that?" I asked.

"I will need a plaintiff."

"Well, you've *got* one!" I replied, meaning me (actually meaning the OMI). I filed a lawsuit to try to get a temporary restraining order to stop the sonar testing in Hawaii; four other organizations—Animal Welfare Institute, Earthtrust, Greenpeace Hawaii and Earth Island Institute—eventually joined as plaintiffs.

We were not able to stop the testing; however, in marine mammal scientist Dr. Linda Weilgart's written statement to the court for the lawsuit, she conveyed her concern that, among other potential effects, such loud sounds might disrupt the mother-calf bond in humpback whales.[21] At that time, I did not believe that would happen, but the increased incidence of humpback calves separated from their mothers in Hawaiian waters since 1998 suggests to me that intense underwater sounds may be affecting the whales in this way.[22]

A research team was working with me in Maui when I heard about the LFAS tests planned for March 1998. It was the end of January and we were getting ready to leave because I had to go back to the east coast to teach. I asked my research team if they would change their plans and go to the Big Island of Hawaii to record the behavior of the whales in February before testing began in order to obtain a baseline of their normal behavior. Then, when they began the sonar tests in March, we could see if there were any changes. My team went to the Big Island.

The scientists hired by the Navy began transmitting low-level LFAS from a ship in March 1998 as scheduled. My research team set up a shore observation site in a deserted area on the west coast of the Big Island where testing would occur. On March 9, they spotted a humpback whale calf in the test area without its mother (a highly unusual occurrence). They observed the behavior of this calf for five hours: the calf breached 230 times, pec slapped (with its pectoral fin or "arm") the water 671 times and tail slapped 42 times in the first four hours. This was a very agitated creature!

After four hours of systematically recording the location and behavior of the calf with a theodolite (a precision surveying instrument for measuring horizontal and vertical angles), my research team stopped writing and just watched for another hour. By dusk, the calf was so exhausted that it just lolled in the breaking surf line. The mother never showed up. The team left the research station, called me on the phone and told me what they had just witnessed.

I immediately called the NMFS office in Honolulu and told them that my team had just documented a separated calf exhibiting unusually agitated behavior. In the permit (required under the Marine Mammal Protection Act) the Navy scientists had received from the NMFS to do the testing, it said that if they saw unusual behavior (like repeated breaching, tail slapping or pec slapping), they would stop the testing.[23] They did not stop. The next day, my research team went out but could not find the calf. A few days later, the head of my research team was on a boat and spotted a lone dolphin calf—very unusual because dolphins live in groups. In early April, a melon-headed whale calf was discovered without a mother. The calf was very dehydrated and was swimming up to tourists, trying to suck on their toes to nurse. This calf was rescued and taken to a sea life park in Honolulu. The calf died there.[24]

Thus, three separated cetacean calves were found in the relatively small LFAS test area off the Big Island of Hawaii during and shortly after testing stopped. Neither the Navy nor the NMFS showed any concern about the agitated humpback calf or the other calves, even though I had faxed to the NMFS the four hours of behavioral data we collected. One scientist hired by the Navy to do the testing later told me that they had ignored the information on the separated humpback calf because I hadn't published a paper on the event. The Animal Welfare Institute tried to stop the testing in Hawaii by taking volunteers near the transmitting naval vessel and putting them in the water. As long as people were nearby in the water, they could not deploy the sonar—it was too dangerous. These brave people managed to stop the tests about one-third of the time.

I spent all of my spare time on the east coast, trying to get the media to cover what was happening in Hawaii. At that time, I couldn't get any journalists to pay attention. The New York Times almost published an editorial but decided not to at the last minute. I vented my frustration to a consultant on environmental stories. "Marsha," she explained, "there are people in high places who squelch stories like this." We have made a lot of progress since then as the press frequently covers the sonar issue now. I later found out that, in the SRP, the Navy never tested the sonar at the full deployment level. Their scientists stated in a Quicklook document after the Hawaii tests that, "It will be difficult to extrapolate from these results to predict responses at higher exposure levels" and "The research did not use the full source level of LFAS."[25]

Even though the humpback whales were exposed to only low-level LFAS sounds, they increased the length of their songs while the sound was on. Some scientists think this may be because the singing whales were "competing" with the sonar sounds.[26] It certainly suggests that the whales were expending more energy singing when the sound was on. Since singing may function to attract mates or repel rivals, this difference in singing behavior could potentially affect reproductive success. In spite of the fact that blue and fin whales decreased their vocalizations, in-shore gray whales avoided LFAS during their migration and humpback whales sang longer songs, the Navy concluded in their final EIS that the behavioral changes observed during their three months of low-level tests were not biologically significant and that LFAS was safe for marine mammals up to a received level of 180 dB.[27]

Anyone who criticized the science behind these conclusions was marginalized by the Navy as well as by many marine mammal scientists. When I walked into the hotel lobby where the biennial meeting of the International Marine Mammal Society was being held in 1998, someone yelled loudly across the lobby, "Boy, Marsha, you really are a controversial person!" I was quite unpopular at that meeting except among the few people who agreed with my attempt to try to stop the sonar tests in Hawaii. One of my research associates said several people came up to her at the meeting and said incredulously, "You're working with Marsha Green?"

The next few years were very intense. I spoke on numerous radio shows and did interviews for magazines and newspapers. At one point, representatives from the Navy and the NFMS withdrew their agreement to be on a radio show after they learned I would also be on the show. During this time, the Navy wrote to the president of Albright College twice, inquiring whether my criticism of LFAS represented the viewpoint of the college.[28] Because of situations like mine, the tenure system was created for professors to protect free speech; unfortunately, the tenure system is currently under intense scrutiny.

A scientist for the Humane Society gave a presentation to the Acoustical Society of America questioning the adequacy of the LFAS research program and the Navy's proposal that an exposure level of 180 dB was safe for marine mammals. She was strongly criticized and had to apologize for her statements that supposedly impugned the credibility of the researchers and which were viewed as misleading by some. Actually, our criticisms have turned out to be valid. The whale species tested cannot be regarded as representative, long-term effects were not studied and the approximately three months of testing were not adequate to recommend the "safe exposure" level of 180 dB cited in the EIS. Evidence from strandings where time-distance analyses are available suggests that intense noise can cause strandings at received levels well below 180 dB.[29]

We now know that they never tested LFAS above levels of 155 dB (and usually exposure levels were well below that), although they claim it is safe up to 180 dB.[30] The Navy mentions this lack of empirical data in only one sentence in Appendix D of the lengthy EIS: "The lack of empirical data in the received level range of 155 to 180 dB is an issue."[31] The Executive Summary for the EIS concludes that the sonar is safe up to exposure levels of 180 dB and never mentions the data gap.[32] We now know, as many of us suspected all along, that 180 dB is not a safe exposure level for all marine mammals. Even the effectiveness of LFAS in accomplishing its major mission of detecting quiet submarines in shallow, confined waters was questioned by the nonpartisan General Accounting Office.[33]

In 1996, there was a mass stranding of beaked whales in Greece while NATO was testing a form of LFAS.[34] NATO eventually issued a report on that stranding and their sound charts indicated the whales were most likely exposed to sound levels of about 150 to 160 dB.[35]

In March 2000, the Navy was using a high-intensity, mid-frequency sonar in the Bahamas.[36] It got a lot of press because the first whale to strand landed on the beachfront property of a marine mammal scientist. He preserved some of the whales' heads in the refrigerators of nearby restaurants and they were then shipped to New England for tests. Computed Axial Tomography (commonly known as CAT scans) was done and bleeding was found around the whales' brains and in their ears. In December 2001, the Navy and the NMFS issued a preliminary report on that stranding, stating that the most likely cause of death was acoustic trauma.[37] There is concern that this single exercise may have decimated most of the beaked whale population in the area since none of the previously identified animals have been sighted since the stranding. Evidence shows that the whales in the Bahamas stranding were exposed to sonar levels that did not exceed 160 to 170 dB,[38] again indicating that the 180-dB safe exposure level set by the Navy is not safe.

This Bahamas stranding inflamed the controversy so much that I organized a symposium on LFAS in August 2000. I invited all the environmental organizations working on the issue as well as representatives from the Navy and the NMFS. I was hoping that we could have constructive discussions. I was surprised when a Navy researcher whom I called hung up in the middle of my invitation. No one from the Navy or the NMFS came to the symposium (at least not in a capacity where we could identify them), but the meeting did serve to initiate more coordinated efforts among the attending environmental groups. After that meeting, we began to have strategy-planning conference calls; those calls continue with expanded participation to this day.

In 2002, there was another high-profile stranding in the Canary Islands during naval exercises involving NATO countries using mid-frequency sonar. Necropsies on these whales showed hemorrhaging in their ears, around their brains and in other organs.[39] Another well-publicized incident occurred during naval mid-frequency sonar exercises in Puget Sound in May 2003. Eleven harbor porpoises were found dead, a minke whale rapidly fled the area and killer whales swam erratically towards the shore.[40] Other strandings correlated with naval exercises occurred in the U.S. Virgin Islands (1999),[41] Vieques (1998 and 2002),[42] Madeira (2000),[43] the Canary Islands (1985, 1988, 1989[44] and 2004[45]) and Hawaii (2004).[46] As recently reported in the Scientific Committee of the International Whaling Commission, there have been a series of beaked whale strandings—10 mass strandings have been reported since the late 1950s and 64 beaked whales are reported to have stranded individually—along the Japanese coast near Yokosaka, one of the primary bases for U.S. naval activity in the western Pacific.[47] Many of us think that this is just the tip of the iceberg as most injured animals will not strand—they simply die and sink to the bottom.

In 2003, the NRDC was successful in getting the court to issue an injunction restricting deployment of LFA sonar to a one- to two-million-square-mile area in the western Pacific Ocean.[48] However, the Bush Administration pushed legislation through Congress that exempts the military from core provisions of the Marine Mammal Protection Act—leaving the military more free to harm whales and other marine mammals while using high-intensity sonars and underwater explosions. Exemptions in hand, the Navy has now filed a motion in federal court seeking to change the terms of the restrictions on LFAS deployment.[49]

While the court's decision restricts the use of LFAS, the formidable task of dealing with the effects of mid-frequency sonar remains. These sonars have been in use for decades and are known to have been in use during or before the strandings and deaths in the Bahamas (2000), the Canary Islands (2002), Puget Sound (2003) and Hawaii (2004).

Strandings and displacement of whales have also been correlated with the use of air guns used for geophysical research and seismic surveys for oil and gas exploration. A well-publicized stranding, correlated with air gun use, took place in the Gulf of California in September 2002.[50] An array of air guns towed behind a ship has a source level of 235 to 250 dB, similar to LFAS. Air guns are a significant source of noise pollution in the oceans (for example, they are a predominant part of the background noise you hear through hydrophones, which are 3,000 kilometers away from the air guns).[51] During seismic surveys off Brazil in 2002, there was an unusual increase in strandings of humpback whales in the region as well as a change in their distribution. Using the Precautionary Principle, the Brazilian Environmental Agency agreed to prohibit seismic surveys when the whales are there.[52]

In 2001, five giant squid were found stranded or floating dead at sea along the northern coast of Spain; in 2003, another four were found. On both occasions, geologists were conducting offshore seismic surveys nearby using an array of 10 airguns. All animals had internal injuries and badly damaged ears. Fishermen reported seeing large numbers of dead fish floating at sea during the surveys. The oil company plans to continue the surveys in 2005.[53] One study showed that air gun use lowered fish catch rates in Norway over a 2,000-square-mile area.[54] Studies not included in the Navy's EIS on LFAS indicate that LFAS has the potential to injure and kill a wide variety of fish at intensities well below the 180 dB "safe" threshold.[55] Thus, the impact of air guns and LFAS may pose a significant threat to the already depleted fish stocks throughout the world's oceans.

Unfortunately, the use of intense, underwater, noise-producing technologies is expanding. Low-frequency sonar systems are being developed by several countries[56] and mid-frequency sonars have been correlated with strandings in coastal waters, which contain critical habitat for marine mammals and other ocean life. Other sources of intense human-generated noise in the marine environment in addition to air guns and military sonars include underwater construction, explosives, ship traffic and acoustic-deterrent devices used in aquaculture. In many cases, there are alternative and realistic mitigation scenarios for reducing and eliminating loud, undersea, human-generated noise. A range of alternative passive sonar systems exist, which sort out underwater sounds using sensitive hydrophones and improved computers. These passive systems give the Navy the ability to listen for sounds of approaching submarines without revealing their own presence the way LFA signals do.

By 2002, it was clear to me that the deployment of intense military sonars and other undersea noise technologies was an issue of international concern. Acoustic energy is not restricted by national boundaries and needs to be regulated by responsible international institutions. I knew I had to start working on an international level because there was not much more I could do in the U.S. That summer, I organized a small delegation to visit members of the European Parliament to urge them to consider the problem of intense underwater noise pollution, especially LFAS and mid-frequency military sonars. I had commissioned a lawyer to research the legality of LFAS deployment under international law and took this legal opinion with me to the Parliament. Very committed members of the Green Party facilitated our visit and encouraged us in what seemed like an uphill battle. There were so many members of Parliament to contact. With the help of the Greens, I learned a lot about lobbying and we gained support from key members of several political parties.

As a result of this first visit, a question, signed by 60 members of Parliament, was drawn up asking the European Commission to address the issue of LFAS in European waters. The Commission replied that it had requested details on LFAS use from member States. Then the European Federation of Green Parties passed a resolution at their annual meeting in November 2002, calling for a moratorium on the deployment of LFA sonar.

In the summer of 2002, I also spoke about the dangers of high-intensity sonars at a whale symposium in Zurich and suggested that Europeans form a coalition of environmental groups to oppose deployment of LFAS. Ocean Care, a marine mammal protection group in Switzerland, consequently formed the ECSO. I have been working with them as their scientific advisor since that time. We returned to Parliament in 2003 to continue our discussions and deliver a petition to the Petitions Committee. The petition requests the Parliament to ask the EU to adopt a moratorium on the deployment of LFAS, to initiate the formation of a multinational task force to develop international agreements regulating noise levels in the world's oceans and to inquire into possible legal remedies to address the use of LFA sonar.

The petition also points out that current deployment may be in breach of Articles 204–206 of the United Nations Convention on the Law of the Sea, which requires states "to assess the potential effects of such activities on the marine environment"[57]; and in violation of Article 194, which requires all states to take all measures "necessary to prevent, reduce and control pollution of the marine environment from any source."[58] The petition was signed by environmental and animal welfare groups in North America and Europe, representing memberships of over 8.3 million people. The petition comes up for discussion in the fall of 2004.

During the second visit, I realized I should start working with the Parliament's Environment Committee on the issue. Discussions that summer and during a subsequent visit in the fall of 2003 set the stage for the Committee's approving a draft motion for a resolution calling upon the EU to adopt a moratorium on deployment of LFA sonar pending a global assessment of impacts, to adopt geographic restrictions on the use of all high-intensity sonars in sensitive marine habitats, to work with NATO and other international organizations to pursue moratoriums and restrictions on high-intensity active sonars and to form a multinational task force to develop underwater noise regulations. The resolution should come up for a vote in Parliament in 2004.

In 2003, I gave a talk about high-intensity sonars at an awareness-raising event in Berlin. For the first time, I went beyond just talking about the scientific, legal and political activities surrounding underwater noise and started talking about the larger issue of ending all forms of violence on the planet. Violence manifests in many ways, but whether we kill whales or other humans, or whether we abuse each other or the environment, violence is a symptom of the loss of a felt sense of connection to ourselves, to other life forms and to the Earth. If we can feel our connection to another living organism, we won't needlessly kill it.

Sigrid Lueber (from the ECSO) and I arranged a meeting with NATO representatives in October 2003 to discuss our concerns and deliver petitions representing over 8.3 million people on both sides of the Atlantic. Our delegation consisted of two members of the European Parliament, scientists, representatives of environmental groups and a Green Party lawyer. We met for over one hour with the Assistant Secretary General for External Relations for NATO and their Senior Scientist in charge of marine mammal risk mitigation.

The delegation explained that 10 years of scientific research on the impacts of high-intensity active sonars on marine mammals has not solved the problem; animals are still stranding and dying. We said that we and the public wanted regulatory action to prevent more needless deaths. NATO representatives replied that this was a hot political topic and the very fact we were having the meeting demonstrated their commitment to working on this issue. At the point of this writing (almost a year after the meeting), we have not been informed of any actions that NATO has taken in response to our petitions, but we continue our communication with them on the issue. Unfortunately, the most recent deaths of beaked whales (July 2004) were correlated with naval exercises involving NATO countries off Morocco.

With the support of the Sierra Club, I arranged a presentation on "Intense Underwater Noise Pollution" as a side event at the fifth meeting on Oceans and the Law of the Sea at the United Nations in June 2004. Representatives from the ECSO, NRDC and I gave an overview of the scientific aspects, the legal arguments and the political activities aimed at placing ocean noise pollution under international regulation. Throughout the week-long meeting, we met privately with the United Nations Secretariat and with delegates from many govern-ments to discuss the growing problem of underwater noise pollution and possible economic impacts—especially for fisheries.

I am currently working with others to formalize the loose coalition of environmental groups that have been addressing the underwater noise issue in the U.S. and Canada to form a North American coalition to parallel the ECSO. A woman in Chile is organizing a similar coalition in South America and we plan to develop a coalition in Asia. We are building to-wards an International Ocean Noise Coalition.

Because of the continued pressure by environmental groups and the public, Congress recently asked the Marine Mammal Commission to appoint a federal advisory committee to study acoustic impacts on marine mammals and make recommendations to them. I am part of the 28-member committee that represents all relevant stakeholders including the Navy, the oil and gas industry, geophysical researchers, scientists, regulatory agencies and environ-mental nongovernmental organizations. Of the 28 places on the committee, six are held by conservation organizations. Our meetings are organized and led by an environmental con-flict resolution team. We hope to have our report to Congress ready in 2005.

We have come a long way since 1998 and there is still much work to do. The increased visibility of this issue is due to the hard and unrelenting work of many environmental or-ganizations and individuals who work together from different angles: the Animal Welfare Institute joined my lawsuit in 1998 and organized the in-water protests in Hawaii; Earth Is-land Institute joined my lawsuit and continues to work on this issue; the NRDC has filed several successful lawsuits and helped write petitions; the Humane Society has worked with Congress and the International Whaling Commission; Seaflow educates people about the is-sue; ASMS–Ocean Care in Switzerland organized the ECSO; and many courageous scientists have voiced their concerns, even though they have been accused of being "unscientific."

Other individuals quietly support the efforts of the frontline people. Earth Island Insti-tute, Seaflow and the Ocean Mammal Institute worked together to develop an International Ocean Noise Coalition website. Organizations from around the world are joining the U.S. groups. We are all working together in an unprecedented, cooperative effort to protect our living oceans. We can always use more help.

Working on this issue for the past seven years has had its ups and downs. As a psy-chologist, I often ask myself why we abuse the environment in the first place. Once we un-derstand what motivates our destructive actions, we can begin the internal work of chang-ing ourselves. Lakota Elder Wallace Black Elk said, "Pollution begins in the mind." I tell my psychology students that they could make an outstanding contribution to the planet if they discovered ways to change our environmentally damaging behavior. The field of ecological psychology is growing and trying to address and transform our relationship with the planet.

The environmental crisis—the plummeting water tables, the extinction of species on a daily basis, the death of forests from acid rain, the chemicals we put in the air and water and the killing of whales with high-intensity sonar—is the result of a constricted, separatist, fear-based world view. Our planetary disassociation is lethal and we are just beginning to see its far-ranging consequences. It is certainly important to stop pollution and the use of danger-ous sonars, but those are band-aid actions. We can sometimes stop one problem, but new problems will always arise and many activists become exhausted.

In addition to working on specific problems, we need to foster an internal change—we must expand our awareness and re-sensitize ourselves by getting our hearts and minds reconnected. Only then will we develop a more compassionate intelligence and make better decisions. We will no longer feel separate from other life forms and the Earth. As a consequence, we will no longer be able to overuse or abuse nature.

If our mind and intellect are cut off from our heart-felt compassion, we can make decisions to start a war, drop a bomb, cut down ancient trees, abuse another person or pollute the planet. We won't feel the consequences of our "reasoned" actions. Nebraska naturalist Dr. Loren Eiseley wrote, "When the human mind exists in the light of reason and no more than reason, we may say with absolute certainty that humans and all that made them will be in that instant gone." Reason must be balanced by feeling and caring.

Our culture encourages us to feel powerful and in control, but the power of nature—both our internal raw emotions and external raw nature—makes us feel out of control and afraid. So, to feel safe, we try to suppress and control both the scary feelings and nature. Internally, we numb ourselves so we don't feel emotions that frighten us; externally, we try to control nature because it makes us feel more in control of our own lives. It's ironic that, in our attempts to control nature in order to feel safe, we have created some of the greatest threats to our survival.

Technologies—such as cloning, creating seeds that won't germinate without special chemicals and the splitting of atoms—are all about controlling nature at the most fundamental levels. It's a self-perpetuating albeit a counterproductive system: as we get more desperate to secure our survival on the planet, we grasp for increased control, which endangers us even more.

To address the root cause of our human and environmental predicaments, we have to commit to reconnecting our emotions with our intellect, and our hearts with our minds, in order to make decisions informed by both knowledge and compassion. We need to develop a reciprocal relationship with nature instead of trying to dominate or control it. Then the energies of nature will support us rather than scare us.

CONTACT
mgreen@alb.edu

SUGGESTED LINKS

http://www.nrdc.org (Natural Resources Defense Council; view litigation issues)

http://www.oceanmammalinst.org (The Ocean Mammal Institute; view petitions for a multinational task force to develop international regulations on ocean noise)

http://www.oceannoisecoalition.org (International Ocean Noise Coalition)

http://www.silentoceans.org (European Coalition for Silent Oceans)

FOOTNOTES START ON PAGE 198.

FRANCES MOORE LAPPÉ

Food and Democracy

> "My daughter and I learned that the heart can grow big enough to hold both the tragedy of this era and hope. From this place, we heal ourselves and the world."

Frances is the author of more than a dozen books and is widely known for her best-seller, Diet for a Small Planet, *which was published more than 30 years ago and has sold over three million copies. She is the cofounder of two national organizations that focus on food and democracy and was the fourth American to receive the Right Livelihood Award (also known as the Alternative Nobel). Her most recent books are* Hope's Edge: the Next Diet for a Small Planet *and* You Have the Power: Choosing Courage in a Culture of Fear.

I have always tried to understand the root of needless suffering. Some of it comes with being human, of course, but so much of it seems avoidable. I have also been intrigued by every aspect of human nature and by trying to grasp "the big picture": how did we get into the mess we're in? Back in the 1970s, I remember saying that the world needed more "professional generalists." Today, so many specialize in narrow fields but are afraid to ask bigger questions out of fear of getting something wrong. One may come up with a right answer if one asks the smallest questions, but that answer may be immaterial and insignificant. I have always tried to ask the bigger questions.

In 1969 (when I was 25 years old), I began asking, "Why is there so much suffering in the world?" I was influenced by the era in which I lived—the birth of the ecology movement and Paul R. Erlich's book *The Population Bomb.* I was a social worker and a community organizer who realized that, even if I were to succeed in what I was doing in my daily work, it would not address the root of the problem. Experts were predicting worldwide famine and arguing that we had reached the earth's limits to feed ourselves. They were touting the use of chemicals and bigger farms to grow more food.

My intuition told me that exploring the roots of hunger would be a pathway, a vehicle of understanding, because food is the most basic need of all. Why hunger in a world of plenty? Through my research, I concluded that the world's population could not only feed itself, but it had more than enough food to go around. More importantly, I began to realize that if we began using the expensive, extractive farming technology being promoted, it might actually make the food crisis worse. I began writing what became *Diet for a Small Planet* in order to share these discoveries.

When I finished the first rendition of *Diet for a Small Planet,* I photocopied it with the idea that I would hand it out as a pamphlet to my friends. The photocopied book got into the hands of publisher Betty Ballantine, who believed that the message had to be heard and published it. During the past 30 years, over three million copies of the book have been sold! I had no idea that it would create my life path.

Much of the information I uncovered during my research was shocking and the future appeared grim. I became very distressed for a period of time. I couldn't imagine bringing children into the world. My attitude changed with my first baby, Anthony—a very wanted child. He and *Diet For a Small Planet* were born the same year (1971)—the biggest year of my life. I loved becoming a mother with its immediate gratification, the feeling of being purposeful and the experience of all-encompassing love—far removed from the intellectual web of historical trends, ideas and movements with which I was familiar. A few years later, I had my second child, Anna. I wanted to be a different kind of mother to my daughter and model a different kind of woman than my mother had modeled for me. I became more motivated than ever to continue my work.

My mother was brilliant and gifted as a writer and thinker. She never had a formal education beyond junior college, but her mind was very alive; however, she was self-effacing and never developed the depth of her talent. On the one hand, I had a wonderful mother who gave me what we all need most: unconditional love; on the other hand, she was unable to express her gifts to the larger world in the way that she could have had she been born in a different era and received more support. I realized how much of her self-effacing personality I had absorbed, and I wanted to overcome those traits so that Anna could see me as a stronger, more self-reliant and effective woman in the world.

Women are now transitioning into their full power, gaining a sense of their personal authority and abandoning the assumption that the other person is always right. My daughter's generation of young women is more evolved than my generation, which is very satisfying.

My husband and I divorced when my children were young, but they remember the shared-custody arrangement. Being a single mother brought me closer to my children and made me even more dedicated to shaping the world so they would have a healthy future.

On the 30th anniversary of *Diet for a Small Planet*, my children sat me down and said, "Our generation needs a sequel to this book and we will help you write it." I was so surprised! Anna was 26 years old at that time, the very age I was when I began *Diet for a Small*

Planet. She and I decided that we would write the sequel together. The timeline for getting the book done was extremely tight (we had one year to travel to five continents, digest all of the information we were collecting and write the book). We met the deadline; in 2002, *Hope's Edge: the Next Diet for a Small Planet* was published.

Traveling and writing *Hope's Edge* with Anna has been one of the biggest blessings of my life. As a team, we went to Berkeley (California), Brazil, India, Banglahcsh, Kenya and France, and found courageous and creative people organizing and taking steps to nurture their natural resources and control the source and quality of their food.

The title *Hope's Edge* was Anna's idea. She told me that she always thought that hope was for wimps and for people who really couldn't come to terms with how bad things are. Now, she and I have come to a very different understanding. We now feel that hope is not something that we seek in evidence by tallying up the negative and the positive. Hope is what emerges within us as we make choices and act.

We found people, many with few options, rising up to gain democratic control over food. In Belo Horizonte, Brazil, we met Adriana Aranha and other city leaders who had been driven by a hunger crisis to make huge changes. They believed that food was a basic human right and that food security meant having enough food to feed oneself and one's family. Belo Horizonte created community and school gardens and set up low-priced fresh produce markets. Dozens of creative city initiatives have had positive effects on the city's residents.

We encountered thousands of women in Nairobi, Kenya, in the Green Belt Movement, which had planted 20 million trees to stop deforestation of their land. They were relearning how to grow traditional crops, which can thrive in that soil and climate. In India, farmers connected to the Research Foundation for Science, Technology and Ecology regained control over their traditional crops, moving away from the use of chemical pesticides and fertilizers and working to keep international corporations from patenting seeds for crops that the farmers have grown for thousands of years.

As with *Diet for a Small Planet*, I discovered that food is personal and universal and directly connects us with the Earth and with each other. Throughout history, food has been an integral part of creating community and human bonds. Food, however, has been commoditized and no longer helps us connect with the natural world. Through our travels, I was reminded that hunger is not caused by a scarcity of food but rather by a scarcity of democracy—by people being cut out of control of their land and their jobs.

Change is underway on every continent. We can choose what we eat and not feel victimized by food corporations. Consciously choosing a diet that is best for us and the Earth has lasting effects throughout our lives and the lives of future generations. After I wrote *Diet for a Small Planet*, many people told me that making the choice to eat a healthy diet gave them the personal power to make enormous changes in the rest of their life.

Fear is often a major obstacle in keeping us from taking necessary action. I recently spoke with a cab driver from Russia and asked him what he thought of the United States. "Everyone is driven by fear. You are all afraid of each other." After the events of September 11, 2001, fear became a dominant emotion here and it continues. Our particular type of market system is based on competitive materialism, which creates fear of losing out; we then impose this cultural value throughout the world.

The only way to counter fear is by acknowledging it and bringing it to the surface. Once we see the fear, then we can creatively work with it. Doing this in a community is vitally important because we are social creatures who find it hard to change alone.

When Anna and I went to Brazil to gather information for *Hope's Edge*, we met with families who had just won the right to land through the Landless Workers Movement (a movement built on a constitutional clause requiring the government to take land that is not serving a social purpose and redistribute it to the landless). Through civil disobedience in which over 1,000 people have lost their lives, a quarter of a million families have now settled on 17 million acres of land. I was inspired by these people who had stood up to land owners and won. Now, many of them—some with only a grade-school education—are successfully building schools and creating cooperative businesses and farms, working to create communities where they can have a choice to grow organic food. In America, we would call such people oppressed; however, against enormous odds, young and old are building a vision that supports a healthy and sustainable future—a great example of what happens when people trust their deeper selves and find courage within the community.

It is natural for humans to want others to eat and corporations are using this natural human empathy to manipulate us. They tell us that genetically modified seeds will prevent world hunger, but research shows that there is currently enough food in the world to make us all overweight.[1] In addition, researchers have found that, by using organic, natural methods, we can increase yields.[2] These findings become a case against risky intervention, such as genetic engineering theories being extolled by corporate food propaganda. We do not have to take these risks with nature in order to grow enough food.

In America, we have been made the guinea pigs for the world and genetic engineering is a symptom of our silencing. Three quarters of the genetically modified seeds planted worldwide are in America, yet we citizens have never been asked if we want our food to be produced in this way.

In France, there was a huge public debate led by the French government about whether genetically modified organisms (GMOs) made sense. The public consensus showed that precautions must be exercised.[3] Most of the world's countries have expressed their opposition to GMOs.[4] The same thing could have happened in the U.S., but it didn't, thus reflecting our lack of democracy.

To feel effective, each of us needs to know that our lives are connected to the bigger planetary challenges. We need to understand why things are the way they are and how our actions affect the whole. During our book tour, we heard people belittle their own efforts, saying, "Oh, I am just a drop in the bucket," but there is nothing wrong with that because drops can fill up a bucket very fast.

Hope's Edge contains stories about courageous people taking major risks to protect their food and farming rights. Each of us can find an entry point to find the larger connection. Look at where you are, who you are and what you love, and you can begin to see this bucket—the larger existing pattern—in order to create change.

Unless we see other people like ourselves rewardingly engaged in solving public problems, we won't believe there is any place for us. We need to hear stories that make us say, "Yes, I want to make a difference. I could do that!" Because our current media diet is so limited, we are unable to get information about important movements that are changing entire communities. If we can't imagine it, how can we create it?

I hope that my children have learned, among other things, to trust themselves and their common sense. When I was writing *Diet for a Small Planet*, all of the experts said that we were running out of food and starvation was inevitable. As a young woman, I put two and two together and said, "no." The book helped others see that human beings, not nature, create hunger.

I love the words by journalist I.F. Stone: "If you expect to see the final results of your work, you have simply not asked a big enough question." If the suffering we see today is a result of hundreds of years of history, then we can't expect to see a complete transformation in our short time on Earth. We must keep asking the questions and passing them on to the next generation.

I was terrified when I began writing *Hope's Edge* and didn't know if I could complete the book. It is natural to feel afraid when embarking on something new. Even though we show up with fear, energies around us change because of our courage. We get the help we need.

When we, as individuals and as a community, choose to leave the pack and challenge the dominant culture, we may feel vulnerable. However, if we act from a deeper sense of self and from our deeper values, we become hope. Hope is not about searching for something outside of ourselves; it is about our inner life. A growing sense of power is another way of talking about hope: we *embody* it rather than *seek* it.

We live in a paradoxical era. The future of the planet is certainly in question as we witness the effects of global warming, species extinction and rising violence; at the same time, people are listening to their deeper needs in order to connect with one another and create real community.

Can we shift away from the destructive tendencies that are bringing down thousands of species? Can we begin to listen to ourselves and, from that place, take the necessary action to heal ourselves, our community and our world? It will depend upon furthering a planetary awakening and consciously choosing our path. We need to challenge today's global materialist ideology and connect with one another, which takes a lot of courage. Courage comes from the French word "coeur," which means "heart."

Courage is demonstrated when a person feels so strongly that they are impelled to take a risk, even though their head doesn't approve. My daughter and I learned that the heart can grow big enough to hold both the tragedy of this era and hope. From this place, we heal ourselves and the world.

CONTACT

frances@smallplanetinstitute.org

SUGGESTED LINKS

http://www.smallplanetfund.org (The Small Planet Fund)

http://www.smallplanetinstitute.org (Small Planet Institute)

http://www.vshiva.net (Research Foundation for Science, Technology and Ecology)

BIBLIOGRAPHY

Lappé, Frances Moore. *Diet for a Small Planet.* New York: Ballantine Books, 1971.

Lappé, Frances Moore and Anna Lappé. *Hope's Edge: The Next Diet for a Small Planet.* New York: Jeremy P. Tarcher, January 2002.

Lappé, Frances Moore and Jeffrey Perkins. *You Have the Power: Choosing Courage in a Culture of Fear.* New York: Jeremy P. Tarcher, May 2004.

FOOTNOTES START ON PAGE 201.

LEUREN MORET

Uncovering the Truth About Depleted Uranium

"Each person has to find their own truth to heal the world.
It is the collective impact that makes the change."

Leuren was born in Camp LeJeune, North Carolina, on March 3, 1945—months before the atomic bombs were dropped on Hiroshima and Nagasaki, bringing an end to World War II and introducing the Nuclear Age. She was one of the first women to graduate in geology from the University of California at Davis in 1968. For the next 10 years, she travelled extensively through Europe, North America and Eurasia, working as a geoscientist.

Leuren worked for Dr. Lewis Leakey on early hominids in Africa; conducted research on expeditions for the British Museum, Kew Gardens and Cambridge University; and periodically lambed 2,000 ewes on a farm in Ireland. After completing her master's degree in Near Eastern studies from the University of California at Berkeley in 1978, she conducted research at the Lawrence Berkeley National Lab on volcanoes, and later worked on the Yucca Mountain project, Waste Isolation Pilot Project in New Mexico and the Superfund project at the Lawrence Livermore National Lab in Livermore, California.

In 1991, Leuren became a whistleblower at Livermore and experienced years of retaliation by the University of California, the Livermore Lab, the Oakland police and local law enforcement. She is working with groups in many countries to establish an international moratorium on the use, manufacture, deployment, storage and sales of depleted uranium (DU) weapons, as well as with communities around the world to inform, educate and empower citizens to protect public health by protecting the health of the environment. Her daughter, Zephyr, is a science major and is as independent as her mother.

I am an independent scientist with a background in the geosciences. My hope and inspiration comes from my work with scientists and radiation specialists worldwide to educate and inform citizens of the world about the health and environmental effects of radiation exposure. In my professional career, I have worked at two nuclear weapons labs: the Lawrence Berkeley National Lab, where the transuranium elements were discovered that built the first atomic weapons; and the Lawrence Livermore National Lab, where nuclear weapons development continues.

After working for two years on the clean-up and disposal of high-level nuclear waste on the Yucca Mountain and Livermore Lab Superfund projects, I realized that something was very wrong. Through my experience, I observed an entrenched pattern of science fraud, theft, graft, corruption, lack of concern for safety and security, blatant discrimination against women and minorities and severe retaliation practices. I drove out of the lab gate one day and never went back. I knew that it would be difficult to survive economically as a single mother of my five-year-old daughter, Zephyr, but also knew that I could not take care of her if I was dead from cancer like so many around me.

I was participating in an industry that I perceived as having an absence of morality and ethics underpinning the misapplication of science and the nuclear weapons project; the apparatus of control and absence of good management; and the sexism and racial discrimination, which had created a completely insane culture dominated by white men. I did not want to remain involved with any aspect of a nuclear weapons lab or the people working there, even if it was to clean up the waste from the project. What species on Earth kills its young, generation after generation? What species on Earth sacrifices its young for the false notion of "security"? What male species kills its young and mates knowingly and repeatedly?

As I approached the gate with my office belongings piled in my car, I felt an incredible lightness of being. I dropped off my badge and beeper and got back in my car, laughing and thinking, "You just got out of jail!" Little did I know what was ahead.

The next 10 years were the darkest of my life and I am lucky to be alive today. My greatest gift was the discovery of my inner strength to be able to survive the retaliation, mobbing and harassment by the Livermore Lab, the University of California and the Oakland police department. Prophetically, an acquaintance coolly said to me a year after I left the lab, "You are in a police net you will never get out of … for the rest of your life." She was right, but I no longer care because now I am not afraid. We are controlled by our fears until we have none left, and that happens when there is nothing left to lose.

The journey to that realization took 12 years of pain, a sense of loss and humiliation, a feeling of abandonment and the lifelong emptiness and absence of being loved—not by anyone, not at any time. The experience and purpose of being mobbed, and what I did not know in the isolation of the experience, is that I was not alone.

"Mobbing" is the purposeful and strategic institutional gathering of all information about an individual by using any method—legal or illegal. Contact for this purpose is made with neighbors, classmates, former partners, family members, former employers, teachers, church members, good friends and even your family tree … everything must be known about the support system around you that makes your life possible.

The assessment of strategic resources and future income (finances, mobility, cars, insurance, credit cards, bank safety deposit boxes, post office boxes, wills, health records, birth certificates, transcripts and photographs) is made without your knowledge. The purpose of mobbing is to drive the target individual out of the job force for the rest of their life; the bigger goal is to drive them to the ultimate self-destruction: suicide. There are now laws made by European unions to prevent this cancer on society and productivity, but it is practically unknown in the U.S.

The University of California, which had contributed so much to the State of California and to the global community through the benefits of education, had become a pathologically dysfunctional institution through its mobbing practices. I learned that more than 500 women and minorities had filed lawsuits against the University of California and had then experienced retaliation by the University of California apparatus of mobbing by employees, alumni and law enforcement.[1]

The lawsuits were for denial of tenure, whistleblower retaliation and theft of intellectual property. These women had similar complaints about the destruction of their own lives and careers. The information gathered by the University of California is used to take your life apart; to destroy all that makes you feel safe; to bankrupt, isolate and alienate you from society and from yourself; and to attempt to make you look crazy. Your children are harassed, they come home with belongings missing and stories of teachers harassing them and a weirdness takes over your lives. Slowly, documents disappeared from my house; porn charges appeared on my credit card; files, my purse and my keys disappeared; mail was lost. I was forced to carry my documents with me at all times. All of my university transcripts and diplomas have been stolen from my house.

Two things kept me going and kept me alive. First, the warrior mother spirit guided me to protect Zephyr. That miracle of life taught me what it means to love unconditionally and completely. I began to learn to love myself. Second, my uncle had told me long ago, "No one can destroy you. Only you can destroy yourself." That information made me fight back. As I fought back, I got stronger, deeper into myself, and slowly left the external validations, which others control, behind and relied more and more on internal validations, which I controlled.

The process during those dark years was horrifying and terrifying; it took me to the edge of my emotions of fear, abandonment, alienation and isolation. In the end, I made the choice to not abandon myself. I knew that those were only feelings and that I could change them or choose different ones, which made me strong and ultimately free. Zephyr is strong and independent from her experience by my side. Perhaps she learned even more than I did.

And let it direct your passion with reason,
that your passion may live through its own daily resurrection,
and like the phoenix rise above its own ashes.
—Khalil Gibran

At the end of the millennium, which gave birth to nuclear weapons, I visited the Peace Museums in Hiroshima and Nagasaki during the 2000 World Conference Against Atomic and Hydrogen Bombs as the guest of Gensuikin (one of Japan's largest antinuclear and peace movement organizations). That visit to Japan changed my life: I finally understood the horrific effects of nuclear weapons.

In 1991, in the first Gulf War, the United States broke a 46-year taboo and introduced DU to the battleground—a radiological weapon that is truly a pernicious weapon of indiscriminate killing and mass destruction.[2] DU is nuclear trash from nuclear weapons and nuclear power projects. I had to ask myself which is worse: the horrific effects of flash annihilation from an atomic bomb or slow, eternal mutilation from DU weapons?

I came back from Japan and wanted to know everything about radiation. A former Manhattan Project scientist, Marion Fulk, who retired from the Livermore nuclear weapons program, had been opposed from the beginning to atmospheric testing. I learned that many scientists in the U.S. and globally, including Andrei Sakharov in Russia, had been united in opposing this insane practice.[3]

Over the past four years, Fulk has taught me everything I know about fallout and the impact on public health and the health of the environment from atmospheric testing. He gave me scientific self-confidence and a knowledge base that was bulletproof when confronting Department of Energy (DOE) and Department of Defense attack dogs who were carefully trained to silence scientists who speak out and tell the truth about radiation. He validated me as a woman as my father never did. He became my teacher, mentor, father, brother and uncle. He changed my life and he changed me. He showed me where the information is and then he showed me how to use it.

I contacted a group of scientists, the Radiation and Public Health Project, who have been collecting baby teeth from children who live around nuclear power plants and identifying the impact on public health from the emissions. I began collecting baby teeth in California and from other countries I visited for their project. The effects of chronic, low-level radiation exposure to populations living near nuclear power plants and facilities were profoundly disturbing to me.

That information and these experiences led me to begin my research on DU. In 2000, I met Akira Tashiro, a Japanese journalist, in Hiroshima, who asked me to write the foreword for his book about DU entitled *Discounted Casualties: The Human Cost of Depleted Uranium.* I began to give talks in small communities, where soldiers are economically drafted, and then for larger events. Soon, I received invitations to travel to other countries and speak.

It seemed as if I were part of a growing global awareness and consciousness that called for a moratorium on DU weapons use, manufacture, testing and deployment. The people I met had a new power and energy based on their spiritual beliefs. They felt that not only was humanity being destroyed by increasing levels of radiation, but it was also a war against the Earth and all life on this planet. I joined a global spiritual army of women warriors and men fighting together.

My first article on DU came out in a small San Francisco newspaper in a mixed minority community. I wanted to write about DU and tell the world about what the U.S. was doing at home and abroad with this horrific weapon. I wrote many articles and that is how I found a voice, *my* voice ... and I found myself.

I discovered something else that was too horrible to imagine. I found proof of the real and deeper purpose for the U.S. using DU weapons beginning in 1991: to deliberately and strategically contaminate entire regions where the world's oil supplies are located. That contamination of permanent, low-level radiation would guarantee the annihilation of populations in those regions who would be chronically exposed.[4] I began to cry the day that bombing started in Afghanistan in 2001. I cried for the mothers, the fathers, the children, the babies, the grandparents and the future generations in Afghanistan who will not be born because of this radioactive poisoning of their genetic future.

In 1943, a then-classified memo was sent to General L.R. Groves from Dr. James B. Conant, Dr. A.H. Compton, and Dr. H.C. Urey (a subcommittee of the S-1 Executive Committee on the "Use of Radioactive Materials as a Military Weapon," working under General Groves on the Manhattan Project).[5] This memo was written on October 30, 1943—nearly two years before the atomic bombs were dropped on Hiroshima and Nagasaki—and was a recommendation that radiological materials be developed for use as a military weapon on the battlefield. It is a blueprint for DU weaponry—dirty bombs, dirty missiles and dirty bullets, which burn and create submicroscopic particles in huge volumes that behave like a radioactive gas.

This memo, now declassified, was given to me by Major Doug Rokke, a physicist and former head of the U.S. Army Depleted Uranium Weapons Project. He is a Gulf War I veteran and is now suffering from DU exposure with severe health effects referred to as Gulf War Syndrome. My work is inspired by the Hibakusha (from a Japanese term for the survivors of the Hiroshima and Nagasaki bombs) around the world who, like Doug, have told me their stories.

It is clear from this memo that the U.S. government and military had known before 1943 that radioactive materials, dispersed as very fine particles on the ground or from the air, would be an effective battlefield weapon. This plan was recommended so that the Germans would not develop similar weapons first from radioactive materials created by the waste from their nuclear weapons development.[6]

In the memo, the scientists recommended dispersing the radioactive materials in very fine particles (0.1 microns in diameter and smaller) from the air, land vehicles or the ground. It would disperse like a radioactive gas—invisible and undetectable to the enemy. They described how increasing the amounts of dispersed radiation would accelerate the lethality, decrease the time until death and increase the numbers of dead.[7]

It was known at that time that it would contaminate the air, water, food and soil. Entry into contaminated environments was impossible without certain exposure both to the enemy and to friendly forces. The memo detailed the fact that no protective methods were possible to develop and that very fine particles would pass through all gas masks.[8]

The memo also described that inhaled particles behave like a gas in the lungs, go directly into the blood and are dispersed throughout the tissues of the body. The gut would also be exposed by ingesting contaminated foods and areas of the gut where the food sat for longer periods would have more radiation exposure and increased damage.[9]

It is clear from this 1943 memo that everything was known about the extreme hazards to health and the environment of radiological materials dispersed in fine particles on the battlefield. The fact that DU burns at high temperatures and forms large numbers of extremely fine particles makes it even more deadly and effective than nearly any other material as a radiological weapon. The half-life of DU is so great (4.5 billion years) that environments where it is used as a weapon will remain radioactive forever.

It is no accident that an international taboo prevented further use of nuclear and radioactive weapons on the battlefield after 1945. The use of DU in Gulf War I was a decision made at the top levels of the U.S. government in order to blur the distinction between conventional and nuclear weapons.[10] Because global opposition to nuclear weapons is strong, the use of DU was used as a strategy to reintroduce the use of nuclear weapons.

Under international law, weapons must pass four tests in order to determine their legality:

1. *Temporal test:* Weapons must not continue to act after the battle is over.
2. *Environmental test:* Weapons must not be unduly harmful to the environment.
3. *Territorial test:* Weapons must not act off of the battlefield.
4. *Humaneness test:* Weapons must not kill or wound inhumanely.

DU weaponry fails all four tests. For that reason, it is illegal under all treaties, all agreements, all war conventions and U.S. military law. It is a weapon of mass destruction by definition under U.S. law.[11]

One military research report summarized the reason why DU was selected by the U.S. Army over other materials, such as tungsten, which are less damaging to the environment: *cost.*[12] Because DU is the trash from nuclear weapons and nuclear power industries, it is a radioactive hazard and a liability to the DOE. The DOE has nearly a million tons of DU to discard. The DOE made the decision to pass the radioactive trash on to the military-industrial complex for the manufacture of weapons. By passing the cost of disposal on to other countries, the U.S. government saves money. In fact, by selling DU weapons to more than 29 other countries, the DOE has made disposal a highly profitable business for the military-industrial complex.[13]

It is impossible for the U.S. government to continue to deny, as they have since Gulf War I, that DU weapons cause no harm or that there are no known health or environmental effects. The 1943 Groves memo and research report summaries of investigations conducted for the military from 1974 to 1999 indicate that the omnicidal (that which affects all life) impact of DU weapons has been known for 60 years.[14]

Learning about DU was a horrible reality from which I could not run. The truth is the truth. Finding a way to communicate this truth, however, and the immense impact that its continued use would have on humanity and life on Earth, was much harder. As I began speaking out, traveling to communities for events and writing articles[15] that came closer to revealing the truth—that the real and hidden purpose of using DU was to achieve geopolitical strategic goals—I came under attack.

I was not alone. Major Doug Rokke, Colonel Asaf Durakovich, Dr. Rosalie Bertell, Dr. Ruth McGill, Canadian Gulf War widow Susan Riordan, and many others who have expressed concerns about the use of DU, have experienced attacks and retaliation. Assassination attempts, break-ins and thefts of critical documents, physical violence, sabotage, guns shot into houses, computer and phone technology attacks, verbal attacks, disinformation and character assassinations are common methods that have been used to thwart and silence us.

The worst thing for me was the kidnapping of Zephyr when she was 13 by her father, with the help of the University of California and Livermore Lab network, assisted by the police and sheriff's departments. I did not see her for five years until she had graduated from high school and came home to "mom." This was the ultimate punishment for a nuclear whistleblower. Compared to that, the other forms of harassment seemed annoying and uncomfortable but bearable—part of the price of opposing government, the nuclear establishment and special interest policies.

My mentor, Marion Fulk, protected me from a credibility attack by showing me where the "official" documents and studies are and how to use them against the very institutions and governmental agencies who had created them. After all, they can't attack their own documents and studies without losing credibility themselves. Other attacks were more personal, such as on e-mail lists and phone calls during radio interviews. Publicly exposing, naming names and posting attacks have been the best responses, where the attackers get attacked by members of the public who provide information and documentation that publicly expose the real intentions of the attack dogs. I just think of the attacks as negative compliments. We must be making an impact if they are responding so viciously to our information in the "court of public opinion."

U.S. government funding for nuclear weapons declined after Gulf War I to the lowest level in decades. From the lowest point in 1995, funding has increased to a level even higher than during the Cold War.[16] The United States has no enemies, yet budget increases continue and nuclear weapons will expand into space in the near future.

Stockpile stewardship of the existing nuclear weapons arsenal is part of the cost, but new and evolving policies are emerging. Enhancing nuclear warhead capabilities are also part of the weapons program. Rebuilding nuclear weapons to improve accuracy, assessing storage capability, altering the ability of warheads to withstand changes in the environment and making modifications as to where, when and how they detonate are also part of existing policy.

"Gold plating the nuclear weapons labs" describes the spending sprees that are a result of large amounts of money pouring into lab budgets. When excessive purchases of instruments and "toys for the boys" exceed what is really needed to conduct competent science, the laboratories become "solutions looking for a problem."

During a meeting in San Francisco where I gave testimony on May 15, 2003, the University of California Board of Regents was informed by National Nuclear Security Administrator Admiral Linton Brooks that the National Labs would be developing nuclear bunker busters. One hour later, he spoke at the Livermore Nuclear Weapons Lab (45 miles away) and informed personnel that they would not only be developing small nuclear bunker busters, but they would be building large nuclear weapons as well!

For 61 years, the University of California has been the manager of the nuclear weapons labs at Los Alamos and Livermore. Dr. Brooks informed the Regents of the University of California at the May 15, 2003 meeting that the management contract will now go up for bid. The University of Texas is perceived to be the favored choice for the new management contract. Is it a coincidence that the Bush family is also from Texas? In November 1991, Richard Berta, the western regional inspector for the DOE at the national nuclear weapons labs, told me, "The nuclear weapons labs exist for the Pentagon and the Pentagon exists for the oil companies."

DU was used in large amounts for the first time on the battlefield during Gulf War I. The use of over 340 tons of DU weaponry in Iraq in Gulf War I has had devastating results over the past decade. The battlefields were far from the cities of southern Iraq, but soldiers and downwind populations could not escape exposure to the invisible war: DU in the wind.

Cancer, birth defects and radiation-related diseases in both Gulf War veterans and Iraqi civilians have increased to alarming levels.[17]

Children born to Gulf War veterans after the war, and children born to civilians living in areas downwind from the battlefields in Iraq, expose the long-term impact of this invisible war. In a Veterans Administration study of 251 Gulf War I veterans, severe birth defects and diseases in 67 percent of the children born after the war were found. They were born without eyes, brains, organs, legs, arms, hands or feet, or they had blood- and other radiation-related diseases.[18] The Iraqi children also have birth defects and a high incidence of leukemia.[19] In the decade after the Gulf War, each month the number of babies born with birth defects and mutations has increased.[20]

Dr. Hari Sharma, an independent researcher, has measured the DU levels in 71 residents of Basra who died after the war was over. He found levels of 150 micrograms of DU per kilogram of tissue throughout their bodies.[21] That would amount to a very high exposure rate, roughly estimated at 10 alpha particles per second throughout the body. (Alpha particles are the most biologically damaging form of radiation.) The radioactive decay products of DU are even more deadly many times over; that is why DU is called the "Trojan horse" of nuclear war: it keeps giving and it keeps killing.

Living in a radioactive environment with chronic exposure to low levels of radiation has a cumulative effect and the entire population in contaminated areas will slowly be destroyed. Genetic defects will be passed on to future generations who will also be exposed to new sources of radiation from contaminated air, water and food. The DU dust will cycle through the environment and be carried in the Earth's atmosphere.[22]

Following the Gulf War, Dr. Doug Rokke was in charge of the DU clean-up team for the U.S. Army. He provided me with documents detailing some of the U.S. Army directives and memorandums regarding DU. Referring to a document dated March 1, 1991, entitled "Los Alamos Memorandum," he said, "I was directed to lie" to cover up the environmental effects of DU weaponry "so that the Army can continue to use it." He told me, "What right do we have to throw thousands of tons of nuclear waste all over any country? [International humanitarian lawyer] Karen Parker considers this to be indiscriminate killing..."

The October 14, 1993 "Somalia Message" is the U.S. Army Medical Care Directive for unusual DU exposures such as "inhalation or ingestion of DU dust or smoke." This directive requires a radiobioassay (the determination of kinds, quantities, concentrations and locations of radioactive material in the human body, whether by direct measurement or by analysis and evaluation of materials excreted or removed from the human body) within 24 hours, nasal swipes and analysis of gas mask filters used by exposed personnel. Hundreds of thousands of U.S. soldiers, Iraqi soldiers and citizens were exposed to "unusual uranium exposures." Dr. Rokke said that nothing was done for anyone.

Under international law of the Hague and Geneva Conventions, after the battle is over, any medical treatment for wounded U.S. soldiers must be provided to wounded enemy soldiers as well. More importantly, any civilians who suffer from war exposures must also receive medical care. If the U.S. provides medical care for its own soldiers and does not treat enemy soldiers and/or civilians equally, it constitutes a war crime.

During the bombings in Kosovo and Bosnia, transboundary contamination by DU was monitored in Hungary and Greece, carried by the winds and eventually incorporated with atmospheric dusts. It is impossible to escape exposure even for populations hundreds and thousands of miles from battlegrounds.

A new study in Germany of Gulf War and Balkans War veterans found significant amounts of chromosome damage in these veterans, which was characteristic of exposure to ionizing radiation and high linear energy transfer particles (alpha particles).[23]

In the 2001 U.S. military invasion of Afghanistan, estimates of more than 1,000 tons of DU weapons were used—nearly three times as much as in Gulf War I.[24] The impact on the wildlife in Afghanistan has been devastating. Not only is the environment contaminated with DU, but the Afghanis have been forced to hunt rare and endangered species in order to eat the meat and sell the skins for money. The devastating effects of DU will occur in all species in contaminated areas. The impact on the animals in the Iraq region was also devastating, yet there was very little reporting on it.

The bombing of Afghanistan by U.S. military forces demonstrates the deliberate use of illegal weapons such as bunker busters, cluster bombs and other DU weapons systems to precision-target civilian populations, water supplies and infrastructure.[25] Afghanistan is a poverty-stricken, underdeveloped country that poses no threat to the United States or to any other country.

In the spring of 2002, an unauthorized, leaked, 7.5-minute video[26] permeated the Internet, showing the destruction from an AC-130 Spectre gunship—a C-130 cargo plane that carries a lot of fire power protruding from the left side—on a combat mission in Afghanistan. In the video, the plane circles a ground target counterclockwise and annihilates it. In the radio traffic from the AC-130 plane, the crew is engaged in combat from a safe distance and without any threat or resistance from the human targets on the ground. The video shows people leaving a mosque and running for their lives as they are fired upon. The AC-130 continues circling and firing on individual Afghanis below. The crew sounds like rednecks picking off varmints on a Texas ranch: "Yeah, I was trying to lead that guy ... he was hiding behind that bank ... he's down, he's still moving ... I saw him fly into pieces ..."

As I watched the video, I was in a state of disbelief followed by extreme sadness for the plight of the Afghanis who, until 2001, had never been conquered or defeated in their long history of thousands of years in the Himalayas. The American gunnery crew shooting the weapons were detached from humanity, the meaning of life, their own military law and international war conventions.

How could the "enemy"—the Afghanis below—respond to the invisible enemy high above? They had no aircraft or military weapons like the U.S. military and no satellite system to direct this unfair war. I began to realize and understand that this was not a war *in* the Third World ... this was a war *against* the Third World. It was a complete annihilation and destruction of the Afghanistan infrastructure, the Afghanis and their genetic future through the use of weapons of mass destruction (WMD)—illegal under the U.S. government's own definition of WMDs.[27] I was completely disgusted and wondered if my father, grandfather, uncles and cousins, who had served in the military, had done the same thing.

DU is a war against the Earth, all life and all living things. DU weapons keep giving and keep killing ... *forever*. There is no way to turn them off or clean them up. DU is the ultimate rejection of life—the gift from the universe for our tiny planet. People do not understand or realize the global impact of DU and other radioactive weapons. The radioactive fallout from these weapons is pernicious, unpredictable and global. There is nowhere on Earth that will escape some form or level of contamination.[28]

Dr. Chris Busby's comments in a recent article posted on a Toronto website sums up the global impact that radiation has had from nuclear weapons testing and nuclear power plants. DU weapons use is adding to the radiation burden, which is the cause of the global cancer epidemic now on the increase. Dr. Busby says, "If you think cancer is a problem now, wait until more DU is released into the world."[29]

The use of DU weapons is a crime against humanity, a crime against all species and a war against the Earth. It is imperative that we demand a permanent international moratorium on the manufacture, storage, deployment, use and sale of DU weaponry. The U.S. has sold it to 29 countries. The message, and maps of contaminated regions from the extensive research I have been doing, are profoundly shocking when they are presented. I think, in the end, people will realize that the truth is being told. As they slowly accept that what I am saying is the truth, they become angry; that anger, once it surfaces, can be used as positive energy to keep us alive. Redirecting the energy from that anger is powerful and liberating. It turns depression, which is anger turned inward, to action. That is what sets us free.

I now have a clear conscience and the satisfaction of acting as a citizen scientist instead of a prostitute for the military or for corporations. I have hope for the future. I know that the people of the world are the only ones who can stop the insanity of nuclear proliferation and radioactive contamination of the environment, which supports all life. With good information, the citizens of the world can make good decisions.

My purpose now, along with other independent radiation specialists who have joined together as the World Committee on Radiation Risk, is to provide good information about the health and environmental effects of radiation to the global community.

Many people have asked me how I could talk about such a difficult and horrifying subject. My answer is that *there is no choice*. For whatever reason, I believe that some power greater than I know has chosen me to be the messenger—one of many messengers—to bring the truth forward into the court of public opinion.

Our planet is being poisoned by the very people and the very entities where I have worked. I have been in their house; I have worked in their dark halls and laboratories. There are more and more of us—insiders who are speaking against ongoing events that will ultimately destroy our environment and ultimately all life.

I am a woman warrior, a warrior mother for all life on Earth. Words are my weapons. I kill with those words and speak the truth for the citizens of the world who have no voice. I am happy now. I feel good and fulfilled—a satisfaction I never had working in mainstream science.

There is a new global spiritual energy, and hope, bringing humanity together and opposing this death knell. In the very darkest hours, when many have thought that all hope is lost, indications are coming forward that there is hope. In April 2004, Spain voted the fascists out because they had sent troops to Iraq when the Spanish electorate had overwhelmingly opposed it.[30] A few days later, Malaysia voted out the fascists who had been in power since Malaysia gained its independence from Britain in the early 1990s.[31] In South Korea, liberals and progressives won overwhelmingly and unexpectedly and are in favor of reunification with North Korea.[32] This is the last thing the U.S. government wanted to happen. Now, encouraged by these small voices in the global dialogue, bigger steps are being taken to remove troops and support for the U.S. policies being carried out in Iraq and other parts of the Islamic world.

I am always inspired by the words of Rev. Martin Luther King, Jr.: "Our scientific power has outrun our spiritual power. We have guided missiles and misguided men." I am just one scientist, but I know that if I step forward and tell the truth as courageous people have always stepped forward and told the truth, others will follow. As Gandhi said, "Even a small lamp dispels the darkness."

CONTACT

leurenmoret@yahoo.com

SUGGESTED LINKS

http://www.mindfully.org (select "Nuclear")

http://www.radiation.org (Radiation and Public Health Project; Nuclear Power Plants and the Tooth Fairy Project/Child Cancer Tooth Project)

http://www.traprockpeace.org (Traprock Peace Center)

http://www.uraniumweaponsconference.de (World Uranium Weapons Conference, Depleted Uranium and other Uranium Weapons: Trojan Horse of a Nuclear War—An International Educational/Organizing Conference, October 16–19, 2003)

http://www.wage.org (We Advocate Gender Equity, University of California)

FOOTNOTES START ON PAGE 201.

SARAH JAMES

Saving the Arctic National Wildlife Refuge

"In order to make change happen, we only need to look down and see that we are standing on the same ground."

A member of the Gwich'in Nation from the Arctic Village, Alaska (on the southern border of the Arctic National Wildlife Refuge), Sarah is a leading voice in the struggle to protect the Arctic National Wildlife Refuge from oil development and defend the rights of her people. Her tireless advocacy work has enabled the voice of the Gwich'in people to be heard around the world.

Sarah is the president of the Native Conservancy. She has sat on the board of the International Indian Treaty Council since 1989, the Gwich'in Steering Committee and the Alaska Action Center. She is special advisor to the Yukon River Intertribal Watershed Council.

As a result of her courageous work, Sarah has been granted numerous awards, including the Alston/Bannerman Fellowship Award, the National Conservancy Trust Fund Award and the Goldman Environmental Prize and the Ford Foundation Leaders for a Changing World Awards.

I am one of the messengers chosen to speak the truth and tell the story of the Gwich'in people. We are also known as one of the "Caribou People" of Alaska. The Arctic Village is located 110 miles northeast of the Arctic Circle—one of the most isolated places and the most northern Indian village in the United States. There is no running water and no road to the Arctic Village; the only way to get there easily is by air. The Gwich'in live in 15 different villages in the northwestern territory, Mackenzie Delta, north of the Yukon Territory (in Canada) and northeast Alaska.

We are long-distance people living in semi-desert conditions inland from the sea. Everyone needs to know how to survive because we live in a very harsh environment. The land is very important to us and, in order for the land to take care of us, we need to take care of it. This is practiced from the time we are born to the time we die. I have been told since I was small to be aware of the environment around me. We live on the edge where any change could be critical to our survival. I was taught that we should always watch out for anything unusual about the sun, the sky or the environment because, if they are not healthy, they could kill us.

Seventy-five percent of our diet comes from wild meat; most of it comes from the porcupine caribou, which migrate thousands of miles each year. When April comes around, they head up north to the coastal plain of the Arctic National Wildlife Refuge, which is 75 miles from my village, to have their calves. When my people were nomadic, we never went to that place because we considered it to be sacred; it has been that way for thousands of years. If the caribou calving grounds are harmed, it would bring an end to the Gwich'in way of life.

The Arctic National Wildlife Refuge, often called the "American Serengeti," is one of North America's last great wilderness areas. It is a rich land, full of some of the most pristine ecosystems on Earth and home to more than 180 bird species and 36 species of freshwater fish and mammals, including polar bears, wolverines, moose and Dall sheep. Rare birds and ducks fly in from all over the world to nest. Polar bears raise their young on the coastal plain; in the foothills south of the coastal plain, the grizzly bears, wolves and other animals raise their young. This is why we call it a sacred birthplace. It's a special time for these animals to be safe and comfortable while the young are nursing. We say, "Gwandaii goodlit gwidehk'it, gwiyin jih rihil'ee," which means "the sacred place where life begins."

Technology and development are not safe for a birthplace. In 1988, the U.S. government proposed the concept of oil drilling in the Arctic National Wildlife Refuge, which was already designated as a refuge. The area slated to be drilled—the biological heart of the entire 19 million-acre refuge—is 1.5 million acres.

The U.S. government set aside the coastal plain and left it up to Congress to either close it to or open it up for oil development. Just as the legendary buffalo herds were vital to Plains Indians, the caribou are the food, language, stories, dances and songs of the Gwich'in Nation. Any industrial development would interrupt the life cycle of the porcupine caribou, which has been the foundation of Gwich'in culture and subsistence for 20,000 years.

Global warming has already disturbed the ecosystems of the refuge. The permafrost on the tundra is showing signs of melting, which affects food supply and migration patterns of Arctic wildlife, including the caribou. Scientists estimate that 200 days of oil may lie under the refuge; even 100 years of oil wouldn't be worth it.

Some of the village leaders asked the elders what we should do. "We need to come back together like we were before the contact with the non-Gwich'in." The last time the elders had come together like that was approximately 150 years ago. Since then, tribes had been kept separate throughout Alaska, the U.S. and Canada by borders that the non-Indians created and we were colonized.

We came back together and the elders took over the meeting. They threw away the written agenda and said, "This is not what we had then and this is not how we are going to operate now." They chose four subjects to talk about: protecting the porcupine caribou herd;

protecting the Gwich'in way of life as it relates to drug and alcohol problems, which exist in almost every Indian Nation; keeping our language; and addressing the boundary problem between other Indian Nations. Only one Native American Indian media group was allowed to cover the gatherings.

The elders brought out a wooden talking stick. "This is what we are going to use to talk and there will be no written notes." We had to speak our native language and 15 chiefs from 15 villages were there. It was like the rebirth of a nation. The chiefs said, "We are making history. It is important that this is happening. The only way the outside world will hear about us is through the black and white, the printed word." Until 1988, no one really knew about the Gwich'in people. We were the last people to be contacted by the so-called Columbus discovery.

The leaders went on top of a hill, created a resolution—to protect the porcupine caribou calving ground and the Gwich'in way of life—and convinced the elders to pass it. The elders decided that, in order for the resolution to work, they had to choose people to go out, speak to the world and tell our story. It was hard for the elders to make this decision because they knew that our tribe would become known throughout the world and others would want to come to our village, which would pose yet another threat to our way of life. They chose four people from Canada and four from the U.S. to represent the resolution. I was one of them.

I felt that it was and forever will be my responsibility to protect the land and my people because I grew up that way. I address environmental groups, churches and university students all over the United States. I have spoken to the U.S. Congress and have met with influential people such as Jimmy Carter, Hillary Clinton and Robert Redford.

When fur trappers first came to our village over 100 years ago, they would shoot the caribou (or any other meat used for bait), skin them and lace the meat with liquid strychnine. Bears and wolves would eat the bait and be poisoned and die. Then the trappers would skin the most valuable pelts. Any meat-eating animal was affected by this, including ravens, blue jays, black-headed chickadees and weasels. Birds that landed on the carcass of the bait to eat the meat would die; anything that ate the birds would die, too. The entire food chain was gravely affected and the health of the ecosystem has never recovered.

Before the trappers came to our village, we were very well organized and many of us could survive off the land. Until then, there were 100,000 of my people; today, there are less than 7,000. We used very little to survive because we were a long-distance, nomadic people. We covered a huge area, so we didn't use up the Earth's resources. Every spring, when the ducks and birds would come in from the south to mate, it was so noisy that people had to stand right next to each other and yell to hear! During the time of the trappers, the bird population was cut in half and it has never recovered.

The non-Indians came to our land for whales, seals, gold and other natural resources and destroyed the ecosystem and the way of life for many native people. Our people are now dying of cancer, heart disease and drug- and alcohol-related deaths—not of old age.

In 2002, after George W. Bush was selected as president, he pushed hard to start oil drilling in the Arctic National Wildlife Refuge. The young people said, "We are willing to put our bodies on the line to stop the oil drilling!" We said we could not do that because the elders told us to do it in a good way. We knew that if someone got hurt or killed, the Gwich'ins would be blamed.

We realized that we should have a demonstration inside our isolated village so we could control it. In June 2002, we called an emergency gathering of the young people to hold a demonstration in the Arctic Village. Luckily, things got better for us because Senator James Jeffords changed his political party, which gave us a lot of support, and the demonstration turned into a celebration.

At that time, the young people said, "We are not going to let this issue go. We are going to stick with it throughout our life." At the same time, they had a ceremony dedicating their lives and future to solar power. They put up solar power panels over the washateria (the only place in the village that has running water, besides the school).

The opposition often implies that Alaska natives want to see oil drilling, but that it is not true. Forty-three villages in the interior have signed on with us against oil drilling and development. We have a support letter from over 200 tribes throughout Alaska. Since 1989, we have a continuous signed resolution with the National Congress of American Indians, which is like a channel for all of the tribes throughout the Nation to have a voice within the U.S. Congress.

This issue affects the entire country because the Arctic National Wildlife Refuge is Public Interest Land. When Gwich'in took the position against the drilling, they were supported by environmental groups. These environmental groups formed the Alaska Coalition, which is now made up of 400 U.S. organizations. Environmentalists have the right to speak on behalf of Public Interest Lands. Gwich'in in the Arctic National Wildlife Refuge see the issue as human rights versus corporate giants for oil.

The opposition also implies that caribou like the oil pipeline because they rub against it and increase in number. This is true of the 40,000 Central Arctic caribou herd, which has the big, open coastal plain that the porcupine caribou do not have. The Central Arctic caribou are less wild and their meat and fur are inferior to the porcupine caribou. Prudhoe Bay used to be the calving grounds of the Central Arctic caribou, but now they stay by the pipeline because it's warm; the oil companies have clear cut trees and planted grass on either side of the pipeline. The open country relieves the Central Arctic caribou from mosquitoes and gives them a clear path to run from predators.

Many of these predators, such as grizzly bears and wolves, have been killed by the trucks driving on the highways built by the oil companies and shot by those who live in the oil development camps. Because they aren't being pursued by predators, the Central Arctic caribou population has increased. Years ago, during a starvation period, reindeer were introduced to the Central Arctic caribou herd, so there are wild and domestic animals living together. For all these reasons, the Central Arctic caribou herd is very different than the porcupine caribou.

The porcupine caribou come through Gwich'in country, migrating thousands of miles every year and making them much healthier and bigger. You rarely see a Central Arctic caribou where Gwich'in live unless it is starving and looking for food. There are 130,000 porcupine caribou, which are sacred to Gwich'in like the buffalo were to the Plains Indians. We have porcupine caribou dances and depend on them for tools and clothing. If it weren't for the porcupine caribou, Gwich'in wouldn't have survived western contact.

Many small children were taken away from their tribes and adopted by non-Indian people or put into boarding schools. When I was put into a boarding school at the age of

13, I had to learn English and live the way of the non-Indian. I saw a lot of greed and waste and learned that I will never again live the way of the non-Indian. Today, many young people are choosing to stay in the village in the way of life that is familiar and natural to them.

We have our knowledge and wisdom, which cannot be taken away from us. When we were faced with the crisis of oil development, my people did not have to follow the system and the law that the non-Indians put upon them after the contact. Instead, we gathered together like we did 150 years ago, but this time to reclaim our ways and make a decision against gas and oil development on our land. We remain committed to this fight. The wisdom we have as a people will keep coming back through dreams and visions and through the exercise of tribal power.

We know that we are the Earth and the Earth is us. We were born with this knowledge and we will die with this knowledge. We don't call the Earth our mother because we know that we *are* the Earth. There is no separation. We don't see ourselves special in any way. We only see that protecting the Earth is our responsibility. We are trying to use the good tools from the western world and use our way of life at the same time. This is difficult but necessary.

Growing up, I learned to respect my neighbors. I use this approach when I speak to many different kinds of people throughout the country. I reach out to grass-roots organizations because we have little money backing us and we are up against multinational corporations. These organizations contact congressional people and create a community of support by making phone calls from their living rooms. We have been doing it in a good way and it has been successful because there has been no drilling in the Arctic National Wildlife Refuge thus far.

I now understand that women need to go out and speak on behalf of the Arctic National Wildlife Refuge because they can relate to nursing and birthing grounds of the caribou and of the Gwich'in people. This year, with the Treaty Council board meeting, I motioned that we address this as a women's issue and that more women should get involved with protecting the refuge. If women take a strong position, it might make a difference. Men should also have a voice about a birthplace because they were also born.

If the U.S. government condones gas and oil development on the refuge, it becomes a human rights issue. The Creator put us there to take care of that part of the world. We are going to stay and we are not going away. We know that the right thing to do is to stand up and speak out against the desecration of the environment. *This is our only chance.*

When my tribe holds the talking stick, we are speaking for the Earth. When I speak in front of Congress and other groups, I speak for those things that cannot speak for themselves. In western culture, "you" means an individual, separate from others. Gwich'in people see that we are not only connected to the Earth but to the entire universe. Everything that takes place in the universe is one whole body.

My vision for the future is that someday we will have clean air, clean water and clean land, and have the life we used to live as Gwich'in people. We will not have peace unless we clean up our act and clean up the Earth. We need to work together, using the right tools to make a change. It is so important to find the common ground of all people.

Some people think that we can't do this because we come from different cultures. In order to make change happen, we only need to look down and see that we are standing on the same ground. We drink the same water and breathe the same air. We all have children and we want them to survive in a healthy and just world.

The Gwich'in word "nan" means "you." It also means land, Earth and backbone. Our backbone is the backbone of life. To all my relations ... "sha lak naii."

CONTACT

sarahjamesav@hotmail.com

SUGGESTED LINKS

http://www.alaskacoalition.org (Alaska Coalition)

http://www.sacredland.org (Sacred Land Film Project)

SARITA CHAWLA

Organizational Learning

"Change in our world will happen with both the individual and the collective; in order to understand the collective, we must understand the individuals who make up the whole."

Sarita is cofounder of Demeter Matrix Alliance and president of MetaLens, which is dedicated to integral coaching, dialogue, organizational learning and diversity. She focuses on developing coaches individually as well as by leading year-long, intensive professional coaching courses with New Ventures West, using the New Ventures West coaching methodology.

Sarita has a master's degree in social anthropology. She has served as a council member for the Society of Organizational Learning, founded by Peter Senge and is a member of the advisory board of Frijoff Capra's Elmwood Institute. She is coeditor of the book, Learning Organizations: Developing Cultures for Tomorrow's Workplace (Corporate Leadership) *and coexecutive producer of the documentary,* BeComing: Women's Circles, Women's Lives. *This video offers a rare opportunity for viewers to experience what transpires in the privacy of women's circles.*

India and Pakistan were partitioned in 1947, the year I was born; the majority of the Muslims went to Pakistan and the majority of the Hindus went to India. My grandparents left all of their land and possessions behind and had to move to India because it was not safe to live in Pakistan as Hindus.

When I was four years old, my father decided to study for the world's most prestigious surgeon's examination and become a Fellow of the Royal College of Surgeons in England. He had a good job as a doctor but did not have enough money to take his wife and child to

England and go to school. However, in his tenacious way, he was able to manifest his dreams, and my mother and I went to England with him for four years.

One of my father's theories of life was, "Don't spend too much time thinking about something; otherwise, your dreams will just remain a fantasy." He did not worry about what it would take to make something happen. Instead, he would say, "We're going to make it work." I learned about making a way out of no way by watching my father. During times when I had nothing, I made it work. This resulted in a resilience for which I am most grateful.

My first marriage was both a disaster (because it was not meant to be) and a gift (because I have a wonderful son from this union). When I was 22 years old, after I received a master's degree in social anthropology, my parents arranged for me to marry a man in the United States—a normal plan in our culture. He came from a good family but the marriage was not a good fit.

I moved to the San Francisco Bay Area and stayed married for eight years because I thought that was what I was supposed to do. When I first moved to the U.S., I dreamt of going to the University of California at Berkeley and getting a Ph.D. in anthropology. When I got my master's degree, I received the gold medal for being the top student that year. A passion for learning had been ignited.

My husband would have nothing to do with my dream, so I let go of it. Money was extremely tight and, to complicate matters, my husband was sending money to India for his family. My F-2 visa (for the wife of a student who had a work permit) did not allow me to work officially for a year. To earn some money, I baby-sat, cleaned other people's houses and became an Avon lady! This was very hard for me because, with my family status back in India, only servants did that type of work, but I did it anyway.

I had an unplanned pregnancy. My husband told me to have an abortion. As a dutiful Indian wife, I went to the clinic and the doctor asked me how I felt about doing it.

"I feel like I'm killing my child."

The doctor said, "Then we cannot do this."

In that moment, I decided that I was going to keep my baby. I called my parents in India and asked them if they would take care of my child for a couple of years because my husband was continuing his education and we were having a difficult time. They agreed. After my son Rahul was born, my husband and I found that we were able to function as a family and Rahul stayed with us.

The marriage continued to be rocky. By the time Rahul was six years old, I made the decision to ask for a divorce. My husband was furious and said he wanted alimony because he was going to college and I was the one who was working. After a much contested divorce, he did not get alimony but we did end up with joint custody of Rahul. Everything had been legally settled, but underneath I felt that something horrible could still happen.

My ex-husband then took Rahul and ran away with him. I had a fear that he would do this because he had threatened to do so earlier. He wanted to show me that he could run away with him (my version of the story). I was terribly afraid for my son's life because I wasn't sure what my ex-husband would do in a moment of anger.

I knew that I would find my son and get him back. Weeks later, I found out by accident that he was in Canada. I called the Federal Bureau of Investigation (FBI), who were already on the case. My father and I immediately took a plane to Vancouver. The Royal Canadian police and the FBI had all gathered but missed them by about 10 minutes. What I didn't know at the time is that my ex-husband had just boarded a plane to India. When I found this out, I went to India and stayed with my parents, continuing the search.

In court, the judge issued a habeas corpus, which gives a mandate to produce the "person" alive or dead—in this case, my son. A few days later, the police located the place where my ex-husband was living and took Rahul in the middle of the night. Through a court order, I had to show up with Rahul every day in court until the matter was settled—a few months from the time my ex-husband ran away with him until the settlement. Finally, Rahul was awarded to me and I went back to the U.S. My ex-husband was allowed to see him but only under supervision until Rahul was old enough and could take care of himself.

When Rahul and I went back to the U.S., my parents came to help us get started again. It was clear that I was welcome to come back to India, but I wanted to take care of my child myself and not go back into the Indian culture as a divorced woman. My parents asked if I was going to remarry, but at that point I was not ready nor did I ever want to get married again. Their support of my decision made all the difference and gave me the strength I needed to be a single mother.

Years later, I realized how difficult it was to be the "mom at home" and support my son's extracurricular activities in addition to saving enough money to send him to college. When I was raising him, I thought of the future and asked myself, "How am I going to do all of this? What is best for my son?" I did not want to become emotionally dependent and live my life through him; I wanted him to have his own life.

I sent Rahul to an Indian boarding school. Initially, he stayed with my parents so he could understand the culture and learn the language. His education was in English but he also needed to know Hindi. After staying with his grandparents, he went to boarding school for five years. He spent the summers with me in the U.S. and then I would spend a month with him during the winter in India. The first year in India was very hard because the children in school would make fun of his American accent. I told him that, for the first six months, he would want to come back because it was going to be a tough transition. I asked him to try it out and, if it did not work, we would think of another plan.

When Rahul went off to boarding school, I felt extraordinarily empty, so I became totally absorbed in my job at Pacific Bell. When I started, I worked as an operator and very quickly moved up the ranks by becoming a supervisor and then a director. I still wasn't interested in getting married because I wasn't ready to trust another man.

Meanwhile, Rahul was thriving in his new environment, becoming an excellent student with a 4.0 grade average and learning to stand in both cultures. He returned for the last two years of school and went to college here. He now works very successfully in the financial arena and still has a spiritual foundation that was richly cultivated during his time in India.

After my son returned to the U.S., I went through a major depression. I had worked so hard at wanting to become "someone." I kept asking, "Am I there yet?" I had worked for Pacific Bell for 21 years and realized that I had sold my soul to the corporation. I was suicidal but didn't know it. I was in the hospital for 10 days, which ended up being the best thing that ever happened to me!

While I was in the hospital, I received a call from a man named Ken with whom I had worked at Pacific Bell. His wife had recently died of cancer and I had supported him through the tremendous grief he experienced around his wife's death. After leaving the company, Ken called me at work and my brother answered the phone. (I had forwarded the calls to my home.) He recognized Ken's name but didn't know that I was no longer working with him. He told Ken that I was in the hospital. The next thing I knew, Ken showed up to visit me *every day*. He became an extraordinary friend, supporting me in coming out of my depression.

Our friendship deepened and developed and we started to date. On one of our dates, he asked me to marry him. The first words out of my mouth were, "Are you *crazy*? Marry a white guy?" At that point, I was not ready, so Ken started dating someone else.

Some time later, I was talking to a close friend. "The truth is that I really do love him."

"Are you going to tell him?"

"No way," I replied. "It's too late."

"Are you going to tell him so he can make a decision?"

I thought about it and called Ken. Being a reflective person, he said that he needed to think about it and would call me back. Three days later, he told me that it was not too late and that he wanted a relationship with me.

"The problem," I said, "is that I'm not sure we could live together for nine days."

He said, "Let's find out!"

We went to Mexico for nine days, had a wonderful time and got engaged shortly after. Now, every nine days, we celebrate by giving each other a card or flower or by going out to dinner. It has become such a sweet practice. We will soon celebrate our 500th nine days! He is my friend, my soul mate and my learning partner, and we love playing and working together.

Earlier last year, when Ken was diagnosed with prostate cancer, I thought my world would be blown away and I was terrified. He is totally cancer free now and I have learned so much about relationships from this experience. A person's deepest need is to be seen, supported and loved; when we are, we want to serve.

Ken and I started MetaLens, a company dedicated to the learning and development of individuals and organizations. We did some work together in coaching, organizational learning and dialogue. I have now embraced my coaching work in a more fundamental way because that is where my passion lies and where I do my best work. It is my vocation. I am leading year-long programs for a company called New Ventures West, which works very deeply and closely in developing coaches; I also have a private practice and do consulting work.

Coaching uses a developmental methodology that supports working on both yourself and others in a systematic and integrated way. I do integral coaching by working with the whole person—their inner and outer world, the environment in which they live and the community of which they are a part. I work with forms of reality that include body, mind, emotions and spirit. These forms are not based on what someone wants to accomplish; they are based on what is next in their development.

I came into coaching with my anthropology background, the experience of motherhood and tenure in the corporate world. There are many streams of development including cognitive, emotional, somatic, relational and spiritual. My task is to help integrate these facets of each person. First, I need to deeply understand the person and provide distinctions and practices to develop their vision. It is not so much about reaching a goal as it is about the skills and competencies someone needs to develop.

In order for me to coach effectively, I need to ponder three questions: What is a human being? What does it take to develop a human being? What is my own theory of change? Based on those questions, I take their current vision and coach them to increase competency, observe where they are and provide practices that will help them become more skilled and developed. The practices are intended to take insight and understanding to an integrated, sustained change.

What work is worth doing and how would I know? What work is not worth doing and how would I know that? These questions helped me sort through what is at the core of who I want to be and what I want to contribute to the world. They allowed me to be in my vocation rather than in my work. Now, one of the ways I talk about myself is that I live in "vocation land."

What is life asking of me? This question is less about me and more about the system and my part in it. I have a deep sense of knowing that we are all connected; what shows up as anxiety is actually the sense of separation that we feel in the world. This is why my work goes beyond the individual.

When I am leading a coaching class, I'm sensing not only what is going on with the individual but what is going on within the entire group. When I work with one person, I come to understand the impact that the person has on an entire group. Understanding and sensing the system becomes paramount to creating change and helping a company or a group of people move towards development.

There is a need for this type of work on a larger level (for example, with our government, with corporations and in countries that are suffering through great conflict). Change in our world will happen with both the individual and the collective; in order to understand the collective, we must understand the individuals who make up the whole.

What is my place in all of this and what are my responsibilities? Why did I come through this manifestation in this life and how can I be conscious of it so I don't get drowned in the sadness of the current world situation? How does one refrain from becoming cynical? I am continually looking for ways to stay balanced, healthy and fulfilled; to keep me growing in my own development; and to be able to help others.

The word "warrior" is about making a way out of no way. The word "mother" is about loving unconditionally and always being a kind of womb that nourishes and is simultaneously compassionate and rigorous. Being a warrior mother is that unconditional dance of both.

My father died in my arms last year. Being a warrior mother means taking on the mantle of responsibility from our elders and stepping into elderhood. We continue to ask questions and remember that mothering and all of our work is a sacred responsibility.

CONTACT

Metalens@aol.com

SUGGESTED LINKS

http://demetermatrix.com (Demeter Matrix Alliance, Inc.)

http://www.newventureswest.com (New Ventures West)

BIBLIOGRAPHY

Chawla, Sarita, coexecutive producer. *BeComing: Women's Circles, Women's Lives.* Videotape available through the Women's Circles, Women's Lives website (http://www.becoming-womenscircles. com/order.html).

Chawla, Sarita and John Renesch, coeditor. *Learning Organizations: Developing Cultures for Tomorrow's Workplace (Corporate Leadership).* Portland, OR: Productivity Press Inc., September 1, 1995.

JODIE EVANS

Giving a Voice to the Powerless

"To make a change, just get up and *do it!*"

Jodie has been a community, social and political organizer for the last 30 years. She has used her skills to protect the Earth, give voice to communities and to people who are unheard and unseen, safeguard human and civil rights, protect the rights of women, raise the minimum wage for farm workers, protect dolphins, work in El Salvador in the early '80s and assist the Zapatista rebels in Chiapas, Mexico, since 1994.

Jodie has led three all-women delegations to Iraq, specifically to research how women and children are fairing under the U.S. occupation. In April 2002, she wrote a mission statement for Bad Babes and their buddies—an organization that educates, inspires and activates women of independent means and their friends to take responsibility for the power they have in the economy of the U.S. and the world—and took it to a gathering, which she helped organize and which became UnReasonable Women for the Earth. Since September 2002, her life has been consumed with CODEPINK: Women for Peace. In 2004, she published the book, Twilight of Empire: Responses to Occupation.*

My activism is constantly in motion. I witness an injustice or hear a call for help and I am moved, literally. Much of my activism involves nurturing and encouraging other activists; I am more attached to the idea that someone is moved to be their own activist than to join my issue.

The seeds of my activism were present from the time I was very young. My parents got together as teenagers and, because of extenuating circumstances, I lived with my grandmother at the beginning of my life. My grandfather sexually abused me; when I was two years old, I hid for an entire day so he couldn't find me.

When I was four years old, my mother married a Mormon. Adopting Mormon beliefs, she decided that my grandmother (who smoked) was the devil, so she kidnapped me and we moved to a Colorado Air Force academy. I was often told that I was bad and possessed by the devil; physical abuse was used. To escape, I would spend time walking on the fire trails behind the house because nature made me feel safe and I wanted to be surrounded by beauty.

At 12 years old, I fled the abuse and travelled 35 miles through the snow over pastures, mountains and barbed-wire fences. By the end of the day, I arrived at the nearest city—Colorado Springs—where I was arrested by the military police, who then took me to a mental ward. I convinced the psychiatrists that I should go back to Las Vegas (my birthplace) and live with my father, who I hadn't seen since I was a small child.

My father said that I could stay with him if I paid my own way. I worked odd jobs and learned what it meant to be "working class." My father held extreme right-wing views, especially about blacks, poverty, the death penalty and the Vietnam War. We constantly fought at the dinner table and, although these arguments made life difficult at the time, they gave me an inner strength and helped me find my own voice. It was the beginning of my becoming a full-fledged activist.

When I was 14 years old, a friend who lived down the street died a couple of months into his Vietnam tour and my stepfather was shot down in Vietnam. These experiences were very close and very real for me and I became involved in the Vietnam antiwar movement. As part of a community of passionate and intelligent activists, I found a place that I could call home. I realized that, through activism, I could make a difference and work through my feelings of powerlessness. I also learned how my own voice could be strengthened and shared.

I became involved with the civil rights movement when the 1965 Watts riots in Los Angeles carried over to Las Vegas. The issue of segregation was personal because I was raised by two black women when I was with my grandmother.

In Las Vegas, parents were seldom home because they were either pimps, musicians, dancers or dealers working the swing shift. My friends and I learned how to survive on our own and, at age 16, I bought a house with my fiancee; however, I reached a point where I couldn't live in Las Vegas anymore. I would walk down the street and pimps would ask me to come work for them; I knew women who were being sexually exploited in the local casinos. I needed to get out and start a life somewhere else.

When I turned 17, I got a scholarship to attend a Los Angeles college and study interior design. It was an election year and the first time that 18 year olds were allowed to vote. I became very active in Democratic presidential candidate George McGovern's campaign. At the same time, I was running a business for a man who was a friend of Edmund G. "Pat" Brown (California's governor from 1959 to 1967). Through that connection, I joined the 1973 campaign of Pat's son, Jerry, who was running for governor of California. I put on Jerry's first fund raiser and tried my best to help him get elected.

When Jerry was elected governor of California, I spent the next eight years working with him and was the youngest member to be on a cabinet. One of my responsibilities as

Director of Administration was to oversee all the programs that came out of the governor's office, including working with a variety of minority communities that needed a voice.

The farm workers' issue was big in Sacramento and Cesar Chavez and Jerry were very close. Because of this, I helped Cesar try to pass a proposition and learned how to be an organizer. We were trying to push through the Farm Labor Bill and we won! It was one of the most challenging and beautiful things that happened while Jerry was in office, and one of the moments where I knew that hard work and integrity really made a difference. I had a leadership position in Jerry's reelection campaign for governor and helped run his 1980 presidential campaign. I got pregnant with my first child the day we went into the presidential campaign, which was extremely challenging because we were running against the sitting president. I delivered my son the day Jerry left the campaign.

With my new son, I decided not to go back to Sacramento; instead, I stayed close to home in Los Angeles in order to create a political office for Jerry so he could run for the Senate. I was managing 10 events a weekend and my baby was in a basket in the back of Jerry's blue Plymouth. He was at the office with me and at interviews, and Jerry even changed my son's diapers! During the last two years of Jerry's administration, I gave birth to my second child. Being a mother and an activist seemed perfectly natural. Everyone loved my new little girl and supported me as I included her in my work life.

In 1983, I went to Cabo San Lucas, Mexico, with my family to meet with a group of people for a board meeting and discuss an action to get a majority of Democrats back into the Senate. My family was standing on the beach when there was an underwater earthquake. A tidal wave washed up onto the shore and took my husband, my two-year-old daughter and me into the water. Disoriented and exhausted, I miraculously made it back to shore, half-drowned; I later found out that my husband had nearly drowned and my daughter's neck had been broken by the impact. In a few hours, she died.

I was devastated, numb and consumed with grief. Everything that had been important to me seemed worthless; I was living like a zombie. I decided that the only way to heal was to create a group with others like myself, so I started a grief recovery center and began leading groups. Witnessing and being witnessed was the only thing that pulled me out of the pit. My husband never recovered from his grief; he died from cancer a few years later.

Eight years after my daughter died (1991), I ran Jerry Brown's presidential campaign. There were some major candidates running, including Bill Clinton. I knew that we couldn't fight on the same monetary level as the other candidates and felt that, if we didn't get money out of politics, we were not going to get anywhere.

Jerry espoused grass-roots issues and people with money didn't want him to be president. I told him that it wouldn't matter who was president if we didn't do something about campaign finance reform. I came up with the idea of a $100 limit for campaign donations and installed an "800" number to take telephone donations. This had never been done before and many thought it was an impossible fund-raising strategy.

It was not about winning or losing; it was about creating a platform for Jerry to tell the truth about money in politics. People who would never have ordinarily financed his campaign donated money because they understood the message. From the eight people in the race, it was Jerry and Clinton at the end. Clinton won the race, but those of us working for

Jerry didn't care. The most important thing is that we had upheld integrity and felt good about ourselves.

Eight years later, George W. Bush was elected and there was huge shift in the country on many levels—the biggest one being that Bush wanted to use his power for a preemptive strike on Iraq. The Democrats had rewritten his resolution but Bush threw it out and moved forward with his own plan.

Several women activists—including Starhawk and Medea Benjamin—were in Washington, D.C. We met at a girlfriend's home and decided to start a movement called "CODEPINK" in response to Bush's "Code Red." We saw Code Red as a call for fear, terror, death and war, and CODEPINK for caring, compassion, love and peace. We gathered other women together, showed up at rallies and marched in pink, which brought levity to a serious situation and joy for the celebration that we were trying to create in the world. When we first suggested pink, we looked at each other in horror ("Anything but *pink!*") but have since learned its power.

In November 2003, we began sitting in all-day vigils outside the White House to protest going to war with Iraq. In the first Gulf War, there were an estimated 100 Iraqi civilians—most of them women and children—killed for every 16 American soldiers. Baghdad is a densely populated city of 5 million people; 50 percent of the 5 million are children under the age of 16. This meant that we were declaring war on innocent children and women.

One day, while we were sitting in vigil, we heard that the weapons inspectors would be coming back from Iraq in January, so 13 of us decided to go to Baghdad. (Unless you go with an official delegation, it is illegal for Americans to go to Iraq.) We flew to Amman, Jordan, and then drove for 17 hours to Baghdad. We wanted to have a personal experience with the women and children and hear their stories; we wanted them to know that there were American women who were against the war. At that time, our perception was that over 50 percent of the women in the U.S. were against the war. We felt that it was a great way to reach the international press, who were all there, and to let them know that not all Americans were for the war.

When we crossed the border, we were shocked at how open the Iraqis were and found them to be generous, kind and curious. Before we left the U.S., our partners and families were very frightened for us; however, the minute we stepped across the border, we realized that we were safe and had come into a community of people with deep values of humanity.

Iraq has a 7,000-year-old culture and I could feel the beauty in everyone I met. They would touch their heart, walk over to me and say, "Here is my heart. Peace." I dropped into a calm curiosity and the Iraqi people held that same place. Instead of being fearful, they looked at the impending war as a question: "Why does Mr. Bush want to bomb us? Why would anyone believe you can bomb a people into freedom?"

When I asked Iraqis how they could be so open to me, they said, "We are not Saddam Hussein and you are not George W. Bush. We know you. You are the people. You are not the power." At a time when the Iraqis were waiting to be bombed, they were grateful that we had made the long journey to learn about who they were as people and that we cared enough to hear their stories. They couldn't leave their country or find enough shelter to save themselves once the bombing started. We returned with their stories and shared them with everyone who would listen—to members of Congress, to gatherings of friends, on the radio and on television. We were desperate to get the message out.

For International Women's Day, we organized a week of actions with a huge march and rally, which ended with 10,000 women in pink circling the White House. There was something very profound and beautiful about hundreds of women in pink representing love and compassion—something that war proponents are afraid will squash the fear they try to instill in the American people: the fear that lets them go to war for oil. I was able to break the police blockade in front of the White House and lead about 25 women inside. They were all arrested, including Alice Walker, Susan Griffin, Amy Goodman and Maxine Hong Kingston.

They arrested Diane Wilson, so I left the group to help her as she couldn't afford an arrest. (Her arrest from our first action in front of the White House meant that she would go to jail for a year in D.C.) Outside the police line, we circled the White House and Starhawk led a spiral dance. Of course, we didn't stop the bombing, but we were able to touch the beauty and visibly mourn what was happening. Because we had done all we could and had stood together, we continued—knowing that this is a long process and what we are standing for is peace, even in the face of the unspeakable.

CODEPINK activists didn't fall into the deep malaise that seemed to engulf so many other activists. We hadn't failed; Bush had. The press often reports that millions of American workers have lost their jobs under Bush's administration; he has put us in a horrible deficit situation. No one is holding him responsible for what he is doing to our country, to the Iraqi people and to those in other countries.

This year, on International Women's Day, we lifted a 40-foot "pink slip" (women's lingerie) in front of the White House, using a 10-foot weather balloon. The pink slip read, "Women say: Fire Bush." We will continue this campaign until he is held responsible—not just by being defeated by John Kerry, but by being held accountable for his lies and misuse of power.

CODEPINK has grown to over 100 local communities of women activists in the U.S. and another 10 or so abroad. I find that women want to be in a community and are very powerful when they create from their own experience and speak from their own knowing. CODEPINK creates the container for networking and holding hands across the country. I have met amazing women this year and have loved my partnership with Medea Benjamin, with each of us learning from the other and growing in our own courage.

We continue to do actions every week and continue our vigils across the country. We have returned to Iraq four more times and are working to help the women there. In July 2003, we set up the Occupation Watch Center in Baghdad.

When I returned home from the trip in July with stories of the U.S. becoming another Saddam housed in his palace, Pilar Perez of Perceval Press asked me to publish them. Friends joined me in the effort and our book, *Twilight of Empire: Responses to Occupation*, has been met with great demand. It provides a vehicle to see and know the truth and to try and understand our role in the occupation so we can be more effective in speaking out against it. After the last trip, which was exactly a year after the first, we returned to give a report to Congress on the status of women under occupation.

Because of the breadth of our experience in Iraq, we have seen the hell that we have brought on the Iraqi people. However, we can share this story and hopefully, in some way, help end it and stop it from happening somewhere else. As the Bush lies become more evident and the devastation we have brought to Iraq becomes more visible in America, this reign of terror can hopefully be ended. To make a change, just get up and *do it*! We are still a democracy and our voice matters. If you do not stand up and take action, then you participate in the atrocities of those in power.

The power of intention is huge. This lesson has resurfaced in my life again and again. When you are up against something that is frightening and confusing, if you stand together with other people and feel the love and commitment versus the powerlessness, magic happens. Once you have done it, you know it is always possible. It looks different every time and you can't force it. Find the courage to begin over again with nothing. Slowly, integrity, courage and beauty surround you. You are in the moment, creating the world that you want.

Being an activist is about living an original life, listening to your own voice and creating the kind of world in which you believe.

CONTACT

85heartofj@aol.com

SUGGESTED LINKS

http://www.badbabes.org (Bad Babes and their buddies)

http://www.bhopal.net (The International Campaign for Justice in Bhopal)

http://www.bioneers.org (Bioneers)

http://www.codepinkalert.org (CODEPINK: Women for Peace)

http://www.occupationwatch.org (Iraq Occupation Watch)

http://www.unreasonablewomen.org (UnReasonable Women for the Earth)

BIBLIOGRAPHY

Evans, Jodie, et al. *Twilight of Empire: Responses to Occupation.* Santa Monica, CA: Perceval Press, August 2004.

LADONNA REDMOND

Food for the Community

"The voices from people of color must be heard in order to create dynamic change—change that will really mean something. I believe that every community … has the intellect to heal itself."

LaDonna lives in Austin, a suburb of Chicago, where she began researching food to figure out how to feed her son, who was having severe allergic reactions. This journey led her to founding the Institute for Community Resource Development (ICRD), which was instrumental in starting the Austin Black Farmers' Market. She plans to open a food cooperative soon.

Austin, with its 117,000 residents, is the largest neighborhood in the City of Chicago; if it were a city, it would be the third largest city in Illinois. It is mostly comprised of African Americans, with some living on government support and some working.

People have characterized Austin as a low-income community, but that label only describes 15 percent of the population. Even though Austin has a huge population base, it did not have a grocery store until March 2002. Cubs Foods (a discount chain store) now sells low-quality, low-cost food, but there still isn't a store in Austin where residents can buy good-quality produce. This became a major issue when my son Wade was born.

Since he was a baby, Wade would get very sick and start to wheeze. In the first few months, we would rush him to the doctor's office and sometimes the emergency room. Wade was hospitalized six times during his second year. He would get well, be exposed to a certain food, catch a cold, get an asthma attack, be hospitalized, be released and then the cycle would start over again. I was spending every sixth week in the hospital with Wade, which was incredibly stressful. The doctor was reluctant to diagnose him because he was under two years old, but we insisted. The doctor relented and gave Wade the medical diagnosis of asthma and a skin test to define his specific allergies.

The results of the skin test showed that he was severely allergic to all dairy products, eggs, peanuts and shellfish. When I found this out, I examined Wade's diet and the way we ate as a family. My husband had been a vegan for two years before Wade was born and that was how we were eating, but we weren't eating organic food. I knew about organic food from friends, but I had never wanted to spend that kind of money on food. I remembered a friend buying two organic tomatoes for $5 and thought, "If it's cheaper with the pesticides, then that is what I am going to buy."

"If you eat pesticides," she explained, "then how can you not be exposed to carcinogens? How can you *not* get cancer if you are *eating* cancer?"

With my baby's allergies to so many foods, I had to figure out a way to feed him. If I fed him the wrong food, it could lead to a life-threatening reaction. The only option was to research food. I searched the Internet and read many books about how food was produced, how much it costs and how it has been commoditized. I tried to figure out how something "nutritious" could make you sick.

Through my experience, I concluded that food labels are inaccurate, that some food is allegedly grown in municipal waste and sewer sludge, and that genetically modified organisms (GMOs) were in much of our food, even though no one had asked us if we wanted to eat that way. When I found out that conventional meat was allegedly produced in factory farms and that hormones were allegedly used in milk products, I didn't want any of it.

As I learned more about how food is grown and processed in this country, I was outraged that our food system had undergone this type of corporatization and chemicalization, and that no one in my community knew about it or was talking about it. During this time, news about mad cow disease was breaking in Europe. Europeans were up in arms about genetically modified foods and sent grain that contained GMOs back to the U.S.[1] I realized that I needed to pay more attention to this conversation about food, but the only ones who were talking about it in the U.S. were upper middle-class white people.

After reading about food, I spent weeks digesting the information and searching for the solution to Wade's diet. With the vegan diet, there was no protection from pesticides or GMOs; we had to buy organic food. I knew it would be more expensive, but it was better to spend more money on food than go to the hospital every six weeks.

We needed to know our farmers and understand the cycle of food so we could buy what was in season, not what was shipped from Mexico or from some other place. Because of the inaccuracy of food labels, we limited heavily processed items (food in cans and boxes). We ate whole grains, naturally raised chicken and fish, fruit and vegetables. Wade made a remarkable recovery and hasn't had a reaction to food since we changed our diet.

In order to buy organic food, I had to travel to Whole Foods, which is located in an upscale white community—a 30-minute drive from my house. When I walked in, I saw black employees and white shoppers; it became clear that organic food was a white person's privilege. Two years later, there were more black people shopping at Whole Foods because African Americans and white people coexist in that community.

There is still a huge number of African Americans from low-income neighborhoods who can't afford healthy food. Even if they have money, like my family, they can't find a ripe tomato anywhere in Austin, much less an organic one. I found out that Whole Foods will not put a store in a neighborhood whose population has less than an annual income of $100,000.[2] I began to look for ways to bring wholesome food into Austin.

When I found out that Wade had food allergies, I was consulting with local community groups and telling them about it. They would listen, but they weren't doing anything about food. "We've got drugs, crime, housing, youth—all kinds of things to work on. We are not going to work on food."

Claire Butterfield, codirector of Faith in Place at the Center for Neighborhood Technology, had an idea of bringing people together from various religious backgrounds. The Austin Interreligious Sustainability Circle was created, which set out to promote health, ecology and economic development. One group decided to work on chemical-free lawns; another worked on the lighting issue that was driving away the night animals; our group decided to explore the issues of food access. I knew that if I bought directly from the farmer, the price of food would be less. I wanted to help small, family organic farms stay alive and vibrant. The result was the Austin Black Farmers' Market.

Years ago, the farmers' market was a big thing in Austin before a federal policy shift from paper food stamps to electronic debit cards. The market was heavily impacted by the shift in policy; low-income people could no longer shop at the market because they didn't have the cash, which caused the farmers to make less money.

The first farmers we contacted were from Pembroke Family Farms in Kankakee, which is a cooperative of African American farmers who run a nonprofit organization and offer financing and group marketing for 12 organic farms. They were the first to bring produce and meat to the farmers' market. The next summer, we were contacted by the City of Chicago because we weren't suppose to start our own farmers' market; we were supposed to go through the city. We ended up going through the right channels and doing it the right way. We have just finished our third and highly successful year!

Most people in our community who buy food from the farmers' market are from the south and had already bought from farmers' markets. They know about growing food and can remember when food was good. I don't have that memory, but my mother and my grandmother do. The point of the farmers' market isn't just about organic food. It's about having access to high-quality food at a low price. The niche organic market focus won't work in communities with people of color because it leans heavily on crisis and the word "organic" is mostly co-opted by the federal government.

We need to talk about health and safe food for *everybody*—not just for people who can afford it. This is a very hard conversation to sell to some of the farmers who specialize in organic foods because they are being paid very high premiums for their produce. In Austin, people pay 40 percent more for conventional food than they would if they lived in a more upscale community. I wanted to find a way to make healthy food accessible to everyone, regardless of their social or economic status.

I continued my food research and realized that no one was talking to African Americans about food sustainability. The conversations that typically revolve around farmers and land stewardship—as well as most environmental movements such as Save the Whales, Save the Earth or Save the Trees—mainly come from upper middle-class white people. Many of their pleas for money are built on crisis. A crisis message is not going to work for most people of color because they already live in a state of crisis.

How could I get African Americans interested in environmental issues, particularly when it affects their food? I looked at food access in my community. Before Cubs Foods moved into Austin, residents had to go to another community to buy food—a huge ordeal for those who didn't own cars and had to take public transportation; they still have to leave the area if they want to buy quality food. Because Austin is a predominantly black community, it is perceived that no one has money or is interested in high-quality produce or organic food, yet everything else is available such as fast-food restaurants, Nike Shoes and Tommy Hilfiger.

Studies show that Austin residents spend over $135 million annually on food and 10 percent of that amount is spent at convenience stores. Unfortunately, that 10 percent doesn't stay in the community because the people who own the smaller convenience stores do not live in Austin and don't bank or shop there. This creates a tremendous economic void as well as a negative impact on the basic survival needs of the residents to feed themselves.

Whether or not you have money, if you live in Austin you are treated as if you are invisible and don't matter. This creates and supports a stereotype around communities of color that allows others to ignore the community. This belief system implies that there are no assets in Austin—only deficits—and leads to the viewpoint that the *people* have deficits.

When my husband and I got married, we decided to stay close to Austin because he had lived there for 35 years. We lived in the building that his parents bought so we could save money and eventually buy our own house. While we appear to be unusual (because we both work, have cars and got married before we had kids), there are many on our street who work for a living and own their own homes; it is not a community of drug addicts and transients. However, the perception that most white people have about Austin is that it is a bad neighborhood. I call this perception "social science under a glass," which holds the idea that black communities should be studied, researched and fixed. The people who do these studies do not live in those communities and wouldn't tolerate those types of studies where they live.

The organic food circles in which I travel are mainly made up of white people, just like the environmental movement. When you hear about organic food, it is primarily suburban white people talking. If there is going to be a message about organic food, then it needs to relate to the lives of everyday people. Urban environments have huge communities of African Americans, but organic food has been co-opted by white communities. Getting food into African American urban neighborhoods often becomes a social service project rather than an effort to provide access to healthy food.

The conversation about sustainability is totally missing in communities with people of color. No one is talking to black people about eating organic foods, using green cleaning products and recycling. The African American community is heavily impacted by environmental hazards, such as soil and lead contamination due to the fact that our children are eating lead paint chips.

We are now entering into the second generation of African Americans who don't know how to grow food. They have no connection to the land and they don't have any idea about the history of black farmers in this country. I am working on a book about the need for African American people to reconnect to the land—a reconnection based on an entire history of plantation farming.

When slavery ended, many black people began working their own farms and growing their own food. The history of black farmers is invisible because they have historically been poorly treated by the U.S. government and the U.S. Department of Agriculture (USDA). A few years ago, there was a settlement in the case of *Pickford v. Glickman* in which 1,000 black southern farmers sued the USDA, charging them with discrimination. It was found that USDA officials intimidated and discriminated against black farmers concerning loans and other support. The loan agent would often lose the loan application or give farmers the loan too late in the season for them to do anything. The farmers couldn't pay their mortgage and they lost their land because of this discrimination. They ultimately won a $300 billion settlement; now, any black farmer who files a claim will get money from that settlement.

Learning about the history of black farmers and black people's relationship to food inspired me to start the ICRD. The Circle for Interreligious Sustainability needed nonprofit status to get funding to continue their work, so the ICRD and the Sustainability Circle came together under one umbrella. The ICRD focuses on issues of sustainability—particularly food sustainability—and has broadened its scope to include land, stewardship, urban farming and advocacy issues in the areas of sustainable agriculture, receiving funds from Chicago Community Trust and the Kellogg Foundation.

We want to start a community-based, cooperative grocery store where the dollars spent will benefit the community. We rented a building to serve as our distribution center and 30 families will buy into the co-op; eventually, we will open a store. I don't want this to be another social service project; I want it to contribute to the economic development of our community.

Childbearing and childbirth prepared me for this work—not my economics degree. Everything I had done in my life came together when I had to figure out how to feed my baby. When I was experiencing the pain and joy of childbearing, I realized I could do anything. I saw my child's potential and understood that my role as his mother was to protect and nurture that potential. I knew in that moment that I had the power to do it.

My husband and I both practice a religion called Ifa, which is thousands of years old from the West African Yoruba system. Ifa is based on divination and understanding of the forces of nature in order to be in harmony with the world. In this system, there is an energy called Iyami Oshronga, which is the mothers of the mothers—the true feminine energy. This energy is feared among the Yoruba and they don't play with the power of the mother because it is the mother who crowns and uncrowns the king. I rest on that realization: there is no power like that of the mother to do what needs to be done for her child and for the world. This power, this sense of being able to make changes and do anything, is carrying over into many social justice actions. People are reawakening to the mother energy, which is creating a reconnection to instinct.

Sadly, I don't see this reconnection happening in my community. I don't see our children reconnecting to the land or their culture because they are being connected to consumerism, which has no respect and demolishes other cultures. What could be saved is being lost, like the legacy of African Americans and farming practices. African American people still carry a tremendous amount of shame about slavery; being unable to connect to that tragedy and heal is a major part of the black community's issues. The whole dynamic of slavery set up a situation in this country that I don't think we can ever overcome without another revolution.

What is going to happen if we don't speak out the way the dominant culture does? While they may be progressive, they still use the slave master's methods and are not being inclusive. I have been involved in many progressive political events where I am usually the only African American in the audience. The voices from people of color must be heard in order to create dynamic change—change that will really mean something. I believe that every community, even those with people who may still feel the shame of slavery, has the intellect to heal itself.

CONTACT

Songobisi@netzero.com

SUGGESTED LINK

http://www.ICRDUSA.org (Institute for Community Resource Development)

SUGGESTED READING

Abelman, Michael. *From The Good Earth—A Celebration of Growing Food Around the World.* New York: Harry N. Abrams, 1993.

_____. *On Good Land—The Autobiography of an Urban Farm.* San Francisco: Chronicle Books, 1998.

Berry, Wendell. *What are people for?* New York: North Point Press, 1990.

Gussow, Joan. *This Organic Life, Confessions of a Suburban Homesteader.* White River Junction, VT: Chelsea Green Publishing Company, 2002.

Lappé, Frances Moore. *Diet for a Small Planet.* New York: Ballantine Books, 1971.

_____. *World Hunger: Twelve Myths.* New York: Grove Press, 1998.

Lappé, Frances Moore and Anna Lappé. *Hope's Edge: The Next Diet for a Small Planet.* New York: Jeremy P. Tarcher, January 2002.

Marcus, Erik. *Vegan, The New Ethics of Eating.* Ithaca, NY: McBooks Press, 2000.

Nestle, Marion. *Food Politics: How the Food Industry Influences Nutrition and Health.* Berkeley, CA: University of California Press, 2002.

Schlosser, Eric. *Fast Food Nation—The Dark Side of the All-American Meal.* New York: Perennial, 2001.

Simontacchi, Carol. *The Crazy Makers: How the Food Industry Is Destroying Our Brains and Harming Our Children.* New York: Jeremy P. Tarcher, 2001.

Steingraber, Sandra. *Having Faith: An Ecologist's Journey to Motherhood.* New York: Perseus Publishing, 2001.

FOOTNOTES START ON PAGE 203.

ELS COOPERRIDER

Leading the Fight Against Genetically Modified Organisms

"If you are going to spend time on an issue,
make sure it is a local issue that secures the
future of your family and neighbors."

Els worked as a scientist for 24 years and now runs the Ukiah Brewing Company & Restaurant with her family in northern California. She and her husband of 40 years live in a 400-square-foot cabin on 40 acres of land off the grid without a phone. When not working at the restaurant or participating in community organizing, they spend time reading and relaxing.

I was born during World War II in a small village in the Netherlands on the North Sea. I was the fourth child in a family of seven who stuck together through hard times. During the war, both my father and mother joined the Dutch Resistance. My parents ultimately hid dozens of Jews and several allied fighter pilots who had been shot down. Years later, my parents were honored by President Eisenhower for their work in the "Underground"; they were also honored by the Canadian and Israeli governments.

In 1955, my father took an oil tanker from Holland to Houston and bought a Greyhound bus ticket, searching for a place to live for our family. Two years later, we immigrated to the San Francisco Bay Area. Soon after that, my parents moved to the small, rural town of Ukiah in Mendocino County, California. My father helped plant a vineyard and worked on a ranch. My mother told my sisters and me that, if we wanted to go to college, we had to get scholarships. I was awarded a partial scholarship for the University of California at Berkeley and worked in laboratories 20 to 30 hours a week to pay for my living expenses.

I graduated with a degree in botany in 1967; 10 years later, I went back for a master's degree in range ecology at Colorado State University. By then, I was raising two sons and still working in research laboratories. My husband earned a Ph.D. in zoology and worked for the federal government. During this time, I also started a country rock band called Mother Country with four other mothers, playing at every honky tonk between Wheatland, Wyoming, and Denver, Colorado. It was a very busy time!

Years later, my husband and I moved back to Ukiah and left our two grown sons in Fort Collins. Our oldest son, a brewer, asked if we could help him start a brew pub in Colorado. We said no, but we would help him start one in Ukiah. He, his wife and their first son moved to Ukiah and, in May 2000, we started the Ukiah Brewing Company & Restaurant—the first certified organic brew pub in the nation. A year later, our youngest son moved to Ukiah and now we all work together at the restaurant and brewery. We went organic because I had been raised in an organic farming family and I as a scientist had serious reservations about the hundreds of toxic chemicals used to grow our food.

In the early 1980s, many of my colleagues went to work for corporations to engineer genetically modified organisms (GMOs)—organisms that are man made in the laboratory by forcing genes from one organism into another, such as putting mouse genes into potatoes, human genes into salmon or human genes into rice. This process has nothing to do with hybridization or cross breeding. These are man-made organisms that have never existed before and never would.

Scientists have taken this shortcut to create new life forms without fully understanding and heeding the unintended consequences. The genes are jumbled in the genetic material and can end up making new proteins that could be toxic. They can create allergens that have never existed and can cross contaminate natural plants that are close relatives. Once GMOs have been released into the environment, they can never be called back.

Like most large businesses, corporations that make GMOs give campaign contributions to politicians running for state and federal offices. Once elected, these politicians make political appointments to "pay their debt." Many of these appointments include powerful positions that regulate commerce, agriculture, natural resources and environmental pollutants. I have a list of 26 people who have been appointed to national and state agencies and who are Monsanto or other GMO biotech company ex-employees. The head of the U.S. Department of Agriculture (USDA), Anne Venemann, is the former vice president of CalGene, which is owned by Monsanto. In 1994, CalGene made the first GMO tomato with fish genes called the Flavr Savr; it was discontinued in 1998 because it bruised easily and was less firm than expected. This characteristic caused production, transportation and distribution problems.[1]

There are two genetically engineered varieties of corn that have been classified as pesticides because they have been engineered for every cell to contain pesticides. When humans or animals eat this corn, they are in fact eating pesticides.

The now infamous StarLink corn, which had not been approved for human consumption, got into the food chain. There was a huge outcry over this "mistake." Large companies were forced to recall thousands of pounds of corn products.[2] In the aftermath of this fiasco, many large food companies have asked their suppliers to deliver only non-GMO ingredients (for example, McDonald's has asked their potato growers to stop using GMO potatoes).[3] Many farmers grow conventional non-GMO crops; however, once harvested, it is often mixed with GMO varieties. In Great Britain, any farmer growing genetically engineered crops cannot get insurance[4]; in the U.S., GMO ingredients do not have to be labeled on food and most people eat GMO foods unless they are eating 100 percent organic.

Studies show that when cows were given GMO corn in one trough, and the trough next to it contained normal and natural corn, the cows avoided the GMO corn.[5] Year after year, geese would fly into a corn field that grew traditional, hybridized corn. One year, the farmer decided to grow GMO corn and the geese completely ignored that field and went to the next field that had natural corn.[6] Rats who are given both GMO and natural seeds will avoid the GMO variety.[7] One has to ask, "What do cows, geese and rats know that we don't?"

In Canada, 73-year-old Percy Schmeiser—a fifth-generation farmer—sued the corporate giant Monsanto. Monsanto discovered that Schmeiser had canola plants that had been genetically engineered to withstand the company's weed killer, even though Schmeiser hadn't bought Monsanto's seed. He said that his farm was contaminated by the genetically altered strain and was likely spread by wind. He had been saving seeds for over 50 years and the contamination ruined a lifetime of work. Two lower courts ruled in Monsanto's favor and ordered Schmeiser to pay Monsanto nearly $150,000 in damages and court costs. This case was just settled in the Canada Supreme Court, which agreed with Monsanto that their GMO canola was found in Schmeiser's fields, but did not hold Schmeiser responsible for the cost.[8] This horror story is part of what has fueled people in Mendocino County to put a ban on GMOs. Here is the story of how it started.

Many of our restaurant customers were interested in organic food and we had long conversations about the fact that the USDA was changing organic food standards. At the end of 2000, four of us (Johanna Cummings, John Milder, Dave Smith and I) formed the Mendocino Organic Network to raise money and awareness about organic food.

With a population of just over 80,000, Mendocino County is known for its rural culture and farming communities. We decided to support the farmers in growing organic crops by starting Mendocino Renegade—a local eco label for Mendocino and Lake County farmers and businesses that have stricter standards than the national USDA or the National Organic Program. We created Mendocino Renegade to empower local businesses and farmers to be certified organic without having to go to the USDA. Political pressures on the USDA have diluted the standards on organic foods at least three times since 2001. Mendocino Renegade has certified four farms and is reviewing more applications. Anyone who meets the standards can apply. One of the standards is that you cannot use bone meal or blood meal—a fertilizer derived from cows—because of mad cow disease. Also, the entire operation must be organic, which is not a USDA requirement.

In March 2004, the citizens of Mendocino County put Measure H on the ballot—the first one of its kind in the nation—prohibiting growing, propagating, cultivating or raising GMOs until Mendocino County voters decide that GMOs have been proven safe.

I came up with the idea to put Measure H on the ballot in 2001 when people were talking about labeling GMOs. I said that we needed more than labels; we needed to stop growing them altogether. I helped create a proactive campaign to inform local citizens about GMOs. No one in Mendocino County has ever grown a genetically engineered crop, so no one was going to go out of business if the measure passed; if anything, it would support the county's reputation for growing organic and pure food.

I decided that, regardless of whether the measure won or lost, the important thing was to educate the public about genetic engineering and let them make up their own minds. I knew that we would have strong opposition to Measure H from the biotech corporations. (The year before, Monsanto and its corporate allies spent more than $5 million on a campaign to defeat an Oregon ballot measure to label genetically modified food.[9])

During the campaign for Measure H, some people asked about their right to grow whatever they pleased on their own property and objected to the ban; many others felt that they should have the right to protect their private property from GMO contamination. The reason the private property right doesn't hold with GMOs is because, if someone is growing GMOs on their land, the wind, bees and equipment can move it onto the neighbor's land who may not want it. Once the neighbor has GMOs in the soil, the whole crop is irreversibly contaminated.

The industry rhetoric states that we need GMOs because it will feed starving people all over the world and cut down on pesticide use. Reliable research has shown that feeding the world is a myth because the yield on GMOs is lower than its natural counterparts and it costs more to grow GMO food.[10] In the last eight years, the pesticide use for GMOs alone has gone up 50 million pounds.[11] A genetically engineered plant cannot adapt to change, but weeds and bugs can. Many weeds have taken up the herbicide-resistant GMO gene and have become problem "superweeds." These superweeds are now spreading across Canada and down into the U.S.

The common, genetically engineered crop has been created to withstand the dowsing of herbicides. Roundup Ready is the most common herbicide-tolerant GMO crop. It is sprayed by a crop duster by Roundup (the herbicide that Monsanto makes) and the plants won't die. When you genetically engineer something, you break up the deoxyribonucleic acid (DNA) to insert the foreign genes, which also include a viral promoter that keeps the gene turned on all the time.

Transgenic (an organism having genetic material from another species) DNA is unstable. It can get into the soil and water and combine with microorganisms in soil, plants and animals. Roundup doesn't kill the weeds growing in a GMO crop because the weeds pick up the genetically engineered trait resistant to herbicides.

The biotech industry was concerned by the national support for Measure H. A lawsuit was filed by an industry consortium of multinational corporations, which attempted to prevent Mendocino County voters from reading key ballot arguments in support of Measure H. The lawsuit named the proponents of Measure H, including me and Marsha Wharf (the local county clerk recorder) because they did not want her to print the ballot.[12] The group behind the lawsuit (the California Plant Health Association) represents some of the biggest names in GMO production and the world's leading producers of herbicides and pesticides, including Monsanto Corporation, Dow AgroSciences, Bayer Corporation, Helena Chemical and DuPont.

The biotech industry's Sacramento-based law firm attempted to strike sections of the election ballot arguments in favor of Measure H before voters had a chance to read the pamphlet. Their attorney told Superior Court Judge Leonard J. LaCasse that, since GMO-contaminated wine is not yet on the shelves, Mendocino County voters should be prevented from reading that GMO-contaminated wine is unmarketable in Europe and Japan.[13]

After it was revealed in court that there are 30 field trials of GMO grapevines currently under development in California, it underscored the need for Measure H as protection for the future of Mendocino County's agricultural economy. The corporations didn't care about Mendocino County; they don't live here, work here or own farms here. These outside corporations are mainly concerned about profit.

We went to court on Christmas Eve 2003 and hundreds of people were in the courtroom. Judge LaCasse decided not to change a single word on the ballot in support of Measure H. His judgment cleared the way for the election ballots to be printed—*uncensored*—in time for the March election. The biotech industry lost!

Not long after the lawsuit (in January 2004), the *Associated Press* interviewed me about Measure H and it went out to a billion worldwide readers. We got calls from all over the world and it didn't die down until recently. It gave Measure H a lot of credibility and it was impacting the nation and the world.

In January 2004, the opposition launched its campaign to defeat Measure H. Radio and newspaper ads and flyers were mailed to thousands of county households—all funded by CropLife America, which represents Monsanto, Dow Chemical, DuPont and other corporations—denouncing Measure H.

Official reports indicated that the multinational corporations outspent the Measure H campaign by more than five to one.[14] Opposition money paid for out-of-county attorneys, unethical push-polling and industry-backed focus groups. CropLife America dumped more than $600,000 into the opposition's campaign.[15] The opposition received only $5,000 in support from the local county; all of the other money came from outside of Mendocino County. The industry-fueled opposition doubled the record for the most money ever spent in the history of Mendocino County elections.[16] In contrast, the "Yes on Measure H" campaign received more than 2,000 contributions, mostly from local business owners, farmers and families who donated between $5 and $99, for a total of nearly $100,000—one of the most successful grass-roots campaigns in Mendocino history.[17]

In March 2004, the voters passed Measure H. We stood together against outside corporations and won! Mendocino County residents refused to be bullied by the corporations. The opposition clearly underestimated the savvy and passion of Mendocino County voters.

The passing of Measure H has created a groundswell. In April 2004, GMO Free Mendocino hosted nine other counties in California in order to learn more about how to ban GMOs from their communities; there are now a total of 14 California counties considering banning GMOs. People abroad had assumed that Americans liked GMOs but, when this story broke, they realized that many Americans don't like GMOs. It gave them a legitimacy to keep American GMOs out of their countries.

People call me an activist. I bristle when I hear that word because I am just an ordinary citizen who cares about what is going on around her. I see myself as a fierce person with a smile on my face who is protective of her family and her environment and who is willing to fight to keep them safe. I don't think I could be effective unless I were optimistic about the future; otherwise, I would just throw in the towel, which isn't fair to our children.

A powerful way to create change and make a difference in the world is by joining a local movement in your community and making your voice heard. If you support local businesses, and the bulk of the community's needs are produced locally, it builds an appreciation of where things come from as well as an appreciation for your neighbors. Once you get to know your neighbors, you will want them to stay in business and you will fight to keep out corporatization. Every person, whether they make a small or a large contribution, makes a difference. Each action becomes part of the whole—the collective—and working collectively is a potent tool in creating change.

CONTACT
ae@ukiahbrewingco.com

SUGGESTED LINK

http://www.gmofreemendo.com (GMO Free Mendocino)

FOOTNOTES START ON PAGE 203.

SUSAN ALEXJANDER

Deepening Awareness Through Music

"I work to protect the diversity of all life and help people remember a deep sense of connection."

Susan has a master's degree in music composition and theory and her compositions have been performed throughout the United States, including collaborations with dance and film companies. Her music derives its data and inspiration from nature's vibrational frequencies such as pulsar spins, elements and water and time cycles.

Sequencia—a unique and lyrical celebration of the miracle of life—is internationally known for its pioneering sound work using the molecular frequencies of deoxyribonucleic acid (DNA). It has been featured on CNN, BBC Radio and Wisconsin Public Radio, and has been on exhibit at the Boston Museum of Science, the San Francisco Museum of Modern Art, the Art Museum of Santa Barbara and the Universal Concepts Gallery in Manhattan.

Susan is currently on the faculty of the California Institute of Psychoacoustics in San Francisco, the Union Institute in Sacramento and Cogswell (Hogswort) College in Sunnyvale, California. Her company, Science & The Arts, furthers scientific research into the "musical" universe of frequency.

My mother and father were wonderful role models. I grew up on the east coast from the time I was four years old until the time I got married. I lived in a New Jersey suburb, right outside of New York City. My father, a gentle man, was an orthopedic surgeon at Columbia Presbyterian Medical Center. He was the first person to drive a Volkswagen into the parking lot at Columbia when all of the other doctors were driving Buicks and Cadillacs. He invented a back operation, a way of using spinal fusion, that is still well known.

My mother was a typical 1950s housewife. When she turned 40, she went back to school and became an artist. Because we were so close to New York, she studied painting with some very famous teachers. I was about 11 years old when she went back to school; shortly before I went to college, she had her first art show in New York City. Before my mother went back to college, she decided to get an aptitude test at Johnson O'Connor, which is a famous New York testing center. I was 19 years old and she took me with her. They said that she had an aptitude for abstractionism and visual imagery, which supported her painting.

When they tested me, they said that my tonal memory was off the charts, I had a great ear and was great with words. I was told that I should be writing musical plays and suggested that I go to Yale Graduate School of drama and music. At that time, I was unable to imagine myself doing that and had aspirations to become an English teacher. I had taken some piano lessons as a child and was impatient with my teachers because I always wanted to improvise. Instead of paying attention to the written sheet music, I wanted to invent my own music. As a result, I was a poor piano student.

I took several English classes at a women's college in Pennsylvania and then transferred after my third year to the University of Utah. Once there, I took music theory classes, sang in the ensemble choir and was involved in recordings. I got married, began teaching high school English and got pregnant, thus ending my career as an English teacher; within five years, I had three daughters.

I spent those years restless and miserable and part of my soul split off. I didn't know who I was or what I was supposed to be doing. I knew that I adored my babies but, on some level, felt that I was not supposed to be just a mother. In addition, my relationship with my husband was unfulfilling. He was hardly around because he was studying to be a doctor and keeping strenuous hours. We didn't have any money to hire a baby-sitter and were not around our families, so it was just me and my three daughters, day in and day out. I really struggled and often felt that I was going to lose my mind.

Somewhere around that time, I had an epiphany. My husband and I had just moved to Boston and I was surrounded by a wonderful community of women. I was doing the dishes one evening, listening to our little plastic yellow radio in my kitchen and feeling really depressed. "What is life about? What am I supposed to be doing?" I silently pondered. In that moment, a Mozart string quartet came on the radio. "That is so beautiful," I thought. "Wouldn't it be fabulous to know how to put that together?" Seconds later, I spun around and thought, "Oh, my God! *That* is what I am supposed to be doing. I am a composer. I am supposed to be writing music!" In that moment, I could see all the pieces, like an engineer can see a blueprint. I understood the joy that I would have in learning this craft.

I called a pianist who lived down the street. I said, almost breathlessly, "I got it! What do I do to get there?" She told me that she knew a great teacher in the graduate music department at Boston University and suggested that I call him to see if he would be my tutor. At the time, I didn't have any money to hire a tutor and couldn't leave my small children, but she insisted that I check it out.

I called him. The minute I heard his voice, I knew that he was my teacher. I told him who I was and what I wanted to study and he turned me down flat. He told me that he was overwhelmed with graduate students and didn't have any time. As he spoke, I felt as if I were dying inside. At that time, I was very shy but somehow found the courage to ask if he would take my phone number, just in case he changed his mind. I thanked him and hung up the phone. I felt absolutely devastated. Thirty seconds later, the phone rang and it was him. "I got off the phone and my wife read me the riot act. She said that I had to work with you. Let's try it."

I paid him $20 a month and went to his house once a month for three hours. He threw everything at me and was thrilled to have a student who was eager to learn. I took in the information like a vacuum. I studied with him for two years and he taught me an incredible amount. I went out, got a beat-up piano for $300 and began composing. I was in absolute heaven and haven't stopped since. It is such a blessing that out of the question "What should I be doing?" came this answer.

After my husband finished his medical training, he was offered a job and we moved to San Jose, California. It was the perfect time for me to go back to school because my youngest daughter had just started preschool. I got my master's degree in music composition and theory at San Jose State University. Sadly, my marriage ended three years later.

Soon after, I got a job with the university teaching in the music department and began to think about frequencies in the natural environment. If everything that vibrated created a frequency, then conceivably it could be creating a sound. That started me on a quest and I started to imagine, "What if?" This quality is called "ideaphoria," which means that a person experiences a rapid turnover of ideas and is able to make multiple connections. Many people wonder how I began writing music. The truth is that I took baby steps by first asking the simple questions and then going deeper. I began to think about the cellular world inside the body and realized that even DNA has a vibration or frequency rate.

One day, I was walking through a bookstore and a book fell off the shelf and landed at my feet. I picked it up and began reading about Dr. David Deamer, who was well known for his work with DNA and the origins of life. I found out where he lived and called him. When he answered the phone, I said, "This might sound really crazy, but I am a composer and I want to know if DNA molecules spin, vibrate and make sound." He was very open to the idea and suggested that we meet.

In our meeting, David told me that he could give me the vibrational frequencies of DNA and then handed me a book with those frequencies written down. I got a computer and a keyboard and began writing music based on the DNA frequencies. It took me a year to do the research for the science part of the composition. Every vibration can be measured with a hertz standard (how many times per second something wiggles, jiggles or goes back and forth).

For example, the reed of an oboe in an orchestra vibrates 440 cycles per second. On western music charts, we call that an A. You can double the frequency and get the A an octave above, or you can cut it in half and get the A an octave below. It needs to be something that happens repeatedly at a steady rate so it can be measured. David had measured vibrating frequencies in the DNA molecule and had given me numbers for these frequencies. Some of the frequencies were so fast (one frequency was 32,000 cycles per second) that they were inaudible to the human ear. Using my computer, I would cut the frequency in half over and over again so that it became the same pitch but in a lower octave.

When I had collected the various pitches from the DNA molecules, I understood the science and could plug all of the hertz numbers into my synthesizer. It was an extraordinary moment when I listened to what I had: one big, clustered glob! Before I started the project, I thought I would get a chime-like sound, but instead it sounded like a huge mess because all the microtones were clumped together.

I spent the next two months letting my hands roam over the keyboard. I would occasionally hit a combination of tones that I liked and would write them in a notebook. Soon I had something to work with that sounded fairly good and it was time to create a musical composition. Two years later, in 1990, I released my CD entitled *Sequencia*.

When I first released *Sequencia*, some people didn't understand it but nonetheless connected aurally. I never heard anyone say they were uncomfortable with it, even though it is dissonant and out of tune to some people's ears. On one level, it has been received better than my wildest dreams. The science of it has been very well accepted. The definitive journal of engineering and biology, *IEEE*, published a prestigious article about *Sequencia* as it relates to sound and health. *Sequencia* is now distributed worldwide and scientists and healers are experimenting with it.

I never really questioned why I was doing this because I was on a hunt—a quest—and it was thrilling. It all arose from my original question, "Is the body vibrating inside?" Now I look back and realize the importance of DNA, especially during this historical time. When people make the connection that there is musical sense in the body (in our DNA molecules), it creates a doorway to go inside and have a very different experience of their own molecular structure. I have watched people listen to *Sequencia* and they are blown away by it—not because of their mind, but because their bodies have a visceral, cellular response. As the resonance relationships come into their ear and go into their nervous system, their body says, "I recognize this. It is very familiar."

This is extremely important because we are creatures of vibration. We are sensitive beings who have so many capabilities that we don't even know how to talk about them. A whole new part of body, spirit and mind is awakened and can be allowed to come out and develop. When I talk about DNA frequencies, I'm talking about all of life. The chemistry that Dr. David Deamer gave me was not just the chemistry of human beings. It was the raw chemistry of all DNA—of people, plants, animals and trees—*all life*. All things have music within them. Stones can be added into this equation because the mineral kingdom is singing as loudly and as beautifully as DNA.

I see *Sequencia* as a doorway into a new paradigm and a new way of thinking about life. It is important to see that our birthright should be connected to every living thing through vibration and common chemistry. We literally are by the vibration we share in DNA. There are more and more musicians working with math, vibration and frequency to inform the art. Math makes patterns visible, so we can see into an inner world that is very abstract and that might otherwise never be seen. You might say that I created an architecture of sound that was beautiful and accessible to the human ear. There is beautiful sound to be found within each inner structure of life and in the molecular world.

In 1994, I was given a fellowship to study the mineral kingdom. I thought I was going to do a second CD based on the crystalline world—I became fascinated with crystals and their inner structure and rhythm—but it was not that simple. I began to study vibrations of water, pulsars and a myriad of different natural elements.

One day, I realized that I should start organizing all of the frequencies. I began making charts and discovered that these natural elements were communicating by sharing frequencies. The frequencies were becoming a kind of language. For example, on one of my charts, I had groups of A sharps, C sharps and F sharps in different corners, which created a triad. Harmonically speaking, this is a very ordered design and it may be important for these groups to be together. When I charted out hydrogen, oxygen, nitrogen and helium, they would occasionally be in the relationship of a perfect fifth (the strongest harmony you can have after an octave). This is extraordinary because it shows that nature loves harmony.

I have researched this for seven years and am beginning to think about the importance of triads in nature, including the Great Pyramids. I have been reading many related books, magazine articles and studies and have been in touch with people worldwide who are working to uncover frequencies and their meaning. I am beginning to unfold a language of vibration that is telling a story about how the Earth is connected to the sun, to pulsars and to all natural elements. There have been studies on the vibration rate of individual living structures, but no one has looked at the larger picture. I am finding out how each one of these individual pieces fit and putting them together into one cosmological overview.

The cosmology that I am piecing together—based on frequency, sacred geometry and science—points to a grand design that connects the Earth and the cosmos. There is some type of communication going on that we don't understand and I am trying to uncover what it means. If I can put something into a musical format, people don't even have to know any of the research or concepts behind it. When they hear the music made from these frequencies, I am hoping that some part of their psyche or body will say, "This music brings me to remember something that I have forgotten."

This memory is very important because it will bring us back to the source. I don't know what the original source is, but it is something divine, within and without, and incredibly beautiful. I think it is the balance we need to touch it in our senses. We need to remember and make that connection once again.

My work is related to being a mother. I work to protect the diversity of all life and help people remember a deep sense of connection. The Greeks studied nature to find their place in it and nature is still our greatest teacher. As awful as the world looks right now, we are seeing the darkness and being given the chance to bring it into the light. We are created with such divinity that nothing is allowed to be hidden if it is not perfect. It needs to be seen for what it is and everything arises to be healed. The Earth and the cosmos are a container … a vessel of total possibility. Life is a response to the gift of life and that is what I attempt to support through my work.

CONTACT
xjander@got.net

SUGGESTED LINK

http://www.OurSoundUniverse.com (Our Sound Universe)

NINA SIMONS

Working for a Restorative Future

"The time has come to model the respectful,
relational connectivity that we know as a
true pattern of life and stand up for that truth."

Nina is the coexecutive director of Bioneers/Collective Heritage Institute. As the coproducer of the Bioneers Conference since 1990, she is a seasoned business manager and expert in community-based marketing. She was the director of regional marketing for Odwalla, Inc., where she designed, implemented and supervised a highly successful and innovative marketing plan. Between 1989 and 1994, she was marketing director and later president of Seeds of Change, a biodiversity organic seed company. Nina was named an Utne Reader Visionary in 1996 for her ground-breaking work in communication, community building and ethical commerce.

Reaching my current work—coproducing the Bioneers Conference and building an organization around our media and communications outreach—has been a long, windy road and utterly unpredictable. If anyone had suggested to me that I might spend my 30s and 40s helping to create an annual environmental conference that's become a communications and network-building organization, I'd have said, "No way!"

As a kid growing up in New York City schools, I always found biology and chemistry classes utterly boring and without any relevance to my life. The arts—and how peoples' consciousness could be affected by them—were what really turned me on. I discovered theater in high school and was later seduced by the avant-garde plays of Harold Pinter and Sam Shepard, which called into question the myths of the American family and illuminated the disparity between our actual lives and our beliefs and values. This kind of theater often left people feeling troubled and uncomfortable. If live theater could reveal some of the short-comings of the great American dream, and get people to question their own belief systems and the foundations of our diseased culture, that was what I wanted to pursue.

After college, I went to work in professional theater and rapidly became disheartened upon realizing that there were only a few places where people were producing that kind of theater. Commercial theater was principally about musicals and comedy—stuff that was entertaining but didn't fulfill my consciousness-challenging aspirations.

After living in New York City and working in restaurants and theater, I moved to Santa Fe, New Mexico. A few years later, I met Kenny Ausubel, who later became my husband and partner. In early 1987, he was completing a documentary film, *Hoxsey: How Healing Becomes a Crime*, which told the story of the politics of medicine and alternative cancer therapies in this country. After his own father suddenly died of cancer, Kenny investigated the largely underground world of alternative treatments and learned how many potentially promising cancer therapies had been railroaded out of the country by the American Medical Association (AMA), leaving a trail of misinformation and grossly limiting options for cancer patients.

I was inspired and began to work with him to support the film's completion. I talked with recently diagnosed cancer patients from around the world. Hearing their panic and anguish—and realizing how badly people needed a responsible and thorough source of information at this pivotal moment in their lives—I knew this was a story that urgently needed to be told. I contributed to the film's completion and then joined Kenny in marketing and distributing it.

The film tells a Mark Twainian story about a coal miner with an eighth-grade education—Harry Hoxsey—who inherited an herbal cancer remedy from his veterinarian father. Hoxsey's father had discovered the remedy by turning his prized stallion out to pasture to die because it had cancer. Observing the horse, he discovered that it was eating a number of roots and barks, which were not a part of its normal diet. Soon after, the horse's condition stabilized and it began to get well. Combining plants derived from "horse sense," minerals and some home remedies of the day, Hoxsey's father devised three formulas. Within a year, the horse was well and the veterinarian became locally famous for treating animals with cancer. On his deathbed, Hoxsey bequeathed the formulas to his son, who began using the treatments, with reputed success, on people.

In its heyday, Hoxsey's cancer clinics spread across 17 states and federal judges upheld in court that the Hoxsey remedy had therapeutic value.[1] Throughout his career, Hoxsey was embroiled in a battle with the AMA—a crusade that went on for decades under the guise of "quack-busting." Though thousands of patients have testified that they owe their healing to his therapies, and Hoxsey himself offered to pay for them, the Hoxsey formulas have never been subjected to clinical trials. The clinic was among the first to open in Tijuana, Mexico, where it still operates.

Making the film was our first experience working together and we really hit our stride in our attempts to market it. We enjoyed the challenge and found that our skills were complementary in a way neither of us had imagined. Our collaboration happened seamlessly and we were quite successful.

The film was released in 1987 and received great reviews in *The New York Times*.[2] It also had a special screening for the U.S. Congress, who reviewed U.S. policy in addressing alternative therapies. It aired on HBO, Cinemax and Bravo, where it received the highest viewer response of any documentary ever shown.[3] *Hoxsey* won a number of film and journalistic awards and was featured at worldwide film festivals.

Distributing *Hoxsey* was a breakthrough experience for me. I learned that I loved helping to get stories widely told that are important for healing. I was enthused and tireless in that pursuit and strengthened by the synchronicity of my emerging partnership with Kenny.

A couple of years later, Kenny was asked to film footage of an unusual garden at San Juan Pueblo near Santa Fe, New Mexico. He went to visit this garden and became fascinated by it. The pueblo had hired master gardener Gabriel Howearth to design and plant the garden. Gabriel had traveled all over Mexico and Latin America, learning about indigenous agriculture and expanding his repertoire of diverse plant families. As people began to trust him, they shared what for them was the most precious gift of all: seeds. Native people often believe that the voices of the ancestors speak through the seeds; we, in turn, become the ancestors for the generations to come in this sacred transmission.

Consequently, Gabriel had amassed an extraordinary seed collection of rare, traditional and heirloom varieties of mostly foods, flowers and herbs, which he then planted in a biodiversity garden at San Juan Pueblo. Gabriel had been hired by the pueblo to rekindle interest in Native American agriculture and this magical garden embodied his unique approach.

After Kenny's initial filming, we learned that this abundant variety of seeds was under threat because of patents and the proliferation of hybrids (new crosses, which were patentable) in the seed industry. We found out that most of the small seed companies were being acquired by the same chemical and pharmaceutical companies that also produce pesticides and synthetic fertilizers. It was ironic to recognize that these were many of the same drug companies that had opposed the Hoxsey remedy.

The experience was a wake-up call for both of us about the danger to our food supply posed by the loss of agricultural biodiversity of the planet and the centralization of corporate control. We came to understand that biodiversity is the very cloth from which life is woven; the reservoir, or library, of all the adaptations that life has made over four billion years. When there is a crisis or a challenge, you go back to that reservoir because it is the source of resilience for evolution itself; yet, here it was, under imminent and escalating threat. We're in the midst of the Earth's sixth great spasm of extinctions, but this is the first one bearing the fingerprint of the human hand. The Earth will regenerate, but it takes 10 million years to achieve the kind of biodiversity we have now—not exactly a human time frame.

Gabriel approached Kenny soon after he'd finished the movie and asked if he would help him raise money to start a health center and an organic farming project. As they talked, it was clear that the most important aspect of the work was the preservation of these precious seeds. They started a company called Seeds of Change, whose strategy was to start a market partnership with backyard gardeners who prize and cherish diversity.

At that time, I was working with the Santa Fe Chamber Music Festival, discovering the beauty of chamber music and developing skills in nonprofit administration. When I went for a walk through Gabriel's garden, it changed my life. I encountered whole societies of tomatoes and peppers of every shape, size and color, and the intoxicating smells were beyond anything I'd ever experienced. There were tall stalks of glowing red amaranth, quinoa and other plants that I had never seen before. As we walked, I was encouraged to taste, so I picked leaves and munched my way through, feeling the utter vitality of the whole environment coursing through my senses.

The richness and fertility of the garden resonated deeply within me; I felt as though the spirit of the natural world tapped me on the shoulder and said, "You're working for me now." The strength of my affinity for the essence of this garden—and the healthy, restorative and vital system it represented—thrilled me and my life took a sharp turn. I quit my job with the Chamber Music Festival and went to work for Seeds of Change.

Having grown up in New York City, I knew nothing about gardening, farming or plant diversity and very little about the biodiversity crisis, but I did know that I was serving something that spoke to me very deeply and had a quality of vitality and a capacity for healing that I had never encountered. I knew that the life force I'd encountered in that garden had a thrilling capacity to renew and heal our world and I threw myself into the work.

Working as marketing director for Seeds of Change, I embarked on the steepest learning curve of my life. While it was daunting to realize how little I knew, it was exhilarating to work for something I believed in so strongly and I felt more alive than with any work I'd ever done. I learned about the loss of obscure kinds of heirloom and traditional food plants, which had been lovingly bred by gardeners for generations but which were no longer commercially available. I learned about how, with open-pollinated varieties, gardeners could save their own seeds from one season to the next, improving their strains through careful observation and selection each growing season.

However, seed companies, which were dependent on annual sales, were increasingly marketing what's called F1 hybrids ("mules" that won't reproduce seeds true to form and require gardeners and farmers to return to the company store each year). To sell them, hybrids were touted as having "hybrid vigor," supposedly being hardier and more productive than the open-pollinated varieties they were replacing. The sad truth is that hybrids were being bred for traits that facilitated mechanical harvesting—like uniform ripening—and not for taste, food quality or nutrition. With Seeds of Change, we were engaging an army of backyard gardeners to help save the diversity and quality of our food system.

As I began to understand these food- and farming-related issues, I saw that this awareness of where our food comes from, how it's raised and how it in turn affects our bodies and our health is a crucial turning point in cultivating our conscious connection to the web of life. I saw that, as we accept convenience as the defining property of our dietary choices, we lose so much of the richness and deliciousness of life's options. More importantly, we stand to lose the adaptability and sustainability of the very food that sustains us.

Most of us, without being aware of how our choices affect our lives, purchase commercially produced foods from the supermarket shelves, which is often out of season and transported an average of 1,000 miles. Many simply rely on fast food; families rarely eat together, losing the entire cultural transmission of cooking and relational intimacy of dining together. Considering the state of family relationships in this country, I began to see how central a role food plays in our culture and our relationship to place, each other and the entirety of the living world.

I learned how to speak to the dedicated world of backyard gardeners who we sought to enlist as our allies in protecting plant diversity through the business of Seeds of Change and who practice their arts from many differing perspectives. Kenny and I were passionate about this work and saw ourselves as working for the seeds—and for diversity itself—and were able to attract a lot of media coverage. We developed gourmet stories for food writers, biodiversity stories for science and environment journalists and companion planting stories for master gardeners and gardening writers. The seeds had found a great ally in each of us.

Following his journalistic curiosity, and as his alarm at the increasing environmental damage grew, Kenny sought to identify people who had demonstrated viable model solutions. One by one, he began to find folks who were effectively working on innovative approaches for conserving biodiversity and bioremediation, which is using natural systems to detoxify soil and water. He discovered that there were many pioneering innovators involved in successful model projects, but no one had ever heard of them and they didn't know each other.

One day, Kenny spoke to a friend, lamenting the lack of public awareness of these promising resources and recognizing the potential of the network they could become to support each other's work. The friend suggested that we produce a conference and offered to help fund it. That was the beginning of the first Bioneers Conference in 1990.

Kenny asked me if I'd help produce it. Although I was ambivalent about its scientific focus, I knew that it was important and agreed. When I heard the speakers who Kenny assembled, science came alive for me and I felt my childlike sense of wonder return. Here were courageous and curious explorers whose experiments with natural systems revealed the complexity and brilliance of four billion years of evolution. Contrary to the arrogant and mechanistic way I'd previously experienced science, these people quivered with the delight of discovery, humbly studying at the feet of a real master: nature herself.

At Bioneers, I first heard Native American people speak about healing from an indigenous perspective—one that included greater relatedness to place, to each other, to the Earth and to all creatures. I understood that their knowledge and experience were essential to our survival as a species; that, having already adapted to thousands of years of change, indigenous people have information about how we are meant to live that must now be reintegrated into our mainstream culture.

Since its founding, the Bioneers Conference has become a preeminent gathering of visionaries with practical solutions for restoring the Earth and its people. This three-day annual conference attracts over 3,000 people, including both professional and general audiences; offers models, resources and networks; and encourages everyone to act as a primary force in the transformation toward a restorative future.

I've come to see restoration as a primary goal and to appreciate that aiming for sustainability isn't nearly as compelling or enough. Paul Hawken points out that sustainability is simply the midpoint between destruction and restoration. Given how degraded our environmental and human systems already are, and imagining how verdant and healthy they could become, I find restoration to be a far more inspiring aim.

This year, 15 satellite conferences (called Beaming Bioneers) will be broadcast in colleges, communities and cities throughout North America, helping local communities organize and network around local speakers and issues. Our award-winning radio series, *Bioneers: Revolution from the Heart of Nature*, is heard on public radio stations in over 120 markets. Half-hour videotaped programs are used by study groups, broadcast on television and shared at schools and libraries. We also have an active membership and a happening website and conduct media outreach to get greater coverage of the Bioneers community.

The Bioneers Conference serves as a focal point for numerous diverse constituencies across a broad span of projects and communities. The gathering provides many opportunities for cross-pollinating information and networks while encouraging collaboration. The conference equips people with models, resources, tools and a community to support greater participation, and nourishes this growing community with inspiration while generating innumerable tangible outcomes.

As a "big tent," Bioneers does not espouse a particular ideology but instead recognizes that, for the system to be complete and most whole, it must include and embrace a multiplicity of approaches. Like any natural system, its health is enhanced by the quality of diversity within it. People are attracted to Bioneers through various entry points, including concerns about globalization, an interest in revitalizing community, alternative energy, seed saving, women's leadership, indigenous wisdom, youth activism, redefining democracy and environmental education.

When I experience Bioneers, I recall the fundamental interrelatedness of the issues we face. We'll never have social justice until we have environmental health; restoring our environmental health must involve addressing social inequality. As Kenny Ausubel's poem says:

> *It's all alive*
> *It's all related*
> *It's all intelligent*
> *It's all relative.*

The Bioneers Conference has assembled a singular, cross-cultural, global gathering of biological pioneers working with nature to heal nature. The unique Bioneers culture focuses on solutions informed by the biological truth of interconnectedness, which is essential to mending living systems and our relationship as human beings with the natural world. The inspiring stories of the successes of the Bioneers illustrate the diversity of ways an individual can make a difference and illuminate a future landscape of hope.

These scientific and social innovators define a coming Age of Biology founded in principles of kinship, interdependence, cooperation and community. They share working models and stories of restoration that can migrate, be refined and spread worldwide as vital keys to environmental and cultural renewal.

Practicing science without art and spirit has gotten us in a great deal of trouble; in fact, they are intimately related. If and when we practice them as a joint discipline, we have a different personal and planetary experience, which leads to different outcomes and requires us to remember how much we have to learn from nature. The current state of the world implores us to rapidly adopt a more cautious and humble stance than science has conventionally done. Once they are rewoven, the hubris assumptions that have led us in so many wrong directions can't continue.

Buddhist teacher and writer Joanna Macy refers to this time as the "great turning." She says there are three elements necessary to assist the great turning to succeed. One of them is revealing the truth of what is actually happening right now—the untold stories about damaging practices to both people and the planet; the second is elevating alternative solutions and possibilities; and the third is a change of heart. Bioneers addresses all three elements and frames the information and networking within the context of our interdependent living system. It gives us a different way of experiencing our story as human beings—being *a part of* rather than *apart from* the natural world.

For me, this work is fulfilling, challenging and exciting. It is well fitted to who I am and uses a myriad of diverse skills that might not be combined in any other position. I spread ideas that have the capacity to help heal nature and culture, help create communications that can reach millions and build connective tissue among diverse constituencies, enabling them to recognize their common ground. Through fund-raising efforts, working with our board and staff, I connect with people who share this vision and offer ways to move the dream into reality through support of this work. I approach most of my days with enthusiasm and a sense of gratitude and celebration at getting to serve our collective healing in a way that I find personally delicious and compelling.

Love is, I believe, a potent driving force in creating change. I have seen many people do extraordinary things with a sense of fierce love and a commitment to protect, defend and serve that which they love. Many amazing women leaders have been motivated by this kind of love, such as Julia Butterfly Hill, who lived in a 1,000-year-old redwood tree for two years. I know that her love for that tree and the forests fueled her through that ordeal.

My affinity with the fertile beauty and healing capacity of the natural world is my primary motivator. In the larger picture, though, I believe there has been an odd disconnect between the women's movement and the environmental movement. Although most women worldwide share a deep concern for the environment, the women's movement has rarely integrated a concern for the Earth.

There is enormous potential in bringing these two movements together. Women are beginning to understand the intimate connection of their own health and the health of their children and loved ones to the health of the planet. Women can effect change by stepping into leadership and demonstrating the power of leading, and acting, through love. Since there are few models for this kind of leadership, we must form and strengthen networks of mutual aid and support, which can increase our capacity and courage to lead in new ways.

At the 2001 Bioneers Conference, activist Diane Wilson closed her speech by saying, "A reasonable woman adapts to the world, an unreasonable woman makes the world adapt to her. So I encourage you all to be unreasonable!" She called Kenny and me after the conference and told us she had a vision that there would be a movement of unreasonable women. She described how, all weekend long, women had thanked her, tearfully, for what she'd said.

I decided that I would help seed this vision by bringing together a diverse group of women leaders to explore what such a movement might look like. I expanded the title of the gathering to "UnReasonable Women for the Earth." I invited 34 women, ranging in age from 23 to 70 years old, and across all disciplines, classes and races. Each of us worked in different domains including environmental health, law, poetry, social organizing, art, writing, seed diversity, urban farming and genetic engineering.

After four days, we agreed that the vision must include and invite all people, although its leadership and design must come from women. One imperative was that we help educate people about the connectivity among issues that are commonly presented in isolation by the media. For instance, in speaking about the need for peace, we must explore the connections between war, environmental devastation and human health; in discussing globalization, we need to address its effects on people, jobs, economics, local ecologies and food.

When we first arrived at the meeting, we spoke about our own feelings of isolation and recognized that we each had a need for more of a community of peers. By the end of the four days, a solidarity had developed—a pledge to stand at each other's backs—that nourished us in unexpected ways. Ultimately, we explored how women come together and strengthen each other.

We have experienced conventional forms of leadership—based on hierarchy rather than relationship and power rather than respect—for 6,000 years, which has left our world in dire shape. The time has come to model the respectful, relational connectivity that we know as a true pattern of life and stand up for that truth. Women all over the world are now leading movements for environmental and societal restoration and are doing it in ways that invite unity and collaboration. This new leadership will not be based on pure logic, rational thinking or mental acuity, nor is it based principally on raw power. It truly integrates the wisdom of body, heart, mind and spirit and organizes it through a shared passion and vision.

Our world has been badly damaged and much of it may be beyond reverse; however, this destruction may have been necessary in order to create a strong enough human response to turn things around. We have a great opportunity to choose either the "doom and gloom" scenario, which perpetuates fear and separation, or the innovators who are walking a healing path and celebrating life's beauty and fertility. It is a time for us to come together and strengthen our alliance with the regenerative capacity of the natural world.

Notice where you have passion and what you feel strongly about loving, and then nurture and feed that within yourself. Most of us have moments where something touches us deeply; for each person, it's different. We all have an opportunity now—perhaps even a responsibility—to notice what makes our flame grow brighter. When we give ourselves over to that passion, to what we love most, it will become our most meaningful and unique contribution towards a healthier world.

SUGGESTED LINKS

http://www.bioneers.org (Bioneers and Collective Heritage Institute)

http://www.bioneers.org/beaming.html (Beaming Bioneers)

http://www.newdimensions.org/special-series/bioneers1.html (New Dimensions World Broadcasting Network)

http://www.unreasonablewomen.org (UnReasonable Women for the Earth)

BIBLIOGRAPHY

Ausubel, Kenny. *Hoxsey: How Healing Becomes a Crime.* Videotape available through the Bioneers website (http://64.45.12.200/shopping_cart/product.html).

Ausubel, Kenny and Chelsea Green. *The Bioneers: Declarations of Interdependence.* Book available through the Bioneers website (http://64.45.12.200/shopping_cart/product.html).

Ausubel, Kenny, editor, with J.P. Harpignies. Foreword by Dr. Andrew Weil. *Ecological Medicine: Healing the Earth, Healing Ourselves.* San Francisco: Sierra Club Books, 2004. Book available through the Bioneers website (http://www.bioneers.org/programs/books/index.php).

____. *Nature's Operating Instructions: The True Biotechnologies (The Bioneers Series).* San Francisco: Sierra Club Books, 2004.

Bioneers: Revolution from the Heart of Nature. Link to radio series available through the Bioneers website (http://www.bioneers.org/programs/radio/series1.php).

FOOTNOTES START ON PAGE 204.

HELEN CALDICOTT

Opposing the Nuclear Age

"There has never been a better time for women
to step forward and take power—and we can."

Helen is the world's leading spokesperson for the antinuclear movement, the founder of the Nobel Prize-winning Physicians for Social Responsibility (PSR) and a nominee for the Nobel Peace Prize. She is the founder and president of the Nuclear Policy Research Institute (NPRI), which was established in 2002 to educate the public through the media about the profound medical consequences of perpetuating nuclear weapons, power and waste.

In 2003, she received the Lannan Prize for Cultural Freedom. The Smithsonian Institute and Ladies' Home Journal *named her one of the most Influential Women of the Twentieth Century and* Condé Nast Traveler *acknowledged her life's work as one of 100 "World Savers." She divides her time between Australia and the United States, where she has devoted the last 30 years to an international campaign to educate the public about the medical hazards of the nuclear age.*

I don't feel that I am a "warrior mother" at all. The work I do is for the children. At age 19, I read Nevil Shute's novel *On The Beach* and it changed my life. I was haunted by the idea of a nuclear war and the havoc it would wreak.

When I was pregnant with my first baby, I thought, "Should I bring a child into this world?" I was a general practitioner at the time before training to become a pediatrician and internist. I had all of the knowledge about the nuclear issue and had to seriously question whether the world was safe enough for my child. When I did have a baby—over 40 years ago—I realized that I was an adult and had to make sure that my child had a future. I am a pediatrician who took the Hippocratic Oath, so potentially all of the world's children are my patients. I practice preventative medicine to make sure that all children have a future. In my work, I am a mother to the world, most importantly as a physician.

I had three children in three years. Being a mother allowed me to experience a new kind of love; for the first time in my life, I knew that I would die to save the life of my child. I became secondary. When I was breast feeding, I was so nurturing that I could have fed the whole world; I was also tired and my appetite was huge. This feeling was immense and hormonal—the result of the love I had for everyone … the love I had for life itself. As the hormones decreased and the baby grew older, I got unhappy because my marriage wasn't fulfilling. I thought, "I know. I'll have another baby!"

My work as a physician and in the nuclear arms race took me away from home. Even still, my children have grown up to be beautiful people and I am so proud of them. What we do as mothers deeply affects our children. We must take a stand and be a model for our children.

My daughter Penny—a doctor with three children—is setting up an alternative medical clinic. She says, "Mom, I am the same as you. I have the same passion and I can do what you have done." My oldest son Philip has trodden gently on the world. He is a waiter and a gourmet cook and has never done anything to damage the Earth. Philip grew up in the U.S. and recently told me, "This country is like an apple. It is rotten in the middle and I am never coming back." He is highly intelligent and very cynical. My third child, Will, is an environmental scientist and received his master's degree from Yale. He is working for a company in Australia called Virotec, which uses red mud to clean up polluted lakes and rivers.

My work is all consuming. I have a photographic memory, which enables me to write books and speak. I know the facts and they are absolutely terrifying. When I give a lecture, it is not to frighten people but to wake them up and do what is necessary to help this planet and the future of humankind. I get great joy in knowing that I have empowered people to change their lives.

Women are much better than men at pulling together the overall picture because we have a larger corpus callosum and therefore our connection between the right and left brain is much bigger. Because of this physiologic difference, we are able to do more things at the same time. Our bodies are built to nurture life because estrogen has a far bigger impact on the psyche in terms of nurturing than does testosterone.

High levels of testosterone have proven to lead to fighting and killing.[1] I spoke at a 1978 women's convention in Houston and made the statement, "Women are the nurturers." Anthropologist Margaret Mead came up on the stage, wearing her cape and carrying her staff, and said, "Yes, women are the nurturers. We nursed our babies in the caves while the men were out killing the saber-toothed tiger, mammoth elephants and other marauding tribes."

We are three million years old and that instinct to kill hasn't changed. Men still kill; women, on the other hand, tend to sit back and do nothing about the men who commit horrific acts of war and create weapons of mass destruction. The killing sickness is now anachronistic because of nuclear weapons. Einstein said, "The splitting of the atom changed everything. Save man's mode of thinking [and *being*], thus we drift towards unparalleled catastrophe." I include *being* because our killing actions are creating a whole new terror throughout the world.

Women can be timid and pathetic and have not stepped into their power. Fifty-three percent of the world's population is women; they do two-thirds of the world's work and earn 10 percent of the income[2]; they have all of the babies and have absolutely no power. In an organization, women tend to vote to support and please the men; however, when their representation reaches a certain percentage, they then tend to oppose the male ethos and instead say, for example, "Let's stop making missiles and vote for milk for our children."

It is time that women take over. The men currently in power in the U.S. are the most dangerous I have ever seen. They need their bottoms smacked metaphorically and should be removed from office. They must be told that they have had their time and they have failed miserably, and now we, the women, are going to run things.

France just passed a parity law in which 50 percent of all people running for office have to be women[3] (it should be 53 percent). I am sick of buttering up to men. For too long, women have been playing second fiddle to men and have been discarded. There has never been a better time for women to step forward and take power … and we can.

Women's instinct to save their children is amazing! I have seen women who are absolute fireballs if their child is sick: finding the best doctor, selling their house and doing whatever is necessary to save their child. That instinct must be extrapolated to all of the children in the world and to the other 30 million species. In 30 years, it has been predicted that 25 percent of the mammals are going to be extinct. That's *us* … human beings! We drive around in sport utility vehicles that get 12 miles to the gallon. How dare we do that? We are egocentric and thoughtless.

Our children know, especially primary school children, that our planet is in a terrifying state and they are desperate. Young children haven't yet developed the instinct for psychic numbing; they have little antennae all over their bodies and pick up everything. When their hormones start surging, they go into the "don't see, don't hear" behavior for psychological protection. The suicide rate in young children is rising dramatically.[4]

Thirty percent of people in America are on antidepressants[5] because they know things are really sick but are doing nothing about it. They seem to be immobilized and, in this paralyzed state, they are encouraged to "buy and fly," as George W. Bush says. Buying achieves nothing except deadness of the soul. People should never watch television; American TV is the most ghastly television I have ever seen. The ads are brilliantly revolting and are brainwashing people to the ultimate degree.

Women need to rise up powerfully. I don't mean by just joining an organization. I mean by taking over and not needing anyone's approval. When I was younger, I felt I needed that kind of approval. I flirted my way through medical school, although I graduated second in my class. My mother taught me to flirt. Part of the hormonal makeup and sociological nature of a young women is that they need to attract the right mate to get their eggs inseminated and have a baby in order to have genetically healthy children. This has to change.

Many women become empowered once they have been through the fire. My fire was devastating but it also made me who I am today. In the late '70s, I moved to Boston to teach at Harvard University. I founded PSR, an organization that now, through its international arm—the International Physicians for the Prevention of Nuclear War (IPPNW)—has over 100,000 doctors committed to educating their colleagues about the dangers of nuclear power, nuclear weapons and nuclear war. On trips abroad, I helped start similar medical organizations in many other countries, all of which became part of IPPNW. In 1980, I founded the Women's Action for Nuclear Disarmament in the U.S.

At PSR, I had problems because I gave older men at Harvard authority over me and, in 1983, I was removed by a group of men from PSR. Simultaneously, Bernard Lown co-opted the international work I'd done to found IPPNW. In 1985, he was awarded the Nobel Prize. Lown had a friend who was a cardiologist in the Soviet Union and who knew Soviet General Secretary Leonid Brezhnev, so he had an "in" with the Russian doctors. Because of his contact, the Russian doctors were all co-opted by the Soviet government to join IPPNW, which meant hundreds of thousands of doctors became members. Lown said that he created IPPNW, but he didn't. I had started all the medical organizations in Europe, all over America and in Japan, Australia, New Zealand and Canada.

When I was tossed out of PSR, I was devastated. Shortly after that—in 1988, when I turned 50—my husband of 27 years left me for a younger woman. My children had also left home and I found myself alone. From those extremely hard years, I got to the stage where I knew I could live alone and be secure and happy.

In 1995, I moved to Long Island, New York, and lived in East Hampton for a few years. I started an organization called STAR (Standing for Truth About Radiation), which is a grass-roots organization concerned about the toxic effects of nuclear radiation. STAR promotes public awareness, medical and scientific investigation, institutional accountability and independent oversight. It is responsible for public health and environmental policies and promotes alternative and renewable energy technologies as the available solution to nuclear-generated power. We closed down two nuclear reactors on Long Island at the Brookhaven National Labs. I recruited supermodel Christie Brinkley into that organization and she is now very powerful.

I went back to live in Australia and finished my fifth book, *The New Nuclear Danger: George W. Bush's Military-Industrial Complex*. I have now started a new institute called the NPRI, which is based in Washington, DC. Its purpose is to educate through the media and mobilize a mass movement of concerned citizens throughout the U.S. to oppose and take on George Bush's extraordinarily dangerous nuclear policies regarding Star Wars and nuclear power in general.

The institute will directly take on the Heritage Foundation, which is the conservative think tank for the American government. They don't believe in free education, free health care, alternative energy or mass transit. Funded by transnational corporations and wealthy individuals (including Joseph Coors, Philip Morris, Amway and Hyundai), the Heritage Foundation's 1999 income was $43.6 million.[6] Lockheed Martin, Raytheon, Boeing and TRW (all major defense contractors) are also financial backers, eager for the $200 billion that George Bush's national missile defense plan has been estimated to cost.[7]

It is no surprise that many Bush appointees hail from Lockheed Martin and the Heritage Foundation. Donald Rumsfeld, the current secretary of defense, was once described by Henry Kissinger as the most ruthless man he ever knew. Rumsfeld is a close associate of Frank Gaffney, a major Star Wars warrior from the Reagan administration, who heads the Center for Security Policy and is behind the demonization of China as the new Cold War enemy.

The Heritage Foundation set up an agenda for the Reagan administration to follow, which they called "Mandate for Leadership—Policy Management in a Conservative Administration." The agenda items included arming America to fight and win a nuclear war and to develop "superiority" over the Soviet Union. During Reagan's second term in office, the Heritage Foundation issued another Mandate for Leadership. The Heritage Foundation is now responsible for most of Bush's agenda in promoting the nuclear arms race and they are actively lobbying for Star Wars.[8] With these kinds of organizations running the world, *we must take action.*

I am a pantheist (named after Pan, the Greek god of nature)—one who believes that God and the universe are the same and that the sanctity of life is nature. I don't believe in life after death, but I do believe that life is sacred. I am absolutely passionate that the creation survives. A few years ago, I decided to retire and spend time in my garden, but I got very depressed and went on antidepressants. I realize now that if I don't serve and do my work, I should be dead and fertilizing the soil. I think that is why so many Americans are on antidepressants: they are not serving.

How can women serve? They can let the knowledge penetrate their soul. If a child had leukemia, their mother would be like the lioness and overturn every obstacle, doing everything in her power to make sure her child survives. Women have to use that instinct to take over. One woman can turn this country upside down. Women come up to me with their eyes full of tears—not because of what I said, but because they know they have to step into their power.

After hearing one of my lectures, a woman in the audience, Joan Bokaer, became so depressed that she couldn't move for two years or get out of bed. One morning, a light went on in her head. She got out of bed, dressed in her best clothes, interviewed for a job with the Heritage Foundation and worked there for one year. At night, when everyone left the office, she went through the files to find the source of their funding and their agenda. At the end of the year, she set off on a crusade across the country, speaking in churches and synagogues and letting Americans know what the right-wing Heritage Foundation was doing.

In between traveling and lecturing, I spend time at home in my 2-acre garden in Australia where I have a profound sense of mysticism and total joy. When I am treating patients or giving birth to a baby, that is mystical as well. I am never happier than when I am in my garden on a still, beautiful and peaceful day, experiencing a total reverence for life. This is an important time for me because this is when I know what I have to do. Every woman has this deep sense of knowing. It will tell you what to do if you listen.

The destiny of this planet, if we continue the way we have been, is destruction. We are killing the Earth and the systems upon which all life survives: the ozone; the temperature-control mechanisms; and the oceans, rivers and lakes, which are terribly polluted. The trees—the lungs of the Earth—are being chopped down at a massive rate. The Earth is going to have total organ collapse, which is similar to what happens to patients in the intensive care unit, and then they die. We are destroying the Earth at a rapid speed. Some of us might survive, but there is little time for evolution.

The other major possibility is that there is going to be a nuclear war. The world is on the brink of one right now with the situation between India and Pakistan and the Middle East. Israel has 300 nuclear bombs.[9] When the U.S. goes into Iraq, the Pentagon says it could use nuclear weapons, which could trigger a global holocaust between Russia and America. Twelve years after the end of the Cold War, the U.S. still has Russia and China targeted with more than 2,500 hydrogen bombs on hair-trigger alert[10]; Russia has a similar number facing the U.S., also on alert.[11]

In contrast, China has only 20 antiquated, liquid-fueled, intercontinental nuclear missiles.[12] Official U.S. policy is still to fight and win a nuclear war, so it maintains extremely accurate, first-strike weapons whose purpose is to destroy Russian missiles in their silos in a surprise attack. Nuclear missile defense weapons would then be launched against the few Russian missiles that may survive an American first strike. This scheme will thus destabilize the delicate nuclear balance among these superpowers, because Russia and China see it as a move to enhance America's first-strike winnable nuclear war capability.[13]

If we continue developing a missile defense system, Russia and China have said that they will build many more nuclear weapons to overwhelm missile defense (called "vertical proliferation"); if the U.S. continues to build more weapons, other smaller countries like Brazil, Argentina, Egypt or even Australia will say, "You are building and testing them, so we will, too" (called "lateral proliferation"). Suddenly, we have vertical and lateral proliferation, which is the nuclear cross on which we will all be crucified. It will happen within the next 10 or 20 years, and most likely before that. In my books, I list all of the near misses we have had with nuclear missiles and nuclear war. I really don't know how we are still here.

Being a mother means a lot to me. I can't stand the thought of my children being killed, but it is deeper than that. I have a reverence for life. I would have done this work even if I hadn't had children. That is why I went into medicine; it's like being a nun. I resent those who create weapons of mass destruction. My life has been stolen and I haven't been able to practice medicine because I spend all of my time getting the word out about nuclear weapons and the arms race.

I am a pacifist, but my feelings are of real anger and hatred towards these men. Imagine spending your whole life making a Daisy Cutter bomb that sucks people's eyeballs out of their sockets! A Daisy Cutter, which got its name for the blast pattern it leaves when viewed from above, is a huge bomb that can cause massive destruction—similar to fuel-air bombs, which have been likened to tactical nuclear weapons without the radiation. They vaporize a fuel in the air and then ignite it. This produces a fireball and a rapidly expanding blast wave many times greater than that from conventional explosives. According to the U.S. Air Force, these have been used on Iraq. The effects are felt over an area reported to be the size of several football fields. Near the ignition point, people are incinerated at a temperature of 2,500 to 3,000 degrees Centigrade.[14] These weapons should be banned and the war machine shut down for good.

When I go into the autopsy room and see a woman, still lactating milk because she's just given birth and lying on the slab just having died from breast cancer, I can hardly take it. The billions of dollars being spent on weapons could be put into medical research and health care. When I read medical reports from Iraq, which indicate that childhood malignancies have increased five times from what they were and that congenital malformations have increased seven times in the areas where the U.S. bombed the most intensely,[15] I become enraged. The worst part is that Iraqi pediatric physicians cannot treat these children because they do not have access to radiotherapy or antibiotics due to sinful sanctions imposed by the U.S. Clearly, the world is out of balance.

Mothers: read all of my books and work out what action you are going to take. Knowledge is ammunition. If you don't have knowledge, you don't know what you need to do to save the future for your children. I hope my books will guide you towards doing what needs to be done. It is imperative to the future of this planet and to the future of all life.

CONTACT

hcaldic@bigpond.com

SUGGESTED LINK

http://www.nuclearpolicy.org (Nuclear Policy Research Institute)

BIBLIOGRAPHY

Caldicott, Helen. *The New Nuclear Danger: George W. Bush's Military-Industrial Complex.* New York: The New Press, 2002.

FOOTNOTES START ON PAGE 204.

PAM PROVINCE

Exploding the Myth About Disability

"Women value life at every level and uphold life in all of its forms. This is the core at the center that makes mothers the caregivers and keepers of the sanctity of life."

Pam grew up in California and is the youngest of five children. She has been married for over 20 years and has two children. She works for a local school district as an instructional assistant in special education. Because of everything her daughter has taught her, she now helps other children with disabilities learn and thrive.

When a woman is pregnant, the feeling of life growing inside her body creates a profound connection to all life. She falls in love with her baby before it is born. She knows that no matter what, she will love her child and do everything in her power to give it what it needs.

I was 32 years old when I got pregnant with Cassandra. My husband Harold and I had been trying to get pregnant for a while. He didn't have any biological children and really wanted a child of his own. When I finally got pregnant and went to a doctor, I let him know that my biggest fear was having another premature baby. (Karma, my oldest daughter from my first marriage, was born three months early.)

The doctor guaranteed that, if I could get past six months, I'd have a full-term baby. The pregnancy was normal and I felt confident. Two weeks past my due date, my husband and I went to the birthing center and the doctor broke my water. Harold and I went for a walk and my cramps got worse, so we went back into the birthing room. I had a funny feeling in my uterus, like a heartbeat in my vagina.

When the doctor came in, I asked him if I could go to the bathroom and he gave his consent. I went to the bathroom and, when I stood up, the umbilical cord fell out of my vagina. I opened the bathroom door and said, "Something's wrong." When the doctor saw the umbilical cord, he put me on the bed and put the umbilical cord back in my body. He called an ambulance and they transported me to the hospital where I had an emergency cesarean.

When Cassandra came out, she was blue from lack of oxygen. When the umbilical cord was exposed to the air, Cassandra was without oxygen for approximately 10 minutes. They took a photograph of her, gave it to me and whisked her away to a children's hospital in Fresno—a three-hour drive. I wanted to hold and see my baby and couldn't understand what was happening. I was absolutely terrified! When Karma was born, she was transported to San Francisco to a neonatal unit because she was a preemie. For three months, we were only allowed to see Karma once a week on Sundays. I was going to leave the hospital once again without my child!

I recovered in the hospital for three days. When my milk came in, I was given a shot to dry it up. I wanted to nurse my baby, but I was told that this would be impossible. I became more frightened every day. When I was released, Harold, Karma and I drove to Fresno Children's Hospital to see Cassandra and stayed there for a week.

When I first saw her, I fell in love, just like any mother. At the same time, I was distraught because she was unable to suck and had a tube down her stomach. Several nurses taught me how to put the tube down her throat into her stomach and it was horrifying. My biggest goal was getting her to suck; after a week of working on this, she started to suck. I felt relieved because I wouldn't have to use the tube at home.

When she was born, the doctors thought she had a seizure and put her on seizure medication, so she had to be weaned off of it. Because Cassandra had been without oxygen for 10 minutes, our doctor thought she had cerebral palsy and said that he didn't know to what extent it would affect her development. I was told that when she turned five, they would have a better idea of how much damage had been done to her brain and how it was affecting her motor cortex. I was also told that sometimes these things happen and we would just have to wait and see how Cassandra developed. I had never been around someone with cerebral palsy and didn't know very much about it, so the information didn't really sink in. I was her mother; whatever happened, I would deal with it.

We took Cassandra home and I was so grateful that she was with us. She was taking a bottle and I was able to hold and feed her, which was extremely gratifying. She appeared normal, but I began to notice that she wasn't developing like other babies: she had a hard time holding her head up, she wasn't reaching out to grab things with her hands and she wasn't able to roll over. Cassandra was missing all of the developmental markers. When she was three years old, her bowels started to fail. She began to have a lot of stomach problems and the doctors couldn't figure out what was going on. I was devastated and thought, "How am I going to take care of her?"

Since she was four months old, she had received therapy from California Children's Services (CCS). When she turned three, she was given a manual wheelchair; shortly after that, she was given a power wheelchair so she could operate it independently. I knew that she would never walk and it was a heartbreak.

At one point, I chose to go to therapy because I thought I was cracking up. My baby cried 24 hours a day and my husband and I couldn't spend any time together. He and I were told by the therapist that our fears were relevant and that we were doing fine, but it didn't feel that way. Through CCS, I joined a weekly group of mothers of disabled children who talked about their stress and their fears.

It is not Cassandra's fault for having cerebral palsy and I wasn't going to deny her an active life. Being disabled in the world is challenging, but she and I have worked together to make it as easy as possible. When she was younger, people would stare at her. She'd want me to tell them what was wrong, but I would say, "Cassandra, I'm not going to stop every person and tell them what's wrong with you. If they want to know, they can ask." When they did ask, I would look them in the eye and say, "My daughter has cerebral palsy," then turn and walk away.

We consulted a lawyer about Cassandra's birth and, after a lengthy consultation, we decided to sue the doctor for malpractice. Over a period of nine years, we went to court three times but never won the case. A friend of mine had the same doctor deliver her baby a year after Cassandra was born. Because of the delivery process, her child came out severely brain damaged. She went to court and won the lawsuit. We did not have the same satisfaction of getting compensation for this terrible medical mistake.

When Cassandra was five years old, she started kindergarten in a public school and was integrated into a regular classroom. The head of Special Services told us that he had everything Cassandra would need to attend school. She was given an aid and a stander, so she wouldn't have to sit in her wheelchair all day. She had not developed any language skills, so communicating with her was difficult for her teacher and her peers. Still, her social life was good. The children included her in everything and she had a lot of friends.

Because Cassandra couldn't speak, she developed signals to communicate. If she wanted something, like a ball, she would look at the ball and then look at me. "Do you want something?" I'd ask. She would shake her head yes. Then I would ask, "What do you want?" She'd look at the ball and then she'd look at her hand, telling me that she wanted it in her hand. It took other people a while to figure out her signals, but once they did, it worked great.

On one of my yearly trips to the Disability Expo in Los Angeles to research new equipment for Cassandra, I saw an Eyegaze computer for $25,000. The Eyegaze System—a communication and control system for people with complex physical disabilities—is operated with the eyes. By looking at control keys displayed on a screen, a person can synthesize speech, control their environment (lights, appliances, etc.), use a typewriter, operate a telephone, run computer software, operate a computer mouse and access the Internet and e-mail. However, there was no way we could afford one.

Two years later, when Cassandra was in the fourth grade, I decided that the Eyegaze was perfect for her. I took her with me to the Expo, walked up to the Eyegaze booth and asked if my daughter could try the computer. They explained to her how it worked and the first thing she typed out was the name of her boyfriend from school. It was the first time in her life she had ever used a word!

Cassandra began screaming and yelling with excitement. She was finally free to express herself with words and really communicate. I asked for a video about the Eyegaze so that I could show it to Special Services. A few days later, I walked in with the videotape and said, "I want you to look at this. It is what I need for Cassandra. Do you have any idea how to get it?" The head of Special Services looked at the videotape about Eyegaze and said, "You're right. This is for her!" He hooked me up with the assistant superintendent and he got the ball rolling.

Our entire community—seniors, families and community businesses—raised money for the Eyegaze. Cassandra was on the local television station, showing how the Eyegaze worked, and the employees in the school district raised money with a "pie in the face" contest and a golf tournament. Within a few months, we had raised $50,000 and were able to buy Cassandra two Eyegaze computers (one for home and one for school).

When Cassandra was in the sixth grade, her bowel problems got worse. She had to have a feeding tube put in because she wasn't eating enough to sustain her. She was extremely thin and her health was deteriorating. By the seventh grade, her body was beginning to fail. The doctor scheduled her for surgery, hoping that it would correct the problem.

The day before surgery, the hospital called and said that our insurance company had denied it. I was livid but said, "I don't care. She's having the surgery. If we have to pay for it, we will, but she's *having the surgery*!" The surgeons and nurses got on the case and, by the end of the day, the procedure was authorized. Cassandra had exploratory surgery and a malrotation of the bowel was discovered. The surgeons were able to fix it, but she became sick again and went back into the hospital for the entire summer. She weighed 48 pounds and her little body was struggling to survive. After five surgeries in one summer, she recovered. Now she is doing great!

We are still dealing with other surgeries for Cassandra. She had an implant put in to help her tremors—an extremely painful and difficult operation—but it wasn't working, so she had to go back for more surgery. Each time a surgery is required or Cassandra needs special equipment, dealing with the insurance companies and the medical system has been a real ordeal.

When she turns 18, she will work with an attendant who will help her with her daily needs such as dressing, showering and eating. I have been doing this for her because we couldn't afford to privately pay an attendant, but this expense will be covered by Supplemental Security Income at that time.

Before Cassandra got the Eyegaze computers, there was some question in the classroom as to her level of intelligence. With the Eyegaze, tests proved that she is of normal intelligence and had been learning all along. She can now surf the Internet and hold conversations with people; without the Eyegaze, she wouldn't be doing much of anything.

Cassandra will be graduating from high school next year as long as her health holds. She is planning on going to Hancock junior college and majoring in computers. She is interested in designing programs and eventually working with the people who make the Eyegaze system.

She spends hours on the Internet looking at group homes in order to move out and be more independent. Unfortunately, these homes are not geared towards someone with her intelligence. She will always have to have an attendant and I am not sure how her living away from home is going to work out. She wants to do what everyone else is doing, but physically she can't. She is a normal person in a lousy body. She's locked in and it's something she's learned to live with, but she doesn't like it. Last Saturday, a group from high school was going to Six Flags Magic Mountain amusement park in Los Angeles and she wanted to go. Since they didn't have the money to rent a wheelchair-friendly bus, I drove her. When we got there, she wasn't able to ride anything and it was quite disheartening.

It is frustrating when someone who isn't disabled parks in a disabled zone. I can push Cassandra if we are too far from an entryway, but I think of elderly and disabled people who don't have anyone to help them. People need to be more thoughtful about disability issues and the daily struggle that disabled people go through.

Cassandra has taught me about patience—mine and hers. She has more patience than I'll ever have. I think about mothers around the world who take care of their children with disabilities and my heart goes out to each one. Women are the caretakers, especially when someone is in need. Two years ago when my mother got sick, I had to take care of her and Cassandra at the same time. Then, my father became ill and I took care of him until he died.

Women have the ability to do many things at once and keep the ball rolling. Having the stamina to keep going, even when we are tired, is a woman's trait. Most parents with disabled children end up divorced. Harold and I have worked together, as a team, to make life as good as we can for Cassandra and our family.

I am very proud of Cassandra. The other day, I found some writing that she did for her class last year. It says so much about who she is as a person, how her mind works and what she can contribute to the world:

"Can you imagine being trapped in a snug tight box? Not being able to move and when you can finally move it's not what you want to do! Wanting to reach out and give someone a hug but only being able to see it and feel it in your mind? Wanting to run and jump, sing out loud? Knowing people look at you like you are from outer space and wanting to yell at them. I'm like you. I have a brain. I have feelings. I can hear and see and I can laugh and cry. I want to speak out loud, give people my thoughts and ideas, but I cannot. I have to type with my eyes on my computer or sometimes count on someone using my white board to single out each letter for me. It may take me some time to type out my words, but will you please listen to me? My thoughts are important for you to know. If you take the time to get to know me, I won't need the computer or the white board because you will be able to read my eyes.

"When I see someone hurting, maybe they have fallen and scraped their knee, I wish I could reach down and give them a kiss. Tell them it will be okay. I may be stuck in this box, some call a wheelchair. I don't want pity. Do not feel sorry for me. In some ways, I have more than others. The will to prove to the world that I am a person. Treat me as a human and take the time to say hello. I don't bite. You may speak to me, I can hear.

"I have so many obstacles in my way, but that has only helped me learn more about life and how to fight for what I want. Some people take it for granted that they can walk and talk. I treasure that I can see and breathe and have the ability to use my eyes to talk, my brain to think, my heart to love and care. What more could a person ask for? Some people who walk and talk don't care, they are dead inside. Their spirit has been broken somehow and killed. My spirit is alive. I have a life and we need to live what we were given and make the best of it. There is a saying, 'Is your cup half empty or half full?' My cup is half full and I plan on making it overflow. What more can a person ask for? Take the time to look into my eyes. They will tell you a lot! It has been said that the eyes are the window to the soul!"

When a mother looks into her child's eyes, no matter what the disability, all she sees is love. I believe that mothers have a bond with their child that no one else has. We don't look at the disability; we look at the child and understand that life is the greatest thing, with or without a disability. This is what keeps us going, even though we may face immense challenges and hard times. Women value life at every level and uphold life in all of its forms. This is the core at the center that makes mothers the caregivers and keepers of the sanctity of life.

CONTACT
karmasmom3893742@aol.com

SUGGESTED LINK

http://www.eyegaze.com (LC Technologies, Inc., Eyegaze Systems)

TERRI SWEARINGEN

Battling Toxic Incineration

"Whether it is working for peace or a healthier environment, the way to make a difference in the world is to *just begin*."

As the leader of one of the longest battles in environmental history, Terri has been called "The Housewife That Roared" and "The Crusader Who Won't Quit"—both apt descriptions of her activism to shut down one of the largest toxic incinerators located 2 miles downwind from her home.

One of Terri's major contributions is to bring moral, ethical leadership back into the debate about corporate toxic waste decisions. A mother and a nurse, Terri has fought the corporate giants whose main goal is financial gain without honoring the value of human health. Her motto has always been, "Whatever It Takes" to "Put People First."

She has been influential in swaying public opinion by helping community members and environmental and social justice organizations work together. She has been featured on CBS's 60 Minutes *and ABC's* Nightline *and profiled in The New York Times. Time magazine selected her as one of their "50 for the Future: A Roster of America's Most Promising Leaders, Age 40 and Under."*

Arrested a dozen times for peaceful, nonviolent civil disobedience and direct actions, Terri has helped to bring about a moratorium against the construction of new hazardous waste incinerators in Ohio and, on a larger scale, to bring to a halt the building of new commercial toxic waste incinerators nationwide.

I became an activist late in life. I was 34 years old when I took a stand against the East Liverpool toxic waste incinerator in Ohio; for 12 years, I have been one of the leaders in the fight to stop the incinerator. It often takes a direct threat before people will get involved and become activists—a threat to them, their children, their immediate family, a loved one or their community—and they take action to stop it, which is exactly what happened to me. Now, when I encourage people to get involved, I tell them, "You don't have to have a member of your family lynched before you know that racism is wrong."

I grew up in an ordinary family from the tiny rural community of New Manchester, West Virginia (in the Ohio Valley) and now live on the outskirts of Chester, just 10 minutes away, near the Ohio and Pennsylvania border. My dad was a pipe fitter in the local steel mill; my mother worked in the hot lunch program when it was initiated at New Manchester elementary school.

The Ohio Valley is notorious for high pollution levels due to the many power plants along the Ohio River.[1] I live within 10 miles of the Shippingport nuclear power plant, which is located alongside of the Bruce Mansfield coal-fired power plant. Air inversions are common in the Ohio Valley where the surrounding hills and mountains cause a bowl effect and where pollution can't rise up and disperse as it might in other areas. The pollution from factories is trapped like a toxic blanket across the entire valley.

After high school, I went to college to become a nurse. I had always wanted to work in the medical profession where I could help people and make a positive contribution to society. I knew that I wanted to work with and for people, and nursing seemed to be a good fit. At age 18, I married my husband, who had already established his dental business in East Liverpool. After graduating, I worked for a time in my brother's family practice medical office. I also worked in my husband's dental office as a ceramic colorist and lab technician, constructing orthodontic appliances.

One day in 1982, while working in my husband's dental office, a client, George Coleman, told me about plans to build a toxic waste incinerator in East Liverpool. It was to be built by Waste Technologies Incorporated (WTI), initially a consortium of four corporations and billed as the world's largest toxic waste incinerator. A Little Rock, Arkansas, company—run by Jackson Stephens, purportedly the wealthiest investment banker outside of Wall Street—first developed the plans for the East Liverpool incinerator. Because of legal, ethical and liability concerns, ownership of the facility has been a critical issue.

In 1990, the permit was sold; Von Roll, a multinational Swiss corporation, acquired sole ownership of the incinerator, but facility construction did not begin until 1991. To sell or trade a permit as a commodity violates the heart of the federal hazardous waste law.[2] Information about changes in ownership was not disclosed by Von Roll until inquiries during a 1992 congressional hearing. The incinerator remains under the control of Von Roll.

In 1996, three executives of Von Roll, including its former managing director Heinz Frech, were found guilty in Switzerland's highest court of illegally exporting war materials to Iraq, which were believed to be for the construction of Saddam Hussein's "super gun."[3] In July 2002, following an extensive German investigation of corruption involving waste incineration projects, René Lüthy (one of Von Roll's chief executives) was arrested on criminal bribery charges and released in August after Von Roll posted a bond of 200,000 Euros.[4] In March 2003, following his resignation from Von Roll, it was made public in Switzerland that René Lüthy was convicted of bribery, reportedly conducted during the past decade while he was a top Von Roll executive and director of the group's major U.S. subsidiaries.[5]

WTI was legally permitted to release 1.28 tons of mercury and 4.7 tons of lead into the air on an annual basis. The lead released from WTI would be the equivalent of about four or five cars pulverized into a fine, inhalable dust sprinkled over the area every year. As a nurse, I knew the ramifications of lead exposure to the human body. It is a well-established medical fact that lead in children causes decreased IQ, hyperactivity and behavioral disorders, and children are especially sensitive to its effect.[6] How could our government allow this to happen?

Lead and mercury emission figures—as cited by George Coleman, my husband's client— were so high that I automatically assumed he was mistaken. I went to the Carnegie Library in East Liverpool (the repository for the Von Roll/WTI permit and other public information on the WTI facility) and found that the information he had given me was accurate.[7] I was pregnant, getting ready to bring a child into this world, and WTI was planning to release toxic heavy metals and other dangerous pollutants into the air! My baby was going to be a victim and that is where my activism started. Any parent hopes to bring their child into the best environment possible. I knew the Ohio Valley was notorious for its high pollution levels and now there were plans to build a toxic waste incinerator that would drastically add to the problem.

I talked to everyone about the toxic waste incinerator. I was quite concerned and very much opposed to it but, at the time, didn't get fully involved in the movement to stop it from being built because a part of me was naïve: I believed the government was there to protect us and, if there were a threat, they wouldn't allow it to happen. There was also a group called Save Our County (SOC), which was working to prevent the construction of the incinerator; I thought they were going to stop it.

At the beginning, I was involved peripherally; my friends and family knew where I stood. Eventually, I went door to door, talking to people and collecting signatures on petitions in opposition to the incinerator. I collected 1,200 signatures in my county in a week. I wrote letters to the editor, to my congressmen and senators and contributed financially; on several occasions, I gave my entire part-time paycheck to SOC and asked my husband to match it, which he did.

There was a dormant period from 1986 until site preparation began in 1990 when the community thought the project was dead because of rumors about financial difficulties on the part of the developer. During that time, it was not uppermost in the minds of people in the community because they did not think it would ever be built.

One day in 1990, as I took my daughter to school, I got behind a big dump truck hauling soil from a hillside. I followed it and discovered that it was taking the soil to the WTI site. They were artificially elevating the site out of the 100-year flood plain in order to legally begin construction. I panicked as I realized they were actually going to build the incinerator! My panic turned into outrage. If I was not willing to put forth the energy and effort to stop it, how could I expect anyone else to do it for me?

It shocked me to see the toxic waste incinerator site—320 feet from the nearest home and 400 yards from a 400-student elementary school. To make matters worse, the elementary school sits on a bluff above the site, so the height of WTI's 150-foot smoke stack would be level with the front doors and windows of the elementary school. I could hardly believe the stupidity—and arrogance—of such a decision.

At first, my activism was inspired by being a fierce protector for my child. That feeling grew into concern for all of the children who had no choice and no voice in the matter and who would be living under the horrifying toxic emissions that would rain down on them daily. It seemed obvious to me that this corporation was more concerned about making money than it was about the health of children and people in the community.

When I first began the fight against WTI, I was known to say, "I can't wait until this is over!" Some people responded, "Terri, this will never end for you. You will always be involved." I look back in amazement because they saw something in me that I didn't see in myself. For the past 12 years, since I got involved to prevent the construction and operation of the WTI incinerator, I have been driven by a passion to right a wrong—to stop a grave injustice.

My drive comes from wanting to protect my community and especially the children. Children are the most vulnerable segment of our society. They are at the core of everything I do in the environmental and social justice movements. I couldn't just sit by while a toxic waste incinerator was being built so close to an elementary school! I never want to look back and think there was more I could have done to try and stop the incinerator.

In 1992, after a 12-year battle—one of the longest, active environmental fights in U.S. history—the WTI incinerator went into operation. An estimated 60,000 tons of hazardous waste is trucked in and burned each year.[8] On some days, I can see the smoke from the incinerator's stack billowing around the school. Von Roll/WTI is located in a poor, minority section of East Liverpool, so the greatest concern for many who live next door to the incinerator is putting food on the table. They can't deal with another problem, so they need someone to speak up for them.

Over the years, I have worked full time to stop the incinerator through many different kinds of actions. It has been an incredible wake-up call and an eye opener to how the government panders to big business and that, for most corporations, the all-mighty dollar far outweighs the value of human life … even the lives of children!

One Saturday, I was volunteering for Youth Appreciation Day at my daughter's school, which is on the opposite side of the river from WTI. The children were engaged in sidewalk chalk art when we heard a deafening explosion and several of the windows on the back side of the school were blown out by the impact. We ran towards the river and saw black smoke rising from a barge that was just down from WTI.

The barge was empty but at one time had contained benzene. Three men on board were cleaning the barge when a spark ignited benzene fumes, causing the massive explosion. It was a serious accident and all three men were blown into the river; one of them died and another lost his foot. I began to imagine what it would be like if there were an explosion at WTI. It became obvious to me that the incinerator was not far enough away from the school. I saw this as a significant warning that, no matter what WTI did to make it safe, it wasn't enough.

Before the incinerator was built, we received a second warning when the WTI construction crew struck a gas main during site preparation. At the elementary school, 400 yards from WTI, the smell of gas was so strong that school officials thought the leak was coming from within the school. Pandemonium broke out as the frightened school children were evacuated. Some of the children complained of headaches and nausea; some threw up from the fumes. WTI officials had neglected to tell the school that they had struck a gas main and that the problem was at the incinerator site. It became obvious that if a far more toxic chemical leaked from the incinerator, it could cause serious health damage—or even death—to children or school staff. Construction continued.

The Ohio congressman at that time, Jim Traficant, suggested that WTI buy the school and relocate it. Citizens protested, saying that even if the school were moved, many of the kids would still live 320 feet away from the incinerator—a much closer distance to WTI's toxic smoke stack. In Ohio, there is a citing criterion (a law that prohibits an incinerator from being built within 2,000 feet of any homes, schools, hospitals, prisons or within the flood plain).[9] This law was enacted four months after WTI got their permit, but nearly eight years prior to construction. Ironically, the property taxes from WTI help fund the school system, which means they are funding the very school they are poisoning.

I started networking. If someone gave me a name, I called them to get all the information I could about incineration and the health effects of toxic pollution. I had a Greenpeace-produced videotape called *The Rush to Burn,* which is about incineration. My husband showed the video in his adult bible study class where they were discussing stewardship of the Earth.

One of the women in his class, Mary Lee Vandevander, was outraged after watching the video. She called and asked me to speak to a local group that she had formed to protest the East Liverpool incinerator. To prepare myself, I went to the library and read everything I could about the incinerator and the toxic waste that was going to be burned there. I also received massive amounts of information from Becky Ammon, a woman who had been involved since the beginning and who had an entire barn filled with some of the earliest documents concerning the incinerator. I went to visit her and brought boxes of material home and read everything. In late 1990, I started speaking about the incinerator to organizations and groups in the tri-state region (Ohio, Pennsylvania and West Virginia).

An East Liverpool neurosurgeon, Dr. Larry Wacaser, asked me to speak before the Columbiana County Medical Association. I had two weeks to prepare, so I called Matt Petrovich, a federal Environmental Protection Agency (EPA) employee who worked at Research Triangle Park and to whom I had talked about incineration. Matt specialized in the effects of pollution on the heart, lungs and brain. He suggested that I read a book entitled *Neurotoxicity: Identifying and Controlling Poisons of the Nervous System.* I read this 362-page book in about two days and the information in it provided the foundation for my presentation to the medical society. My hopes were to obtain the support of the medical community and perhaps an official resolution of opposition, which we could use to support our position. After my presentation, they offered the resolution and made a generous financial contribution.

I learned about other chemicals found in incinerator emissions, which no one mentioned. WTI was going to be burning hundreds of different chemicals, including chemical warfare agents, pesticides and herbicides such as Agent Orange.[10] In addition to carcinogens and mutagens, incinerators emit about a dozen pollutants known to be endocrine-disrupting chemicals, which disrupt the hormone messenger system and which can have devastating effects on human health, especially the reproductive system.[11]

We spoke to city councils and met with county commissioners about the dangers of incineration. We prepared and disseminated fact sheets and fliers, issued press releases and held press conferences, which were covered by radio and television. We held community meetings up and down the Ohio River, telling people, "One of the world's largest toxic waste incinerators is being built not very far from where you live. We want to share what we've learned about incineration and its impact." We warned them that pollution knows no boundaries and can travel for hundreds of miles.

Over time, groups opposed to the incinerator began springing up around the region. In 1990, I cofounded the Tri-State Environmental Council to join forces, coordinate activities and unite efforts. Representatives from each of the groups in the tri-state area would meet to plan our strategies.

Even though we were speaking to government officials from various offices and agencies, not much headway was being made to stop the incinerator from being built. Corporations try to do everything behind closed doors and secure a certain path before they make their plans known to the public, which is exactly what happened. I began to question democracy. We escalated the issue from the local to the state and then to the national level. This battle started in the early 1980s and we have been keeping up the pressure ever since.

Over the years, especially when things got really active and our fight picked up momentum, I received threatening phone calls. One night, my then nine-year-old daughter, Jaime, and I were home alone and having dinner. The phone rang and I decided to let the answering machine pick up the call. A husky, deep male voice said, "If you don't stop this, you're going to end up dead."

My daughter cried for three days; she was very scared and didn't want me to leave the house. It was tough enough to have to make the kind of sacrifices necessary to stop a grave injustice or right a wrong, but it's heartbreaking when you see such fear—planted by a sick mind—in the eyes of the very child you are trying to protect. How can you explain to a nine-year-old child who is afraid that she's going to lose her mom that the sacrifices being made are an effort to protect her and other children? How could I explain to her how important it was to stop the incinerator?

As much as possible, I included Jaime in my work and took her to local rallies and marches. In the spring of 1993, I went on a month-long, Greenpeace-sponsored, cross-country bus tour, visiting 25 toxic hot spots in 18 states. We traveled on the Green Bus, which runs on soy diesel fuel and has solar energy panels. During that month, I came home for a visit, and my daughter and I drove to Michigan to meet the bus and attend a march and rally. She thought it was a lot of fun, especially since she got to take her little dog, Maggie, who trotted alongside her in the 5-mile march!

One of the first actions of the Tri-State Environmental Council was to take over a U.S. EPA public hearing concerning the addition of a piece of equipment called a Spray Dryer to the incinerator. Both the state and federal EPAs govern the incinerator because it is operating under a federal Resource Conservation and Recovery Act permit. The EPA was holding a public hearing for the community to comment on the Spray Dryer; however, most information about the equipment was deemed confidential by WTI. These hearings are held in order to comply with the law that mandates public participation. From past experience, we learned they are used to placate the public; the EPA allows the public to "vent" and then they rubber stamp the permit in question.

On the night of the public hearing regarding the Spray Dryer, we filled the auditorium to capacity, each of us signing up for the five minutes the EPA had allotted per person to present comments or testimony. We had an EPA whistleblower, Hugh Kaufman; Matt Petrovich, from EPA's Research Triangle Park; and several incineration experts, including Dr. Paul Connett and Dr. Mike McCawley, who were going to speak on our behalf.

We knew that five minutes would never be enough time for them to present the information they had gathered, which proved that the addition of the Spray Dryer would cause problems without further modifications. One by one, each citizen went to the microphone and relinquished their five minutes to one of our experts. When all was said and done, one of our experts had the floor for nearly two hours! Frustrated and angry at the way the meeting was going, the EPA changed the rules in the middle of the hearing, telling us that there could be no more relinquishing of time; however, by this time, it was too late. All of our experts had already testified.

It was totally to our advantage because our experts had said everything they needed to say. They had testified that the addition of a Spray Dryer to WTI's facility would cause an increase in harmful, toxic emissions of mercury and dioxins. WTI's expert, a representative from WTI's sister facility in Germany, was late for the hearing because his flight was delayed, so he arrived after the EPA changed the rules about relinquishing time and only got to speak for five minutes! For the first time in years, the citizens were in control. However, after the meeting, we heard nothing for months. The EPA never disputed or refuted the testimony of our experts.

Imagine how a community feels when experts testify that there will be serious problems at the incinerator and the EPA does nothing except tell the community that they will issue the permit. As a result of the citizen outcry, the EPA scheduled another hearing on the Spray Dryer, but we knew from experience that the EPA wouldn't listen to us.

The first night, the EPA was scheduled to have a public information session where citizens could ask questions. Citizens boycotted the meeting inside. We gathered outside and wore skeleton masks and T-shirts that said, "Don't Be Happy, Worry!" (a play on the words of a popular Bobby McFerrin song, "Don't Worry, Be Happy"). We held a funeral for democracy, complete with a minister, a bugler playing taps and a eulogy. We passed out flyers explaining exactly why we were boycotting the EPA hearing.

The second night was the official EPA public hearing and 800 people against WTI showed up. We smuggled in five electronic bullhorns and, when the meeting started, I stood up on a chair and shouted, *"This hearing is a sham. We demand democracy!"* All 800 of us chanted for 45 minutes. Even with a loudspeaker to try and quiet us down, the EPA chairman couldn't be heard, so he wrote across the blackboard, "This hearing is adjourned. If you would like to make comments, send them to the EPA." The next day, there was excellent coverage of the issue in Ohio's largest newspaper, *The Plain Dealer*.[12] It seemed to be a turning point in our battle and media interest in the WTI incinerator case swelled.

In late 1990, I consulted with a good friend of mine, Jonathan Wishon, who was an effective North Carolina activist. In our conversation about how to stop the incinerator, he said, "You just have to do whatever it takes." I adopted his words as the motto for our fight: "Whatever It Takes." We have large, bright, neon green and yellow buttons with our motto on it, which shows "WTI" in the center of a circle with a slash through it. We always carry a large, professionally made yellow banner with our slogan (the circle/slash WTI with "Whatever It Takes" in a semi-circle around it). We've always used signs and buttons very effectively. When WTI asked for permission to burn lab packs, which are problematic because they contain mixtures of various pure chemicals that can and have resulted in explosions at other incinerators, we made a button with a picture of dynamite on it that said, "Lab packs are a blast."

When we publicly released information about the money man behind the project, Jackson Stephens, we made a red, white and blue button that said, "Avoid the middle-man; vote Jackson Stephens for President." *The American Spectator* magazine thought it was so clever that they asked us to send them one and they used a photo of the button, in full color, in their article about the WTI incinerator.[13] We've had coverage from both sides: *The American Spectator* is a conservative publication, yet they presented the WTI case in our favor; at about the same time, *Mother Jones*, a liberal publication, reported on the case.[14]

One day, in 1992, we got word that the incinerator was going to begin "shake down" (an initial start-up period in which the incinerator begins to burn hazardous waste during a trial phase), leading up to approval for full commercial operation. With every step WTI took, I knew they were getting closer to getting the green light to begin full commercial operation. Our job was getting harder and harder. I looked back at how long I had been working on this issue and was flooded with emotion.

In February 1993, EPA scientists found that the dioxin emissions from the incinerator would build up in livestock and in food grown on local farms and gardens.[15] Richard Guimond, the U.S. EPA's senior public health officer, wrote a memo to EPA Chief Carol Browner, detailing a strategy to avoid acknowledging the serious health threat from dioxin emissions from WTI. Guimond wrote that the risks due to consumption of contaminated beef raised in the vicinity of WTI could be 1,000 times greater than those considered in the inhalation-only risk assessment, which meant that the cancer risk posed by dioxin alone would be 130 times greater than EPA's "acceptable risk" standard. Cancer risks from eating beef contaminated by just one year of incinerator operation were predicted to be 42 per million—well over the agency's acceptable risk standard for a lifetime.[16] These facts supported my battle and I felt an overwhelming need to keep working to shut down the incinerator.

As the months went by, new information emerged proving that the incinerator was a greater threat than previously acknowledged. In March 1993, the incinerator failed its trial burn, emitting four times more mercury than allowed, and toxic dioxin emissions were two to five times the expected amounts.[17]

I was brought up as a law-abiding citizen and taught to respect the law. Now I realize that if I need to break the law to prevent something that is legally and morally wrong, I'm keeping with the historical tradition of activism in this country.

Some of my actions have landed me in jail. My first arrest was with actor Martin Sheen and 32 other activists who climbed over the eight-foot-high chain-link fence surrounding WTI. The police were a bit star struck with Martin Sheen. As they moved in to arrest us, they first shook Martin Sheen's hand and then cuffed him! One by one, they arrested the remainder of the group and hauled us off to jail.

During their 1992 presidential bid, Bill Clinton and Al Gore made the East Liverpool incinerator a campaign issue. After they were elected, WTI became the very first environmental issue addressed by the new Clinton/Gore administration. They promised they would stop WTI until all safety and permit questions were answered. It was a huge disappointment when they backed off from their promise. I found it very telling when we discovered that

Von Roll, the owners of WTI, had donated $10,000 to the Democratic National Committee just prior to the presidential election.[18]

To protest the Clinton administration's failed pledge, we posed as tourists visiting the White House. Near the end of the White House tour, in the hallway just after the State Dining Room, we formed a circle, joined hands, dropped to our knees and began to sing and pray. I was arrested with seven other WTI opponents and we were taken to a cockroach- and flea-infested jail in Washington, DC. We were proud of the charge: "Failure to Quit." That was shortly after I had borrowed a ball gown to sneak into the Tennessee inaugural ball to question Vice President Al Gore about not keeping his promise to keep WTI from going into operation.

In another peaceful, nonviolent direct action, nearly 60 of us handcuffed and linked ourselves to a 24-foot-long truck, which was fitted with a smokestack releasing mock emissions from a fog machine that blew towards the White House. The truck was painted to resemble the WTI incinerator and carried a giant sign that read, "Clinton-Gore keep your promise—shut it down!" Our group was made up of 35 Ohio Valley residents and people from the Washington, DC, area; a dozen citizens from communities around the U.S. where incinerators were being built; and actor Martin Sheen and Barbary Dudley, executive director of Greenpeace. The "mock incinerator" was parked in front of the White House and, after snarling up traffic for approximately six hours, 100 police and 20 firefighters gathered around us. It took almost eight hours for the police to remove those of us who were connected to the truck by steel conduits anchored to several thousand pounds of concrete. Of course, we were arrested, but we felt that this was an important act to show Clinton that we were holding the Clinton/Gore administration accountable to their word. We felt that we would do whatever it took, no matter what the risk, to get justice and protect our children.

Shortly afterward, the U.S. EPA declared an 18-month nationwide moratorium on new commercial hazardous waste incinerators and reduced the levels of heavy metals and dioxins that existing plants could release[19]—the very steps that we had proposed in an earlier petition to the government! However, it was nearly meaningless since the permit process for new hazardous waste incinerators takes at least that long.

This battle has had personal consequences. I have been arrested a dozen times and spent more than two weeks in jail. WTI filed a $1+ million defamation lawsuit against me,[20] which was very stressful for both my husband and me. There are times when citizens in my situation have felt like Sisyphus—condemned to roll a heavy stone to the top of the hill, only to have it fall back down each night. I know I have felt this way, but ours is *not* meaningless work and we *are* making progress.

In our struggle with WTI, we've had many reasons to celebrate. We've helped prevent other communities from having to face the kind of struggle we've been forced to endure. No new commercial toxic waste incinerators have been built in this country since 1992, and existing incinerators have been forced to comply with more stringent pollution standards resulting from national policy changes brought about by citizen pressure. Each time we take action, it opens the door for change. I honestly believe I can do more good to protect people's health with this work than I could in a lifetime of nursing.

This fight will continue to be a tribute to grass-roots activism. I am proof that *anybody* can do it. I am an average, ordinary housewife who decided to take a stand for my beliefs and speak out against injustice. You don't have to have letters following your name or be an "expert" to get involved.

My favorite quote is by Calvin Coolidge: "Nothing in the world can take the place of persistence. Talent will not; nothing is more common than unsuccessful men with talent. Genius will not; unrewarded genius is almost a proverb. Education will not; the world is full of educated derelicts. Persistence and determination alone are omnipotent."

If you want to make a difference or right a wrong, *get involved*! The government is not always going to protect your best interests. We need to keep our elected officials in check by letting them know that we, the people, are watching their every move. If we don't hold them accountable, they will spin further out of control; eventually, we will face even greater threats to our environment, our civil and First Amendment rights, our democracy and our society. I often question what it takes for people to stand up against injustice. Blanket trust in our government creates a dangerous apathy. We often use a saying in our efforts: "If you're not outraged, you're not paying attention!"

Whether it is working for peace or a healthier environment, the way to make a difference in the world is to *just begin*. Learn everything about your issue. Read. Talk to people and find others who share your passion. Organize. Once you get involved, it will change your perspective and entire life forever.

I have found that the environmental and social justice movements are comprised of the most brilliant, dedicated, compassionate, courageous, hard-working and inspiring people on Earth. The more you learn, the more you will understand why you can never go back to a place of ignorance. Your mind will be expanded forever. Your passion will be your driving force and you will find boundless energy. You only need to begin … to take that first step … and you can make a difference.

CONTACT
tswearin@weir.net

SUGGESTED LINKS

http://www.cwwg.org (Chemical Weapons Working Group)

http://www.greenpeaceusa.org (Greenpeace)

http://www.iPEN.org (International POPs Elimination Network)

http://www.movementech.org (Movement Technology Institute)

http://www.no-burn.org (Global Anti-Incinerator Alliance/Global Alliance for Incinerator Alternatives)

http://www.rachel.org (Environmental Research Foundation)

FOOTNOTES START ON PAGE 204.

SATSUKI INA

Voices of Japanese American Children of the Camps

"All of us wept for the entire three days. We were just beginning to tell the stories that we had never shared and that we never fully understood."

Satsuki is a professor emeritus at California State University in Sacramento. Having recently retired after 20 years of university teaching, she continues her private practice in marriage and family psychotherapy.

Her first documentary, Children of the Camps, *which was released in 2000, tells the stories of three men and three women who were children in a Japanese American internment camp after World War II, and describes their journey from the trauma of racism and imprisonment to healing.*

Satsuki is currently working on her second documentary, From A Silk Cocoon, *which is based on the letters her parents exchanged while imprisoned in two separate American concentration camps during World War II. The public television broadcast is anticipated some time after September 2004. Satsuki is also writing a children's book,* My Name is NOT Sandy, *about appreciating one's ethnic identity. She makes monthly visits to Seattle to be with her new granddaughter, Skyla.*

I was born in Tule Lake, a World War II Japanese American prison camp in a remote and desolate northern California agricultural area, far from San Francisco where my parents had both been living as a newlywed couple. My parents were Kibei—the second generation born in the United States, but partially educated in Japan. Like many Kibeis, my grandparents registered my parents' birth in Japan; consequently, my parents held dual citizenship. Because of losses in their family, my parents were sent back to Japan for a period of time when they were young children. They returned to the U.S. as young teenagers.

In 1939, my mother went back to Japan to take care of her ailing grandmother, who had raised her. Japan was entering the World's Trade Fair for the first time to exhibit their silk industry. My mother was a beautiful young woman who could speak English as well as represent Japanese culture, so she was selected as one of the four "Silk Girls" and sent to the Golden Gate International Exposition in San Francisco to demonstrate Japanese silk reeling. Young Japanese American men living in San Francisco waited excitedly for these beautiful Japanese Silk Girls to arrive. When my father saw my mother, he fell in love immediately. The World's Fair ended in 1940 and my mother went back to Japan, promising to return to marry my father and make her home in San Francisco.

December 7, 1941: Pearl Harbor was bombed. Within months, my parents were removed from their home and placed in an "assembly center" in the Tanforan race track just outside of San Francisco. After living in horse stalls for several months, they were sent to Topaz, Utah—one of 10 American prison camps. My older brother, Kiyoshi, was born there. While in Topaz, my parents were required to respond to what was referred to as the "Loyalty Questionnaire," which would eventually determine who would be eligible to be drafted into the military. In this questionnaire, my parents were asked whether they would be willing to bear arms against the enemy and disavow their loyalty to the Japanese emperor. Betrayed by the country of their birth, and with hopes that they might live a life of dignity back in Japan, my parents answered, "no-no."

As a result, they were sent to a segregation camp for so-called "disloyals" in Tule Lake, California, where I was born. This was an ominous beginning for me. My parents had been instructed to renounce their American citizenship if they wished to go to Japan. Then designated as "dangerous enemy aliens," my father, mother, brother and I all had Federal Bureau of Investigation (FBI) files on record. My file was started when I was two months old. My father, who was now considered a "dangerous pro-Japan loyalist," was taken from us and put into a Department of Justice prison camp in Fort Lincoln, North Dakota, with German Enemy Aliens.

When Japan lost the war, relatives wrote to my parents and told them not to come to Japan because there was a terrible shortage of food and housing. Fearful for their young children, my parents withdrew their request for repatriation and we were sent to a camp in Crystal City, Texas, where we were finally reunited with my father. My family and I were released after being incarcerated for four years. We were advised not to go back to the west coast because of the continuing public hostility against Japanese Americans. My parents moved to Cincinnati, Ohio, where relatives had relocated after the camps. We stayed there for a couple of years and eventually moved back to San Francisco.

We lived through a very difficult and hostile time of rampant discrimination against people of Japanese descent. We weren't allowed to live in certain neighborhoods; after four years of imprisonment, my parents had to start their lives all over again. We lived in a ghetto with other poor minority groups. I went to elementary school where I have many memories of being called names and being bullied for being Japanese. My parents could only get blue-collar jobs. It was 11 years after their release, in 1957, when my parents received a letter from the Department of Justice reinstating their citizenship. A class action suit had been filed by Attorney Wayne Collins on behalf of the renunciants; it was eventually determined that renunciation of their American citizenship, made under duress, was null and void.

After the war and resettlement, no one in the Japanese community talked about the internment. I believe that they had decided to put it behind them and assimilate as much as they could. My parents never talked to me about the prison camps or their renouncement of citizenship. They did everything they could to forget about the suffering and humiliation they had endured.

Pressure to be a good and loyal American was the focus of our lives. Teachers told my parents that, if they really wanted me to be a good American citizen, I should have an American name. Although my birth certificate states my birth name as Satsuki, my parents felt it best to call me Sandy. When I was in my 30s, I found my birth certificate, realized what had happened and reclaimed my real name.

As I reflect now, signs of trauma of being in the camps as a young child began to surface. In junior high, independent of any school assignments, I became very interested in the Jewish holocaust. I remember riding home on the bus from a downtown San Francisco library, carrying an armful of books loaded with information about what happened to the Jews in Germany. At the time, I didn't have any idea that what I was reading about was so closely related to my own past.

I attended the University of California at Berkeley in the 1960s and was greatly affected by the civil rights movement. I was incensed by the racism and oppression directed towards African Americans and, even then, I could not consciously identify the similarities I had experienced with those of my African American friends.

By the time I graduated with a degree in social work and psychology, I was married and moved to Oregon. I gave birth to my first child—a son—and lived the life of a stay-at-home mom while my husband attended graduate school. When he finished his degree in physics and engineering, we moved back to Sacramento and I began working as a counselor for minority students at Sacramento State College.

With the advent of ethnic studies programs on campus, I began to learn about the Japanese American internment history and was consumed by issues of human rights and the psychology of racism. I took a job as a counselor in the Educational Opportunity Program on campus, which advocated for Native Americans and African Americans who were unable to meet standard college admission requirements.

During that time, I had a second child—another son. Being a mother inspired me to learn more about what it means to be an ethnic minority in America. I decided to enter a doctoral program in Oregon. I wanted to dedicate myself to weaving together all of the issues that were fragmented inside of me. My marriage was strained and my husband decided that he didn't want to move to Oregon. My need to learn and grow was so intense that I decided to leave my marriage and my home behind.

With my two sons, ages two and 10, I left for a four-year stint as a single mom and graduate student. Leaving an 11-year marriage was a family and cultural fracture and I went through an extremely emotional time. My parents had known my husband's parents from the camps and felt that our marriage was made in heaven. Our divorce brought a lot of shame to my family. There wasn't a job or a familiar face waiting for me in Oregon; all I had was a letter admitting me into a doctoral program. I quit my job at Sacramento State, cashed in my retirement account and just pushed forward.

With my two sons, I began a life-changing journey to heal and strengthen myself. We arrived in Oregon in June and settled in. My boys went back to visit their father for the summer and, for the first time in many years, I was alone. I went to a garage sale, picked up a bag of different colored yarn and decided to crochet squares for a granny quilt. As I sat in a rocking chair, crocheting and reflecting, I was depressed, fearful and uncertain about the direction my life was about to take. I had to support my children and make my own way.

One morning, after two months of sitting in my rocking chair, I woke up with a tremendous sense of will. I looked at the bags of squares I had crocheted and knew that I didn't have to join them together. I gathered them up, put them in the closet and realized that the pieces of my life had fallen into place. I realized how much I enjoyed being with myself. I was ready to move forward.

By the time my children came back at the end of the summer, I had my sleeves rolled up and was ready to go to work. It was an incredibly challenging and exciting time. My father passed away and I inherited a little bit of money, so I was able to buy a small house. As my sons learned to cook, sew, clean and do whatever was needed to keep up a house, a new way of "being with" them emerged.

My oldest son was a fishing fanatic and I promised him that, no matter what, every Sunday we would go fishing. Every Sunday morning, we would get up, make tuna and peanut butter and jelly sandwiches and drive to Deschutes County to the river. In the winter, it would be so cold that my youngest son and I would sit in the car, wrapped in a sleeping bag. I would read from my stack of books and wipe the frost from the car windows. I could see my other son standing at the river with a big grin on his face and icicles forming on his fishing rod. He has worked as a professional fishing guide in Alaska and now works as a freelance copywriter for fishing and sports magazines. My youngest son is an artist, writes graphic novels and now has his own internationally distributed comic book. I had followed my passion, so perhaps my sons learned how important that was. To this day, my children claim that those early years were some of the happiest times of their lives.

After I received my Ph.D., we moved back to California because it was important to me that the boys lived in a multicultural community. I got a job teaching at California State University in Fresno with a focus on multicultural counseling. I continued to be interested in the impact of culture and the experience of racism on mental health issues. A few years after my oldest son was in college, I got a job teaching overseas through Boston University, and my sons and I went to live in Europe for a year.

We moved back to Sacramento where I was eventually hired by California State University, Sacramento, in the Counselor Education department. Upon my return, I had a moving experience while attending a therapist's training workshop. People were directed to form small, simulated family groups. Each person took a turn in the center and imagined lying in a crib, looking up at their mother and father. Then they talked about what that image evoked.

When it was my turn, I had the experience of being surrounded by webbed, woven material. When I tried to imagine the face of my mother and father, I saw fear. In that moment, strong emotions emerged and I wept for hours. Much later, of course, I realized that I had had a post-traumatic response. After the workshop, I asked my mother where I slept as a baby. She told me that there were no cribs in the prison camps, so she put me inside of a willow basket. I realized that I had retrieved an actual memory! I asked her what it was like being a young mother of a newborn in a prison camp. She told me that it was both a blessing and a burden of fear because she lived with so much uncertainty about our future.

I began talking to other Japanese Americans who were my age and asked them if they thought their early childhood experience in prison camps had affected them as adults. There were similar stories to my own—feelings of not belonging, being on the outside looking in, as well as self-esteem and depression problems. I decided to get a group of people together for a three-day weekend to share our stories and explore the connection between our prison-camp life and our current lives. Before the weekend, I asked members of the group to talk about their childhood to a family member who was with them in the camp. It was a deeply moving, disturbing and emotional weekend. All of us wept for the entire three days. We were just beginning to tell the stories that we had never shared and that we never fully understood.

After that experience, I decided to facilitate groups for other Japanese Americans who wanted to process their childhood camp experiences. Their stories were not unlike my own—low-grade, chronic depression; achievement-related stress; stress-related somatic problems; and the intense need to be accepted. Many of us were overachievers and had multiple college degrees. Our lives were anxiety ridden as we strived to be the perfect model minority. Today, I believe these behaviors and feelings are directly related to the internment trauma. Like children in an abusive family, we were all afraid of the perpetrator and had spent our lives acting out the "good child" role in order to avoid further abuse.

On my 50th birthday, I signed up to go on a pilgrimage back to Tule Lake, the site of the prison camp where I was born. Over 250 former internees attended, including elders. It was clearly a very moving moment as memories were recalled and stories were told, yet the emotions were self-consciously kept in check and the discussions did not delve deeply into the pain and suffering. When I arrived at the prison camp site, it was as if the incomplete gestalt had finally come together and formed a more complete picture.

When I saw the remnants of the stockade and barracks, I felt anger, sadness and outrage. All that remained were fragments of memories to mark such a horrific time in our history. The most moving place for me was a huge concrete slab with holes in a line that had been the latrines. My mother talked about how humiliating it was to go to the toilet because there were no walls or doors, so she would take a towel to cover her face. There was also a stockade—a prison inside of a prison—for participants in the pro-Japan movement. My father was imprisoned there before he was shipped off to Fort Lincoln. I could see the writing on the walls from the prisoners as they lay in their beds. The experience was disturbing and extremely meaningful.

Once home, the images of Tule Lake stayed with me. I knew that I wanted to do something with my family's story, but I wasn't sure what. One day, while teaching in a multicultural counseling class, one of my students showed a video, *The Color of Fear*. It was about racism. I was so moved by the resulting class discussion that I went to my office and called the producer of the film, a Chinese American man named Lee Mun Wah. I left a message on his answering machine, thanking him for making the film. I briefly mentioned that I had been facilitating group discussions for Japanese Americans who had been children in World War II prison camps. He called me back and strongly urged me to document what I was doing through video. I had never been involved in film, but he convinced me to meet with him to further discuss the idea. After our meeting, I decided to do one more group and have it filmed.

Candidly sharing one's life is counterculture for Asian Americans, yet the people who showed up for the group openly talked about their families and the personal suffering they endured in the prison camps. Three men and three women, who were children in the camp, shared their personal stories and discovered ways in which that experience impacted their adult lives. When the cameras started rolling, I don't think anyone really knew what would surface in the process. An emotionally honest, heart-rending story of each participant's journey from the trauma of racism and imprisonment to healing was revealed.

The *Children of the Camps* documentary was released in 2000. What began as an effort to make a video for use in my classroom eventually led to a national broadcast on public television. I have had the privilege of traveling all over the country with the film, screening it at over 100 events in Japanese American communities. The documentary has become a safe vehicle for former internees and their families to begin a dialogue about the impact of the camp experience.

Many people have written to me after participating in a community screening or viewing the documentary on television to tell me that it has opened a door for sharing stories about the internment with their children, their parents, their students and their teachers. Many came to realize that this experience was about an unjust historical event as well as a psychological community trauma. In this way, I believe the documentary has helped others in the healing process. It was our hope that *Children of the Camps* would serve as an educational tool to prevent similar injustices from occurring.

I have recently been asked to present the documentary to stimulate discussions about the connection between the current stereotyping of Arab and Muslim Americans and Japanese Americans. Current government language, regarding the necessary means to maintain national security, echo experiences of World War II and the ultimate internment of over 120,000 Japanese Americans. History has shown that when there is intense societal anxiety, the identification of a scapegoat serves as a means to manage that anxiety level, often without addressing the true underlying cause of the problem. This was true for the Japanese Americans after Japan bombed Pearl Harbor.

I am now taking a break from traveling to work on a second film, *From A Silk Cocoon*, and to write a book about my parents' experience in the prison camps. After my father's death, my mother and I discovered a box of letters that my father had received from my mother while he was in the Fort Lincoln prison camp. The amazing thing is that my mother had also saved the letters he had sent to her—a total of 180 letters sent back and forth over an 18-month period. Some of the letters, written in Japanese, were censored and parts were left in shreds. My father wrote haiku every day and my mother kept a daily journal. I am weaving together their personal story with documents that I retrieved from the National Archives, which include my family's FBI files and other government documents regarding the prison camps.

Many people today have some knowledge about the injustice of the Japanese American internment; however, my hope with *From A Silk Cocoon* is to put a human face and real emotions to the story. The letters, diary entries and poetry reveal the suffering and strengths of one family coping with separation; fear for their lives; their children's survival; communal, primitive living conditions; and their hopes, dreams and will to survive.

The American government imposed a crisis of loyalty on Americans of Japanese descent when their patriotism was suddenly in question, which could then justify their imprisonment. This propaganda was used to rally support for the war. It has now been determined that there was not one case of espionage or fifth-column (traitorous insider) activity committed by a Japanese American.

We were American citizens. My father bought war bonds; he was on the civil defense patrol; he was saving money for his children to go to an American college. He was working hard to achieve the American dream, and trusted that his government would protect and advocate for him and his fellow citizens. What happened to Japanese Americans was not a "crisis of loyalty" but rather a "crisis of faith" in their own government.

We need to heal these wounds through education and person-to-person dialogue. In the end, the Japanese American experience can serve as a great teaching tool about the dangers of racism and the violation of human rights in the midst of war-time hysteria. After talking with hundreds of former internees, a common thread that contributed to their trauma was the absence of the voice of dissent on their behalf. Witnesses to their unjust treatment remained silent; for many, this was the greatest betrayal. My hope is that, through the medium of documentary films, people will be moved enough to speak out and take action to prevent the repetition of this tragic history.

CONTACT

satsukina@aol.com

SUGGESTED LINKS

http://www.children-of-the-camps.org (Children of the Camps)

http://www.tulelake.org (Tule Lake Committee)

BIBLIOGRAPHY

Children of the Camps. Satsuki Ina, producer; Stephen Holsapple, director; National Asian American Telecommunications Assn., distributor, 2000.

From A Silk Cocoon. Satsuki Ina, producer; Stephen Holsapple, director; Hesono O Productions, distributor, 2004.

RHONDA ANDERSON

Community Organizing for Justice

"Building community for the world at large means that we have to get to know one another and open ourselves up to each other through communicating, sharing ideas and making necessary changes in our lives."

Rhonda is a native, lifelong Detroiter who has worked in labor and the social services sector. She is the environmental justice organizer for the Sierra Club, based in Detroit, as well as a member of the Michigan Environmental Justice Coalition—an organization of environmental groups and activists. Rhonda became a Sierra Club employee in 2000 after having worked for Wayne County Juvenile Detention as a guard and with Warren Conner Development Coalition as an organizer. She also has experience with Detroiters Working for Environmental Justice.

I grew up during the civil rights movement, down river from Detroit in a very small city called Ecorse. If you had a third leg, you could stand in three cities at the same time—Detroit, Ecorse and River Rouge. Most of the people came up from the south; black people lived on one side and white people lived on the other. Up until high school, I was sheltered in the segregated north. My community had its own theaters, stores and everything else we needed, so we never had to leave. The only time we got to see a white person was when we went shopping at Sears department store, which was cordial and polite due to our southern ways.

On weekends, when my father was home from working his two full-time jobs, my parents would constantly yell at each other and my father would beat my mother every weekend night. There were many times when my mother would grab me by the arm to flee the house and find shelter with friends.

When I was seven years old, my mother died as a result of domestic violence. It was a terribly hard thing to go through as a little girl. I knew that what had happened was wrong, but I didn't realize the immensity of it until later in my life. Even though my mother was a victim to one of my father's rages, we kept living with him. He could have easily given my brother and me to another relative, but he chose to raise us himself. (I have often wondered if it was part of the guilt he carried about my mother's death.) Violence in our home was an ongoing occurrence and I thought every family lived like us. As I grew older, I realized how dysfunctional we were.

When I was 14, my girlfriend knew a boy who wanted to date me, but I was not interested. Finally, with her prodding, I went to a party with him. He was much older and ended up dragging me into a bathroom and telling me he wanted some "satisfaction." I was a virgin and had no idea what he was talking about, but I knew that whatever it was, I wasn't going to give it to him!

He threw me into the bathtub and beat me so hard that I lost my back teeth. I staggered home, ashamed and bloody. When I walked into my house, my father was waiting with a 12-inch hose because I was late. Without even asking what had happened, he beat me repeatedly. That night, as I lay in bed, I resolved that I would never let anyone hit me again. That promise gave me an immense sense of strength, which has carried me through the years.

While I was struggling with issues of domestic violence in my own household, the U.S. was buzzing with the fire of the civil rights movement. Marches occurred in all of the major cities and segregation, voting rights and other laws were being challenged. I knew there was a difference between black people and white people, but I didn't understand the magnitude of it until I started high school in 1962—the first time I had gotten up close to white people by sitting next to them in class.

Being black, I experienced the painful effects of bigotry and prejudice from my white classmates. My brother and his best friend joined the Black Panther Party. They were fired up about the Black Power movement and I heard a lot of news from my brother about the radical left. Even with all of this going on around me, I hadn't yet stepped out to make a commitment to any one cause.

When Martin Luther King, Jr., was killed, the black high school students were discussing whether or not they were going to walk out of the school as a protest. Finally, we made up our minds that we would. On the way home that day, I saw a mass of students marching down the street and a wave of black faces yelling, "Black Power!" with a girl leading the march. All of the students at Detroit's South Western High School had walked over 10 miles to the high school in River Rouge; when I saw them, they were on their way to my high school in Ecorse. It was a major step for young black people to make this kind of statement and it gave me a sense of hope that people coming together could have a voice.

Because I lived so close to Detroit, when riots broke out in the city center I saw the Special Weapons and Tactics team with their rifles and tanks coming across the railroad tracks in my neighborhood. Martial law was instated and, at night, we became prisoners in our own homes. Even still, there was an amazing surge of energy and a great feeling of unity among black people. It was another moment in my life where I finally got what civil and human rights were about, and I felt the power of the people and the community.

I was 15 years old at that time and got pregnant. By the time I mustered up the courage to tell my father, I was too far along to get an abortion. Back then, if you were a young woman and had a baby out of wedlock, you were usually kicked out of school. Instead, my teachers supported me any way they could; some even came to my home to give me lessons. I loved being a mother. I missed my own mom and was reliving the love that she had given me. After my son was old enough to be left with a baby-sitter, I went back to high school. One year later, I got pregnant with my second child.

The hardest part of being a young mother was how my peers shunned me. In high school, I was branded a "bad girl." I knew that many other girls my age were having sex, but they had never gotten caught or become pregnant. No one would date me; when the prom came around, I wasn't invited. It was difficult, but I learned to hold my head high. With two children, I stayed at home and studied as much as I could to keep up with my high school credits. When I was 18, I had one credit left for a high school diploma, so I went to night school and was able to graduate. At the graduation ceremony, I was handed my diploma and then ran home because I had two little boys waiting for me.

With my high school education behind me, I began working full time in the billing department at the hospital where my father worked—a place that took care of people in the black community—and I felt very comfortable there. I was also a full-time student at a community college. It was incredibly challenging to juggle work, school and motherhood, but I was driven to make the best of myself and give my children the best that I could provide. My father graciously took on the role of grandfather and helped me with parenting responsibilities.

While I was working at the hospital, I became involved in the union by sitting on the bargaining committee. Some of the guys from the labor union saw the way I performed on the committee and asked me if I wanted a job as a union representative for Local 79 Service Employees International Union. Affirmative action came out in the late 1970s and doors seemed to be opening for minorities. By the time I was hired, there were only two other black women working at Local 79. I represented over 600 union members in contract negotiations and grievances and led trainings. I saw the union as an extension of the civil rights movement—a grass-roots organization fighting to give rights to the people.

During my employment with Local 79, I was taken out to lunch by the president of the union, who had close ties to the Teamsters Union. He told me that a very good black friend of his had told him that I was a racist and that I had made some statement against white people. With the few black people at work, I had talked about certain issues between whites and blacks, but I had never made a specific racist comment.

I started to realize that there was a major difference working in a place where the majority of the people were white. I spoke black English and my white co-workers had a hard time understanding me. At first I thought they were making fun of me because they were always saying, "Huh?" every time I would say something, so I changed the way I pronounced certain words.

Changing something as personal as language was a major issue for me. In many ways, I felt as if I were giving up a fundamental part of myself to keep my job. Because my white co-workers had never worked with black people, their guidelines were *their* guidelines and I had to conform. The whole issue of the civil rights movement while retaining my identity in the midst of being scrutinized became a major part of my daily life.

Three years later, the president and vice president were having an internal battle. The staff felt the tension and worried about a shakedown in the union. An anonymous employee got copies of the payroll and sent them to all of the staff. It was obvious that every white worker was paid more than every black worker, regardless of seniority; in addition, all of the men were paid more than all of the women. Being a black woman, I was at the bottom of the pay scale. All this time, I thought I was working for a progressive grass-roots organization—Labor—but I found out about the incongruences inside the organization.

Many employees said that they were going to file charges with the Equal Employment Opportunity Committee (EEOC) but were afraid. Another black woman, a white woman and I filed charges. I felt that it was the *right* thing to do and the *only* thing to do given all I had been through. After we filed charges, all hell broke loose because we were going up against one of the largest and fastest growing unions in the country. We became known as the "Detroit Black Bitches," including the white woman because she was married to a black man.

During this time, I got pregnant with my third child and became the first woman to carry through a pregnancy while on staff. Before that, if a woman was pregnant—even if she had an abortion—she had to leave her job at Local 79. Because I had filed charges with the EEOC against the union, I was treated with kid gloves. No one was going to ask me to leave, pregnant or not. During this time, we also formed our own unprecedented union, a Staff Association. When the president heard that we had done this, he was very upset.

Even though the union administrators didn't want to rock the boat, they pulled out every trick they knew to try and make my life on the job miserable. When I was seven months' pregnant and driving to Lansing, Michigan, to do some union organizing, I noticed a man following me in another car. Whenever I switched lanes, he switched lanes; if I slowed down, he slowed down. It was obvious that he was trying to scare me. I panicked, pulled off to the side, quickly backed up to an exit and drove off the expressway where I lost him. There were many other incidences like that where local officials were out to scare me.

Taking on the union was overwhelming. The two other women and I were working with pro-bono attorneys, who would at times not show up in court, and the judge would say that we only had so many days to come up with some information for our case. We would have to drop everything, run out and find another attorney to meet the deadline. We finally understood that the union was getting to the attorneys and that's why they would suddenly stop handling our case. It took everything we had to stay with the fight.

To add to the stress, my father died and then my oldest son was killed. He was 19 years old and attending a Ohio university—a miracle because the odds for a black male raised by a single mother to make it to a university were extremely low. I was so proud of him and he was very excited to be at a university.

The night he was killed, I was attending a Local 79 dinner for the governor of Michigan. I had an overwhelming feeling that something wasn't right and felt that I should go home. My cousin, not having the slightest idea where I was, found me and told me that my son had been struck by a drunk hit-and-run driver while crossing the street in front of the university and was in the hospital. I collapsed to the ground and my cousin drove me home. I called a girlfriend and she came over to give me some support.

It was two o'clock in the morning and I was trying to figure out some way to quickly get to Ohio. I asked my girlfriend if she would drive me, but she said it would take too long. Then she told me that she knew a French man with whom she had been taking flying lessons and that he might be able to fly me there. She called him and he told her go to the Detroit City airport where he would meet us.

On November 1, we drove as fast as we could through the fog and mist. We went into the airport and found a man standing outside of his private airplane with the propellers going—just like a movie. I went up to him and pulled out my credit card to pay for the flight, but he told me that we didn't have time for that. We jumped on the plane and he flew us to Ohio. All the way there, I felt that I was in another dimension, filled with disbelief and fear. When the plane landed, we were met by a state trooper. He told us to get in his car and drove us directly to the hospital.

When we arrived, we saw my son's friends standing outside of the intensive care unit, crying their eyes out. The doctor came up to us and said, "Your son isn't going to make it." If I had any hope, the doctor had just taken every ounce of it away. I broke down and started crying harder than I had ever cried in my life. The doctor brought me into my son's room and I couldn't believe what I saw. His arm had been torn off and he had all kinds of internal injuries.

"You get up from here," I said to him, "and come home because your sister and your brother are waiting for you! *Come on!*" Of course, he didn't get up. He just lay there, unable to talk or open his eyes.

A nurse said, "He is going to die. Do you want to be with him when he dies?"

I looked her in the eye. "Of course! I was with him when he was born and I will be with him when he dies." I had always thought that I would die if I lost one of my children but, in that moment, I felt that I was handling it fairly well.

The nurse showed me the television screen that monitored his heart. "When that line goes flat, he will be dead." She left the room.

I sat there and held him, watching the line on the screen go up and down. I could feel his breath growing more shallow. Suddenly, the line went flat. I kept holding and rocking him. He was my baby … my first born. He was so peaceful, so beautiful. In an instant, it hit me that he had left. My son was gone forever. I sobbed and sobbed.

For three years after that, I lived in denial. I kept telling myself that he was away at school and would be back. I was still working full time at the union and fighting the legal case. When my daughter was almost three years old, I began to look for a school that would support her. I didn't want her to be called "black" in a negative sense. I wanted her to go to a place where she would have positive reinforcement.

I found an African-centered school in Detroit. When she was in first grade, there was a dispute between the director of the school and the teachers, so the school split: half the school went with the teacher and the other half went with the director. I went with the teacher and we found ourselves with no school for our children. We believed in the idea of African-centered education, so we started our own school, which still exists.

My daughter was growing up with a Labor mom and spending most of her time on a picket line; while I was negotiating contracts, she was walking under tables. The women at those meetings would help take care of her. During the summers, I would run a booth for Local 79 at the state fair and she would work the booth with me. She handed out pamphlets and was successful because people wouldn't refuse a child; if they did, she would stick the pamphlets in their back pockets as they walked away!

One day at work, I was given my first bad employee evaluation. In all the time that I had worked for Local 79, I had never been given a write-up. I broke down and cried uncontrollably. All of the grief around my father's death, my son's death and the stress of the lawsuit came flooding through me. I left work and checked myself into a hospital. I thought I was suffering from premenstrual syndrome but the doctor said it was depression, which surprised me. I was working no less than six days a week, 12 hours a day and raising my daughter and teenage son. I thought depression meant you couldn't do anything.

I stayed in the hospital for seven days, but couldn't stay any longer because I didn't have anyone to take care of my little girl. My son was having an extremely difficult time. After his older brother passed away, he went into a downward spiral and began selling drugs on the street. He had already been struggling with learning disabilities, so being in the world was difficult for him. I couldn't afford to be away from home; I needed to get back to my children.

I had worked 19 consecutive years without missing a day of work, but the depression overwhelmed me. I quit my job with Local 79 and stayed at home for three years. Without a job, I found myself poorer than I had ever been. I didn't have a car and could barely afford food. In exchange for my daughter's tuition, I worked at the school. Without enough money for the bus, I had to walk in the rain and snow 2 miles there and 2 miles back.

My main source of income was Aid to Dependent Children, which was dehumanizing. The title "Aid to Dependent Children" is now called "Family Independence"—as if a family can live independently on the money they get from the government! When I was getting Aid to Dependent Children, my $230 a month house note was paid as well as a portion of the electricity and gas; I also received $30 cash twice a month. When someone heard that I was receiving Aid to Dependent Children, they immediately judged me as a lazy mother who leaches off the government and who refuses to get a job. They didn't know that I had worked for almost 20 years as a single mother.

During this time, I got pregnant with my fourth child. I was sick for most of my pregnancy and considered a high risk because I was 41 years old. I walked 2 miles to the health clinic for my regular checkups, which made my blood pressure rise (it was already high). I had never planned to be a single mother. I had always dreamed of getting married; it was one of the only things that I had ever wanted to do. I had marriage proposals but not from the man I loved, so it was heartbreaking. Being a single mother, pregnant and poor was hard; however, in the face of it all, I learned humility.

My friends pulled me through this challenging ordeal. They took care of me and my children, brought us food, baby-sat and gave me emotional support. After two years of being unemployed, the settlement with Local 79 ended and I received enough money to buy a raggedy car and pay a few bills. A dark cloud lifted from my shoulders and I began to come out of my depression.

My first thought was to help someone else the way people had helped me. There was a home for teenage girls called Alternatives for Girls, so I decided to work there as a volunteer. I could relate to the girls because many of them also came from dysfunctional families and troubled backgrounds. I supported them and, at the same time, gave them strict boundaries with set limits. I volunteered there for one year and then joined the staff full time. It was very satisfying work.

Part of my job was helping the girls with employment and education, which meant getting them back in school. Many of the girls had never had positive adult role models but, with someone believing in them, these girls blossomed. My 10-year-old daughter took care of the baby while I was working the afternoon shift. She had a lot of pressure put on her, but it was the only solution.

After one year, I got laid off due to budget cuts. I started working for a friend of mine whom I had met while working in Labor. She had an organization called Detroiters Working for Environmental Justice and, a few months later, she recommended me as a community organizer for Warren Connor's Development Coalition.

Detroit's population is made up of approximately 80 percent African American who live in a heavily polluted industrial environment. My job was to go out into the community and help black residents who lived in extremely poor neighborhoods form block clubs in order to empower them and give them the tools to come together as a community. My task was to get the basics done, such as cleaning up the neighborhood and disseminating health information. It was a tough job because I was working to organize families that could barely put food on the table and asking them be concerned about cleaning up their neighborhood. Most of them could care less about their community because they were worrying about their next meal.

This led me to work for the Sierra Club as an environmental justice organizer for residents in a neighborhood that boasts two major industrial plants: Continental Aluminum and Chrysler. The two facilities sit across from each other in a residential African American neighborhood. Continental Aluminum is now shut down; Chrysler continues to operate.

When Continental Aluminum was in operation, it emitted many pollutants[1]; finally, the plant had so many violations against it that the City of Detroit forced it to close.[2] Continental Aluminum has moved to another part of Michigan and opened up a brand new facility in an all-white neighborhood. The now-defunct plant site is ugly and the surrounding soil is still full of contaminants, primarily lead.[3] The health of the people in this area is very bad. One of the major pollutants—lead—affects their children's learning abilities, behavior and predisposition to violence.

We went to a meeting about this and a woman doctor said, "If the children eat healthy food and parents read and talk to them, they won't have these symptoms." One of the biggest problems in this neighborhood is that there is no access to fresh fruit and vegetables. Most families go to Burger King and McDonald's three to four times a week because the women are so tired and depressed from working two jobs that they don't want to come home and cook—an equation that makes it almost impossible for these women to do anything.

One of my primary jobs is to go door to door and educate people about what is happening in their neighborhood. In the community where I work, over 50 percent of the households are headed by single women who are working two jobs and struggling to raise a family.[4] Part of my job is to help them understand the magnitude of what is happening and how the corporations are polluting neighborhoods throughout Detroit. These women need a personal touch in order to feel like they have the power to take action. When I talk to an overwhelmed mom, I say, "I know your plate is already full, but you have another problem, and it is going to impact you and your children for the rest of your lives." If you help a black woman's children, she will be forever grateful and loyal.

As I struggled with methods to help get the women organized, I went to a concert with some friends and we had to wait in a long line. There was a woman next to us wearing a red African outfit. We complimented her, telling her how good she looked. We started talking about the color red and how African American women don't often wear it because we were taught that dark women don't look good in red; at the same time, it is a powerful color and represents the "blood" or connection among African American women.

My friends and I decided to start Sisters in Red. One day out of the year—the Juneteenth Day, which celebrates the emancipation of slaves—African American women across the country wear red and don't shop. African American women are big-time consumers. Our message is that there is unity among African American women to make a statement to corporations that are controlling us through consumerism and disinformation.

I am going to be leading Sisters in Red in the neighborhood where I work as a community organizer, creating a place where these working moms can step into their power together. The residents of this neighborhood are way down at the bottom of the rung and they need to come together to find their way out. Instead of waiting around for a leader to show up, every woman needs to be a leader, find her voice and let it join the voices of other women.

Building community for the world at large means that we have to get to know one another and open ourselves up to each other through communicating, sharing ideas and making necessary changes in our lives. When you listen to others, you see them as no different than yourself. We all share the dream of living a happy, healthy life. By breaking down stereotypes, we can look beyond our prejudgments and see our neighbors as our community and the larger world.

When we separate ourselves, it is easy to think, "These are people of no value. We can bomb them and it doesn't mean anything." It becomes easy to remove ourselves from someone else's suffering—just like people remove themselves about the social impact of lead poisoning on the City of Detroit.

It is easy for people on the outside to say that blacks are genetically inferior. When are we going to enforce the law that says every child on Medicaid must be tested for lead poisoning? (Right now, only one-third of all of the children are tested for lead poisoning.[5]) What about the mothers in Iraq? If our government doesn't care about the mothers and children in Detroit, they surely don't care about Iraqi mothers and children.

How can people drop bombs on a city or village? It is the same type of mentality that comes into play when a factory is located next to homes and spews lead far beyond regulatory standards. Human life is devalued on all levels and people become disposable. The drop-out rate of children in Detroit schools is on the rise.[6] It is easy to think that they are medically inferior and something is genetically wrong with them, but it is being proven that lead and other pollutants add to this crisis.[7]

We will begin to change our world when we change our communities. All of the work I have done has been based on that premise. We can build community one family at a time … one person at a time. Through community, we can heal ourselves and our world.

CONTACT
rhonda.anderson@sierraclub.org

SUGGESTED LINK

http://www.sierraclub.org/environmental_justice (Sierra Club)

FOOTNOTES START ON PAGE 207.

ANNA MARIE STENBERG

Protecting the Redwoods and Timber Workers

"My motto for action is: 'Without sharing there can be no justice; without justice there can be no peace; without peace there can be no future.'"

Anna Marie is the proud mother of three sons: Zack Stentz, 35; Will Stenberg, 24; and Jesse Stenberg, 21. Leah (Zack's wife) is a labor attorney and the mother of Sophia, 5, and Ian James, 1 year. Anna Marie has worked as a shoe-shine girl, a dishwasher, a car hop, a waitress, a department store clerk, a factory worker, an assembly line worker, an airport security guard, a cook, a natural food restaurant manager, a gardener, a laborer, a business recycling consultant, a day care center owner/operator, a paralegal, a law clerk, a personal assistant, and has had her own business called Wallpaper Rose.

In the 1990s, Anna Marie spearheaded and organized a group that took on Waste Management, Inc., when they tried to establish a monopoly of the garbage in Mendocino County, California. She has sat on the board of the California Communities Against Toxics and helped organize the migrant farm workers in Kettleman City against the incinerator. Anna Marie has sat on the boards of many nonprofits for peace, justice, homelessness, health care and environmental issues. Recently, she passed six college-level examinations, giving her enough college credit to enable her to read for the bar and become an attorney. She has finished and passed the first year's law studies exam and is planning to take the bar without having attended law school to become an attorney to fight injustice.

She is currently an active member of United Farm Workers of America, Industrial Workers of the World (IWW), American Civil Liberties Union, Greenpeace, CODEPINK, National Lawyers Guild, Stop Prisoner Rape, Veterans for Peace, Common Cause, Direct Action to Stop the War, A.N.S.W.E.R. and Friends of Enchanted Meadow.

I am a Romni (a Gypsy) and a survivor. My grandparents, who were very poor, were from Lebanon and Macedonia and moved to the United States before I was born. When I was born, my mother had a two- and three-year-old son at home and was a single parent. Life was very hard growing up; obtaining basic needs such as food and shelter were a constant struggle.

My brothers and I were street kids and I had to be my own mother and father. My mother was angry at her life and much of the time took her anger out on me, her only daughter. From the time I was two until I was five years old, we were put in a series of foster homes. When we were reunited with my mother, she warned me never to speak of being a Gypsy because that is why we were taken away.

In my culture, children are taught to be keen observers. My family moved from town to town and across the country many times while I was growing up. My mother didn't send us to school and I only went when the truant officer dragged me there. Romanes and Arabic were my first languages and, when I did go to school, it was difficult. When I was about seven, we lived in Buffalo, New York, where I spent a good deal of my time in the library because it was warm and safe. The librarian was kind and taught me the basics of reading; I have been an avid reader ever since.

When I was 10 years old, on one of our trips across the country from New York to California, we stopped in Ohio to visit a man that my mother knew; I ended up staying with that family for the next seven years. The man was sexually and physically abusive. He told me that my mother had sold me to him for $500. I worked hard cooking, cleaning and caring for his eight younger children. As I got older, I also worked nights at various jobs and had to sign my paycheck over to him.

When he enrolled me in school, my records indicated that I had only gone to school a total of three weeks. He sent me to a strict Catholic school. When it was time to graduate from high school, the administration claimed I couldn't because I had missed so many days. After I protested by pointing out that I had all As and Bs, they made me take a General Equivalency Diploma test, which I passed, and then I received my high school diploma. I set out on my own at 17 years old without any connection to my real family.

I married early and settled down to have children; I had 11 miscarriages and one stillborn child. I had two children and was pregnant with my third child when I went to a high-risk pregnancy clinic because I was afraid I would miscarry again. They did many tests to find out why I was miscarrying but couldn't find anything wrong.

One day, while I was driving home from the hospital after the doctors reported that there wasn't any reason for my miscarriages, I started thinking about Rachel Carson's book, *Silent Spring*. The symptoms inside my uterus were similar to what had happened to the birds and their eggs as a result of dichloro-diphenyl-trichloroethane (DDT) contamination. The shells were very thin and they were unable to hold the baby birds.

I had spent a portion of my young childhood living and working in the fields as a migrant farm worker. I remember the planes flying overhead and spraying the fields while we were working. I would eat the strawberries I had just picked, which I thought were covered with "powdered sugar" … it was DDT. We drank the well water and lived in the fields like all migrant farm workers do. We weren't just exposed to the chemicals when we were working; we were surrounded by them 24 hours a day.

I called the doctor and said that I thought the miscarriages were related to my DDT exposure. They ran tests and found many times the normal amount of DDT in my body fat. I also had cervical cancer in my 30s that I believe was a result of DDT exposure. In my adult life, I have worked to help migrant farm workers who are still being poisoned.

In the early 1980s, my husband and I moved to Fort Bragg, a small timber mill town on the northern coast of California in Mendocino County. Soon thereafter, I got divorced and started a day care center that served 46 families, including loggers, doctors, lawyers, mill workers and Native Americans. The families were a wonderful cross-section of the community and I loved it. At the end of the day, I would cook dinner and the parents would sit down and have dinner together with all of the children. I also became a foster parent for several teenaged children. We were all one extended family.

Like so many people, I thought that government agencies set up as a result of 1960s activism, such as the Environmental Protection Agency and the Occupational Safety and Health Administration (OSHA), were dealing with the problems of protecting the environment and worker safety. In 1986, I found out that the government *is* the problem. I learned that, in order to get to the polluters—the "bad guys"—you first had to get through the government agency that is, in reality, set up to protect them.

My education about these issues started when I began fighting the unjust practices of timber harvest corporations. One afternoon, while listening to the news, I heard that there had been a so-called harmless polychlorinated biphenyl (PCB) spill at the Georgia Pacific (GP) mill in downtown Fort Bragg and the mill was closed for three days. Many of my day care kid's dads worked at the mill. When one of them came to pick up his child, he was very upset and told me that he had been doused with PCBs. He said that his union, the International Woodworkers of America (IWA), was protecting GP instead of the workers and asked for my help.

I investigated what had happened and learned that the workers at the mill were poisoned by the PCBs. To make matters worse, they were bringing that poison into their own homes, my day care center and the community because it clung to their boots and clothes. The workers had been told by the GP power plant to put the PCB-contaminated sawdust onto the conveyer belt and burn it in the power plant at a low temperature; unfortunately, this created large molecule dioxins from the PCBs. The huge GP smoke stack had spewed that poison into the air and it fell within half a mile from the mill onto the Fort Bragg neighborhoods. The dioxins were poisoning the entire community where the children played, including my organic garden. After doing more research, I found out that all kinds of toxins were regularly being emitted into the environment by GP. [1] *I was furious!*

I went to bat for the workers and a five-year battle ensued—my first community organizing effort in Mendocino County. I turned to my day care parents and others in the community for help. After a year, we had gotten GP cited for willfully exposing the workers to toxic PCBs, which in a criminal court would equate to attempted murder, and for seven other violations[2]; GP appealed it. It was going to court in San Francisco, four hours south of Fort Bragg. I insisted that OSHA issue subpoenas to 28 of the mill workers who were going to testify, so GP would have to let them off work and pay them. The workers and a big part of the community were going to get on rented school buses to go down for the hearing. At the eleventh hour before the hearing, we learned that OSHA and the IWA had worked out a settlement with GP without even talking to the affected workers.[3]

When the OSHA settlement was proposed, we were told that nothing else could be done as the union agreed with the settlement. That night, on a local television station, I saw a debate about logging between Don Nelson—the head of the IWA, the sell-out union for GP—and Judi Bari. I didn't know who Judi was, but it was clear to me that she was smart and had experience dealing with unions. She was giving Don hell!

After the program, I called Judi and explained my involvement and intention. She came over and we ended up forming an IWW Local Number 1 (Wobbly).[4] This was a long, drawn-out and hard-fought case, which went all the way to Washington, DC, where I wrote and submitted a brief in support of the workers. We lost because the IWA is a closed shop and OSHA ruled that, if the IWA was satisfied with the settlement, there was nothing the IWW/workers could do.[5] In some ways, we won, because we fought it and brought attention to the matter, even though the IWA had sold out. Later, we also helped the workers win their fight against a union dues increase and Don Nelson was replaced as president of the union.

This battle made me realize that governmental agencies protected business entities. It enraged me. I paid taxes! I was supporting these governmental agencies and they were subverting any attempt by the people to protect the environment, the air, the water and the Earth on which my children were living. I was upset because I hadn't been paying attention. The general public in this country thinks that someone else is going to take care of the problem. We give a doctor or a lawyer our money and say, "Take care of it," but they are most likely going to take care of their own problem first: making money. I learned that you cannot give away your role or your power in any situation. This launched me into a lifetime of activism.

Judi Bari was involved in stopping the destruction of the redwood forest and I was involved in protecting the mill workers. Judi explained that the timber companies were practicing liquidation logging—clear cutting everything in the forest, including the undergrowth. Later, when I saw my first clear cut, it took my breath away and tears began to stream from my eyes. It was unbelievably violent. Judi told me about how she was trying to save the forest and about Earth First! (a movement whose followers believe in biocentrism where life—the Earth—comes first with a practice of putting their beliefs into direct action). As she spoke, I suddenly realized that GP was treating the forest the same way they were treating the workers: they didn't care about anything but the almighty dollar.

Judi and I worked together for the forest and the workers, and organized Redwood Summer to bring public attention to the liquidation logging and to the plight of the workers. After Judi's car was bombed and she was severely injured, I was the key organizer for the summer of protests we had planned. During the Redwood Summer, the hearings about the PCB spill were ongoing.

GP tried to paint me as an environmentalist who hated the timber workers, but I was trying to protect them! Timber workers met in my living room and made slogans and signs for the rally. A week before the Redwood Summer rally, 11 timber workers' families pulled their children out of my day care center. They were told to either do that or lose their jobs at GP and Louisiana Pacific (LP). One dad, who was a supervisor at one of the mills, cried when he told me why he had to pull his child out of my day care center. We were all very close.

I fought against the overcutting and logging of old-growth redwood trees in every way I could. I began organizing my community to stop this destruction and to take direct action. I was arrested numerous times. As my children grew older, they would occasionally join me in organizing and at protests.

During Redwood Summer, Earth First! activists had joined with a local group, Friends of Osprey Grove, to save a small grove of old-growth redwood trees. The community had been negotiating with LP to save the grove. Save-the-Redwoods League, whose primary purpose is to acquire and protect redwoods, had offered LP fair market value for the grove. I helped raise money to pay the loggers for lost wages if we were successful in stopping the cutting of this small and rare old-growth grove.

Without warning and while negotiations were progressing, LP sent loggers to cut down Osprey Grove. Friends of Osprey Grove rushed to get a temporary restraining order (TRO) and several of us went down to see if we could stop LP, but the loggers were frantically cutting down as many redwood trees as they could before the TRO got there.

I watched the terrible destruction of a beautiful grove of old redwoods and sobbed because there was nothing I could do. In the grove, there was a huge, old, hollowed-out redwood tree called the Grandmother Tree, which Earth First!ers had stayed inside during a protest several months earlier. A woman who had videotaped that protest for local television wanted to get one last videotape of the Grandmother Tree before it was cut down. To protect this woman while she was filming, I followed her into the grove.

The loggers charged at us from every direction. The woman ran out of the grove, but I jumped into the Grandmother Tree. It was damp and safe—like a womb—and smelled wonderful. Five of the loggers came to get me out, but I couldn't abandon the tree or let them cut it down. This event was on the local radio station and my oldest son, Zack, came down. He convinced the loggers to let him come into the grove to talk me out of the tree. The loggers had surrounded the tree and Zack told them to step back. He asked me if I was coming out.

"No."

Zack said, "I can't talk you out?"

"No," I said emphatically.

"OK, I'll come in with you!"

The loggers were infuriated, but we wouldn't leave. As they were threatening us, Zack and I sang. It was his 21st birthday and the day before my 42nd birthday, so we sang "Happy Birthday" and "The Internationale." We were going to stay there and protect the Grandmother Tree until the TRO came.

A logger with a chain saw said that he was going to cut the tree next to us, which was very close. He told us that we'd better leave because the tree he was cutting could fall in any direction. I looked at Zack and said, "I'm staying. If they murder this tree, they'll have to murder me."

Zack said, "Me, too."

I was so scared for Zack and for the Grandmother Tree. The logger put that tree down very close to us and our eyes were affected by the flying sawdust. We finally got the TRO and the logging was stopped. Our direct action saved the Grandmother Tree, but only 13 out of

55 old-growth trees were left by the time that massacre was stopped by the courts. It was heartbreaking.

In the news coverage that followed, I asked to be contacted if any of the few remaining old-growth groves in Mendocino County were on the chopping block. Zia, a single mother, contacted me and explained that she lived above the Albion River and had spent many family times in an area she named Enchanted Meadow. This sacred place had a pristine, old-growth grove that she called Raven's Call.

For several years, Zia had been doing everything she could to save this area from being cut. She spent a great deal of time documenting and educating people on the importance of the area to the forest's health and to the endangered salmon, spotted owls, osprey and other wildlife living there. Over the years, she had filed several lawsuits to stop this area from being cut; one of these lawsuits was still pending. We went to see Enchanted Meadow and Raven's Call and I did what I could to help.

When the lawsuit was lost and LP was free to cut, Zia mounted a public campaign to demand that the California Department of Forestry (CDF) make LP file a new timber harvest plan on the area before they could cut. I joined in her efforts and helped to document and publicize the environmental issues and the importance of saving Enchanted Meadow.

As a result of the intense public pressure that we generated, CDF agreed and issued an order not to log the Enchanted Meadow area until a new timber harvest plan was submitted and approved. LP took it to court and got the local judge to lift the order. At 5:30 in the evening, we learned that LP was going in the next day to cut. There was no time to organize any protests. There was an occupied osprey nest in an old-growth tree in Raven's Call that needed protection.

The next morning, right after dawn, I went into the grove to try and keep the trees in the ground while Zia worked to get a lawyer to file a TRO and alert the community. I was hiding, praying and crying. Four logging crews showed up and started to cut. The osprey were making a racket, trying to warn them to stay away from the nest. I felt so helpless. When the third old-growth tree came down very close to me, I took action. I jumped out of my hiding place and ran up and down the steep ravine, hiding behind trees and bushes, yelling about the osprey and making it hard for the loggers to know where I was.

They stopped logging and the sheriff's office was called. When the officers came, I stayed in hiding but yelled, "Listen to the nesting osprey screaming. The cutting of this grove is illegal!" The Department of Fish and Game came and issued a stop order for Raven's Call as logging was not permitted around a nesting osprey. The community came together and a six-week forest occupation of the rest of the Enchanted Meadow area ensued. Many people were arrested before the court finally issued a stop-logging order. LP tried to stop the protests by filing a Strategic Lawsuit Against Public Participation (SLAPP) against me and more than 100 other community members.[6]

Most of the defendants settled with LP early in the lawsuit; three held out (Zia, Beth Bosk and I) and we worked very closely with our attorney. This lawsuit cost us almost five years of our lives and much pain and anguish. Zia was pregnant when LP started cutting and during the first months of the SLAPP. At full term, her baby was born dead as a direct result of her stress. Hundreds of thousands of dollars in legal fees were spent. Enough was enough.

I had an idea to end the lawsuit and turn it into something positive. The three of us met and agreed upon a strategy and tactic for what I called "composting the SLAPP." Each of us would agree to stop the legal battles if LP would agree to give us something back. I called LP's Western Regional Manager Tommy Thompson and he agreed to meet with me. When we sat down together, I said, "Look, Tommy, this lawsuit has been going on for almost five years. No one is winning but the lawyers. I will never give up because I didn't do anything wrong. I will stop if Louisiana Pacific stops. We can settle this by LP dropping the charges against me and using the money saved in legal fees to work with me on a forestry restoration project."

It worked! We created a restoration project on the banks of Greenwood Creek, which saved the Town of Elk's wells. Zia and Beth followed my lead. Zia, having lost the most, managed to settle by getting LP to agree to deed Enchanted Meadow and Raven's Call to her; Beth couldn't get her demands met by LP, so Zia agreed to give her the meadow and the SLAPP finally ended.

The California Anti-SLAPP Project (CASP) represented us in this lawsuit. After the lawsuit was settled, the director hired me as the CASP paralegal and organizer. For the last 12 years, I have been working for CASP, defending people and organizations who have been sued for exercising their First Amendment rights and helping them transform their SLAPPs, as I did, into a weapon to help win their battles.

At the height of my activism, I was arrested 16 times. Some of my direct actions were very dangerous. I have always believed in telling my kids the truth. For instance, when they were school-aged children, I would tell them, "I am going into the woods tonight to save some of these big, old-growth trees that I have shown you. You know how important they are to us, to the forest and to the Earth." They would always ask me when I was coming back and if I were going to jail. I would tell them that I didn't know. I would tell them that it was dangerous, but I would try and be as safe as I could.

I have asked my grown sons what it felt like to hear those words coming from their mother. They told me that they felt pride, fear and gratitude. At the height of it, they had to deal with negativity at school because my name was famous and I was high profile and not necessarily popular with everyone. In grade school, my sons would often get hassled by other children about their mother: "the environmentalist who was out to destroy jobs in the community."

With the media coverage of my activism, hostility towards me was growing in my community. In the early '90s, I decided to run for supervisor so that people could hear from me directly. People in town were told that I was trying to take their jobs away. When I ran for supervisor, I had a half-hour, call-in radio program every week on the "redneck channel" and was involved in seven televised debates. The main goal was to have people hear me and not the stories filtering through the media.

The first debate was at the IWA hall, sponsored by Women In Timber. The hall was totally packed and I was really scared. I am not comfortable as a public speaker, but I got two standing ovations. I didn't get elected, but I got my voice out and talked about the real issues in our community. Three quarters of my campaign organizers were timber people who didn't buy the corporations' lies; about one quarter were misfit radicals.

When my mother died, I embarked on a major healing to reclaim my heritage as a Romani woman (Gypsy). After all these years, I am working for and with Romani women, men and children who are still living with severe discrimination in every country. Roma have no homeland, which means that they have no government to protect them. As an adult, I took my mother's warning seriously: until she died in the late 1980s, I never spoke of being Roma. I now know that there is a tremendous amount of negative stereotyping of Gypsies and resulting prejudices.

A year before the U.S./North Atlantic Treaty Organization bombing of Kosovo, I helped found Voice of Roma (VOR), a nonprofit public benefit corporation. There were at least 150,000 Roma living in Kosovo before the bombing; at least 125,000 are now living as displaced persons without refugee status and protection in camps outside of Kosovo because it is too dangerous for Roma to return.[7] They are the forgotten victims of that war. VOR is dedicated to eradicating the stereotype of Gypsies by educating the general public about Roma and their plight in the modern world. We also work hard to empower Roma in and from Kosovo with the needed tools and economic development in order to have a strong voice in their lives.

For the rest of my life, I am 100 percent committed to work for justice, peace and reclamation of the planet's health by sharing the world's resources with all of its inhabitants. My motto for action is: "Without sharing there can be no justice; without justice there can be no peace; without peace there can be no future."

Surviving the pain of my childhood has taught me to take the negative and create a place for healing, both personally and in the world. I believe in the ancient wisdom that all living things are connected. I don't believe that one living thing is better than another. I believe in Gaia, the Great Spirit, Jesus, Mother Mary, the Great Masters and Teachers, the Saints, the Angels and Maitreya. In order for darkness to disappear, it has to come into the light. I think that concept is coming to the surface everywhere, in all of our institutions, even in the Catholic church. Mainstream America is starting to understand that the government doesn't speak the truth and does not protect the people.

All spiritual teachings have their root from the same tree. The number one truth is "Love one another as you love yourself." I am taking what I learned from my healing work and applying it to myself. To heal the planet, we must heal ourselves. Start from the base of loving yourself and then move out into the world from that place. This has been forgotten in our government and in our world at large. So many systems are now based on "power over" another, which is very destructive.

I am not an activist who connects to other activists; I am an activist who connects to other people. When I see an injustice in my life or in my extended family, I take action. There is no doubt in my mind that "warrior" and "mother" are synonymous. Today, most of the real activists in the world are women. Every woman activist I have ever met cares deeply about the state of the world and its children and gets her strength from that caring. Often, if a man is at the front lines, a group of women is standing behind him, giving him strength and doing the work.

As mothers, we need to confront the corporations, our government, George W. Bush and the whole lot of them. Mothers can wield fury to bring justice to the world. Women need to take the helm. We bring life into this world and it is up to us to protect life, no matter what the cost.

CONTACTS
ams@casp.net
ams@mcn.org

SUGGESTED LINKS

http://www.casp.net (California Anti-SLAPP Project)

http://www.friendsofenchanted.org (Friends of Enchanted Meadow)

http://www.iww.org (Industrial Workers of the World)

http://www.voiceofroma.com (Voice of Roma)

FOOTNOTES START ON PAGE 207.

PATTI BOUCHER

Healing the Wounds of Childhood

"I believe there is a resiliency in
human nature—a huge reservoir inside us
that helps us rise up and bounce back."

Patti is a marriage and family therapist with years of experience in the movement arts, Buddhist meditation, somatic psychotherapy, compassionate communication skills, wilderness adventure and gardening. Patti teaches Pilates exercise classes and mind/body/spirit integration practices to groups and individuals. She has recently begun a consulting business and coaches adoptive parents of children who have experienced early childhood trauma. She and her husband Jan are raising their two adopted sons in their energy-efficient home made of recycled materials in the Richmond hills of California.

Patti received her bachelor of art degree in psychology at Temple University in Philadelphia, Pennsylvania, in 1974 and her master of science degree in counseling at California State at Hayward in 1978. She became a marriage family therapist in 1986.

For the past 20 years, the premise for my work as a therapist has been that healing people and healing the planet are part of the same challenge and enterprise. As I write, I look out my west-facing window and see a young neighbor busily landscaping his yard. He moved in a few years ago and transformed a shady, weed-filled hillside into a lovely haven with recycled materials and a huge variety of plants. It is now a lush, orderly and aesthetically pleasing piece of property.

In my work with clients, families and friends, I use the metaphor of an inner garden and a real garden. I help individuals be their own inner and outer landscape architects. If I can guide one person a month to recycle, compost and buy pesticide- and hormone-free food, then I am helping the planet to heal. If I teach someone to differentiate emotions from judgment, that is the same as weeding one's garden to allow the roses and jasmine to flourish. Three years ago, when my husband and I adopted two young boys with a traumatic family history, these guiding principles became a full-time practice.

I am the fourth oldest of 14 children. My father was Irish Catholic from the Philadelphia area; my mother was a Methodist and half Choctaw Indian from Oklahoma. I grew up mothering my younger siblings. By the time I was in high school, I made dinner five nights a week, did the family laundry, helped my brothers and sisters with their homework and cleaned the house. I was a huge asset to my parents.

Beatings with a strap were a way of life while growing up. I have memories of my father lining up my brothers on the couch with their butts in the air, going down the line and hitting them all. We were chased around the house many times with a strap or broom. I didn't get beaten very often because I was "good." Eileen, my sister who is one year older than me, was depressed and often lay around, so she got beaten often. I did not want to have to be seen with bruises, so I did my work and often hers so she would not get hurt.

During high school, I made plans to attend college, even though my parents wanted me to stay home and work for them. When my father wasn't around, my mother would secretly tell me that she wanted me to study home economics at college; however, in my father's presence, she would say that it was best if I stayed home. I wanted to be a medical doctor from the time I was very young. In the 1950s, a daughter of a working class family did not become a medical doctor. My parents would laugh and say, "Don't you mean you want to be a nurse?"

Against my parents' wishes, I enrolled in a local junior college. I was a scholarship student, working as a waitress on weekends and working for my parents when I wasn't at school. The pressure was immense because I was studying for the first time in my life and barely had time to sleep. I didn't have the financial support to move out of my parents' house, so I was stuck under the grueling work schedule of managing a family of 14 children and carrying a full class load.

I started to slack off and rebel at home. One evening, I did not finish the dinner dishes and instead left the dishes in soapy water overnight. I crawled upstairs to my room and passed out from exhaustion. The next morning, my parents screamed at me to get downstairs. I was so tired that I couldn't get up. My father dragged me out of bed, pulled me down the stairs and put my face in the dirty dishwater. Some time after the dishwater episode, my father came up to my room and demanded that I do my chores. I was too fatigued to move. He insisted and I fought back. He kicked me in the face and broke my nose.

Soon thereafter, I went to stay with my girlfriend Carol and her family, who were willing to stand by me in the face of my father's threats. They lived on the Delaware County side of a street in Bryn Mawr, Pennsylvania. The community college I attended was in Montgomery County, just across the street. My father found out that I was attending school in the wrong county and tried to get me expelled.

At the time, I was working as a secretary for the law enforcement program of the community college and showed up with two black eyes and a busted nose. The head of the department listened to my story and sent me to the school dean, who was planning to ask me to re-enroll in my county's school. When he saw my face and heard my story, he allowed me to stay.

Not long after that, Carol and I found our first apartment, which was a haven for me. I spent every free moment going to thrift stores and refinishing furniture. I became passionate about learning and studied late into the evening. The apartment was over a pizza shop and I delivered pizzas for them. In our living room, I placed a huge, funky lamp that I found at a garage sale. I put a red light bulb in it and covered the hand-me-down couch with a red bedspread. To add to the design, I painted the woodwork black.

After living there for one month, my father and mother came to visit. Shocked by the décor, my parents marched down to the pizza shop and screamed at Jake, the shop owner. My father shouted that my apartment was a hen house and in a red-light district. (I was a virgin at the time and had no idea what he was yelling about.) He accused Jake of running a house of prostitution. Jake defended me, but my father threatened Jake's life and his business. The next day, Jake asked me to find another job.

All through school, my parents made snide remarks about my pursuit towards a college degree. When I finally graduated, I was first in my family to receive a bachelor's degree. My father's response to my finishing college was, "So, what now? All you know how to do is waitress!"

In my late 20s, I earned a marriage family and child counseling license and began working as a therapist. When I finished my academic training, I decided that all I wanted to do was dance. To support myself, I became a massage therapist. Within a few years, I was specializing in chronic pain using body-oriented psychology and dancing whenever I could. In my late 30s, I trained in martial arts, engaged in annual wilderness experiences and embraced meditation. The culmination of years of my own wilderness experiences, 10-day meditation retreats and connection to my Choctaw heritage directed me in my early 40s to take women on vision quests, which were solo spiritual wilderness journeys.

When I was 40 years old, I found my life partner Jan, began crewing with him in sailing races and got married. Our relationship jelled the day we discovered our mutual passion for environmental issues and our visions of having a house built of recycled materials.

Four years ago, Jan and I decided to dedicate the eighth day of a 10-day backpacking trip to our relationship. At this point, we had our dream home built, were married and owned a sweet, high-energy dog. I was 46 and perimenopausal. Since I had 20 nieces and nephews, I did not feel a burning desire to reproduce, yet I did want to have the experience of raising a family. My body was running out of eggs and I didn't want to spend our savings on modern means of conception.

When we woke up on that eighth morning in the eastern Sierra high country, we started brainstorming about adoption. We were euphoric in the creative process of exploring a new vision together. At that point, we thought that we should adopt one boy because, in this country, boys are easier to find when you are not attached to getting an infant. One year later, after extensive research, classes and getting the Catholic Charities foster parents certification, Jan won a set of bunk beds at a raffle. We felt that this was a sign and decided it might be easier to adopt siblings rather than go through the whole process again in few years if we wanted a second child.

Within a few days of telling our plans to the social worker, meetings with three sets of brothers were arranged. We ultimately chose two Hispanic brothers: Valencio and Valentino. We knew a little bit of their history and were told that they appeared to be developmentally on target. There was a picture of the brothers—two and three and one-half years old—and a paragraph about each. We were informed that substance abuse issues with both parents were the primary reason they were in foster care. When I met them, I fell in love. There was a two-month transition period where we visited them three or four times, took them to the Santa Cruz boardwalk for a day trip and started having weekend overnight stays; they moved in one month later.

Before meeting the boys, we were told what to expect, yet I don't believe that we were adequately trained or informed of how all encompassing it would be. Through my varied experience with delinquent/wayward teenagers, homeless folks and my own family, I thought it would be much easier; in hindsight, I believe I was star struck with idealism and naiveté.

One month later, after the boys moved in, their biological parents tried to regain custody. It had been one year since the boys had seen their biological mother and father. Now, it was ordered that they see their bio parents on a weekly basis, which was very difficult for us. It was a two-hour, round-trip drive on a congested freeway and the boys yelled and cried every time we went. After two visits, my older son screamed, kicked and refused to enter the room where his bio parents were waiting. With a slight smile, the social worker finally announced that she was not in the business of forcing children to see parents and lifted the visiting requirement.

After several weeks of intense waiting, the judge did not return custody to the biological parents and the bio parents filed for another appeal. We were called into mediation with the family who was foster-adopting our boys' older brothers. We tried to convince the biological parents that we could give their children a better life. It was very useful to meet our sons' biological parents and give us more of a feeling for their past. As we sat with their bio parents, we saw a family full of dysfunction, poverty and suffering.

A deeper appreciation for our boys has grown as a result of that meeting. For the first year, Jan and I were involved in intense bonding and connection with them. The boys tended to have regular nightmares in the beginning—often three times a night. I made up short lullabies with their names, which I would sing over and over while rocking them. Every morning, we would rock them awake for 20 to 30 minutes with classical music. Jan would connect through drumming, tickling and wrestling.

Since they were in a full-time Montessori program, we made a conscious effort to have long, daily, intimate rituals at dinner and at bedtime where we would light candles, say grace, talk about our days and discuss the food we ate. At bedtime, besides reading stories, there was massage, cuddling, holding, singing and humming. I believe that this was all soul retrieval work as well as a crucial part of bonding. We could tell that the boys knew they had been rescued and seemed deeply appreciative.

With Tino, at age 2, the physical connection was quick, warm and satisfying; however, I was aware of how difficult it was for him to maintain eye contact. He was extremely aggressive at times and could not suck but only bite. We bought baby bottles and pacifiers and held him to teach him to suck. Now, at the age of 5, he is again requesting the bottle to soothe himself.

With Valencio, the older one, it took a while for his little body to release and receive while being held. After about two months, he sobbed one day in my arms for over an hour; from then on, he was able to melt his body into mine. It took much longer for him to trust and attach to his dad. Jan started to massage his feet every night and slowly, over months, Valencio allowed Jan to give him affection without stiffening up or emotionally detaching.

The adoption/foster counselor advised that I have limited contact with any of my family members who have substance abuse problems since that was a traumatic factor in our sons' early lives. Like many Irish Catholic families, most of my nine brothers and one of my sisters choose alcohol to cope with life. The need to control our sons' environment, protect them and keep them safe unfortunately meant eliminating visits with members of my immediate family.

During holidays and other family celebrations, losing contact with my family has been sad. At times, it has been a welcome excuse to say that we do not want to attend gatherings where alcohol is abused because of the boys' history, even though we just might want to stay out of the soup. This has been a difficult yet conscious decision for Jan and me. Because of the confusion, lies, denial, minimization, broken promises, incomplete communication and verbal attacks that inevitably come with alcohol abusers, I find it wiser not to have contact. There is relief knowing that family members who drink will not be at my door; with it comes the grief that my siblings aren't available to help and witness the lives of my children.

For the first year and one-half, we were not allowed to take the boys to therapy because the county social worker would not approve of it while we were still foster parents. I think she was afraid that we would change our minds about the adoption if we uncovered the boys' trauma through the therapeutic process. This meant that I was a new mom, a healer, a friend and a therapist. A great deal of the time, I felt like an overstretched rubber band. Thanks to friends, my weekly meeting with Quirk (a women's improvisational movement group that has met for 20 years) and the boys' school, I survived and was given great counsel during stressful situations. I tapped into the resources of the intuitive mother and wise warrior within myself.

Eventually, after the finalization of the adoption, I found a wonderful therapist, Dr. Joan Lovitt, who specializes in early childhood trauma and uses eye movement desensitization and repatterning. One day in her office, while I was playing and holding Valencio, he crawled into my lap and began to wriggle and groan. I felt an eruption of emotions throughout his body and his breath was strained. He wrapped his body with my long, scarlet-colored scarf and tied it around my waist. Slowly, painfully and intensely, he moved his head between my legs and began to work his way down towards the floor. Until that moment, I thought he was playing, but then I realized that he wanted to be birthed by *me*, his adopted mom! I was swollen with emotion, full of joyful and sad tears. He held on to me as if to cling to *my* life force, and untwisted and uncurled his tense little body towards the floor. I felt myself breathing deeply to release him and stay grounded.

It was such a profound experience to feel both elation and deep grief for never having physically given birth. He pulled the scarf as if it were the afterbirth and reached up as if from Mother Earth to have me untie the cord. When the birth scene was completed, he jumped into my arms and let me hold him with the intimacy of a newborn baby. He cried and cried, then smiled and looked into my eyes with such appreciation and gratitude that I cried, too.

I realized in that moment that the healing work I had done in my own life was a preparation for my sons' healing. It is clear that, as I help my boys heal, they contribute to the continued healing of my past. As I approach each challenge with my sons, another dormant layer of my own traumatic past is uncovered. The warrior mother adopted two sons, knowing of their traumatic start in life. The warrior mother now sees the path ahead—full of obstacles, challenges and never-ending moments of frustration and elation. It is a path that I will need to bushwhack with my sword.

I have had to be my sons' advocate with the steadiness of the warrior and the heart of the Divine Mother. When applying to schools for the upcoming year, I was aware of the need to protect, advocate, encourage and prepare them for possible disappointment. Sure enough, after testing and interviews at one private school, my sons were not accepted. I received a notice saying that they did not think one was ready and that they could not meet the special needs of the other. Both boys took the rejection quite hard and had a few months of regressed behavior. It was truly hell to witness Valencio's feelings of low self-worth and rejection and Tino's anger and oppositional behavior.

My boys need the depth of love and nurturing from their mother as well as the discipline and consistency of the warrior. The warrior part of me takes a step back and scopes out situations. With a deep breath, I move forward. Whenever I sense hesitancy from my boys' caretakers, I stand firm to get their needs met. Whenever I sense rejection or doubt about my boys' needs and desires from educators, medical people or neighbors, I try to take everything into account and stay tuned to the most effective course of action. I anticipate our differences in skin color as a possible reason for discrimination, so I often use the mantra to stand firm and calm and keep my heart open.

During the past three years, Jan and I have woven together everything we have ever learned and experienced to have our sons bond, heal and flourish. We have had to give regular "holding times"—a technique developed by Dr. Margaret Welsh—in which the complete synthesis of warrior mothers is needed. There are three stages: first, you hold the child and confront them with the undesirable behavior; next, you hold them through an intense resistance stage until the third stage of resolution, when the child and mother (or other holder) receive the blissful love bond. My youngest son, who tends to have oppositional behavior, will need to be held in the resistance stage for sometimes up to an hour or more while he tries to kick, punch, bang his head, pinch, bite, spit and thrash himself with anger. It requires all my physical strength, compassion, endurance and patience.

Having children has enhanced and strengthened my view of the world. I am an environmentalist and an artist. I am in love with nature and desperately want to share this with my sons and lay the foundation for their appreciation of this planet. I want to do my part in preserving our resources for my children's children. I believe that the maternal and warrior energy in all of us comes from love for our incredible planet, including the discipline to take care of it and the patience to heal the air, rivers, forests, agricultural fields and endangered species.

I try to be a role model for my children. We are not just here to take up space or to take and consume the world's precious resources. We are also here to give back and I strive daily to help my sons adopt this practice in their own lives. My strong belief to respect others and honor the Earth has been deeply planted in their psyches. The boys are tuned into nature and seasonal rhythms and are beginning to identify local birds and plants. I teach them yoga poses and other calming methods. We eat healthy foods and talk about where food comes from and how it is grown and distributed. At our evening meal, we say a simple prayer by thanking the farmers, the truck drivers, the storekeepers and the cook.

The most basic job of a mother is nurturing and feeding her children. Earth is what gives us our food. Our dear Mother Earth suffers from repeated abuse. I read daily about the biosphere's devastation due to modern factory farming, the bulldozing of rain forests and mad cow disease. Pesticides, artificial flavoring and coloring, hormones and antibiotics land on dinner tables and leak into our rivers and oceans. There is a huge amount of work to be done and I often get lost in the question of which battles to choose. As a mother, I am sworn to this challenge and do everything I can to educate my children so they will grow up living lightly and giving back to our Mother Earth.

Since I have become a parent to young boys with a traumatic start in life, I have felt the desire to shift gears in my work as a psychotherapist. I am now interested in working with other parents who have children with trauma. Clearly, my future work will include healing attachment disorders and trauma in order to have complete, intimate and healthy relationships.

I am particularly interested in working with the many woman, like myself, who were busy living life with the freedom we grabbed after the women's movement but did not get around to having babies. I believe there are plenty of couples who want children and have experience and wisdom that would qualify them to handle the millions of children in foster care. I lead workshops and classes and teach important survival skills including the art of play, ways to cultivate compassion, deep and reflective listening, how to share one's passions with their children, healthy cuisine, kind discipline, the difference between protective and punitive use of force, emotional encouragement and spiritual guidance.

I am deeply involved in the tapestry of motherhood. My adopted sons have required a good deal of healing to build the needed bond in our family. Their traumas have left scars that need my patience and understanding as well as all the tools and interventions I have ever used as a therapist.

It has often been challenging for my boys to gain confidence and mastery at some of the simplest tasks. The weaving is thick, lush, colorful, intricate, hardy and substantial. I realize that, as a mother, I will be forever weaving, learning and praying for patience. Telling the truth without blame and judgment and protecting our children are maternal warrior stances. We must tell the truth about our food, our schools, our involvement in other countries, our environment, our treatment of animals and our own personal histories. Mothering is all encompassing and can be relentless and incredibly rewarding. It is the ultimate creative process and an ongoing opportunity to love, nurture, teach, perform, celebrate, do ritual and ceremony, clean, organize, manage, share and receive. It is the opportunity to apply all of one's quirky, wacky ways and wisdom.

A deep realization hit me after the September 11, 2001 tragedies: It is time for the sacred feminine to take the helm of life in all countries. Women need to take over in order to save this planet. It may not come to full practice in my lifetime, but I see it happening in small ways. On a daily basis, I am aware of instilling the ways of the sacred feminine consciousness into my sons. Cultivating a strong connection with nature, eating healthily, recycling and having respect for all beings are our basic principles.

Before adopting my boys, I believed that love could cure all and that maternal energy was the ultimate healing. I have since learned that discipline and courage of the warrior archetype is also needed. Being a mother goes beyond her children; it directly affects the world. I have no doubt that our children are the future. In many ways, I feel that helping my sons heal their wounds heals the planet's wounds. Having children has helped me realize that I cannot give up hope. If I can't give up hope on my children, then I can't give up hope on the world.

CONTACT
Hydrophilos@earthlink.net

SHERRY GLASER

Activism Through Comedy

"The truth of a person's life is very political. Each of us is truly an anarchist who is able to govern ourselves if we realize that we have that power and that it is our responsibility."

Sherry is the star and author of Off Broadway's longest running one-woman show, Family Secrets, *as well as her visionary and revolutionary comedy,* Oh My Goddess! *Her latest multicharacter comedy is* In Touch With Reality. *She has performed with Whoopi Goldberg, Mo Gaffney and Kathy Najimy and has won numerous performance awards including the Los Angeles' Outer Critic's Circle Award and The New York Theater Award for Best Debut. She is a strong environmentalist and human rights activist. Sherry shares her dramatic personal story of being a mother of two young daughters when her husband, Greg Howells, mysteriously disappeared and never returned.*

I find it appropriate that I was born in the Bronx, New York, in June 1960. It gives me an attitude of strength and humor and provides me with a rich cultural sense of history—from Grandma Rose's kitchen on Decatur Avenue to the Catskills for vacation to the Beatles at Shea Stadium to high school on Long Island.

I became a "mother" figure when I was about four years old. My mother was battling mental illness and I had to take on a lot of responsibility. By the time I was nine, we had moved to Long Island where everyone blended together into a big, Jewish Jell-O mold with weird colors, wiggly boundaries and very little substance. I refer to them as the "wonder years" (because I constantly wondered what was going on), but even during my adolescence in Oceanside, when I began a downward spiral of self-abuse with drugs, sex and bulimia, there was always a voice … an angel … a will at work beyond my limited scope and belief that my life was doomed. This voice told me to move to California.

Under the guise of attending college at San Diego State University, I found the light of the Pacific Ocean, the sunset, alfalfa sprouts and avocados. My life was saved! College felt like summer camp. I discovered the art of improvisation under the generous tutelage of Professor Jerry Farber. I could, for the first time in many years, play like I was supposed to when I was a child. I had found my art, so I dropped out of school and got involved in street theater with the likes of Whoopi Goldberg, Kathy Najimy and Mo Gaffney. I was a founding member of a feminist comedy troupe called Hot Flashes.

In Hot Flashes, I became aware of the mighty role of women in the world, especially mothers who held down jobs, raised children and sustained the community. We would research, study and impersonate women of the world and bring them to the stage. It was my first real education.

I met my husband Greg Howells through my comedy career. He was a fan and a friend of my next door neighbor. Greg offered fresh and funny material for one of my characters, Bernard Gluck, a schmaltzy Borsht Belt comedian. Our chemistry for comedy spilled over into great love and affection, and soon our daughter Dana was conceived. With the pregnancy, we chose to marry and immediately created a monologue based on having a wee creature growing in my body.

On the occasion of Dana's home birth in San Diego, I gave birth to a monologue for *Family Secrets* about home birth and have reenacted my labor pains over 3,000 times to hysterical audiences all over the country. Greg and I were in the habit of running the whole show—from the ticket taking to the lights and the sound—and because we had our new baby, I put Dana in the show for about nine months and actually nursed her on stage during the introduction to the piece. Audiences were awed and delighted at the sight of mother and child in such a tender pose. *Family Secrets* ultimately became the longest running one-woman show in Off Broadway history.

After a 15-month run in New York, followed by a six-month tour of eight shows a week, I decided to stop performing and have another child. I had always wanted two (so they could have someone to talk to about their crazy mother). Lucy was conceived on our wedding anniversary in August and was born on May 6. During labor with her, one of my most wonderful characters revealed herself: "Ma," the great Jewish mother of us all—loving, big, delicious and wise—who is half of my show *Oh My Goddess!* "Ma" is unconditional love and acceptance. I haven't totally integrated these qualities as a human, everyday mother, but she helps me get better at it.

When my husband of 10 years vanished on June 18, 1997, it became an almost insurmountable obstacle but has somehow become my salvation. Greg was fully established as my director and co-writer and we were at the peak of a very successful debut of *Oh My Goddess!* in Carmel, California. It was a Tuesday, our day off. I decided to go to the farmers' market with my cousin Linda, and Greg decided to go golfing at Rancho Canada. We had had a beautiful morning together and the last thing I said to him was, "I love you. You're a genius. Have fun."

I didn't start to worry about Greg until around 11:30 PM that night. It wasn't unusual for him to have a twilight round of golf (on practically the longest day of the year), then go to the Rio Grill for a burger and beer and watch a baseball game. I took Lucy to bed with me around 11:30 PM. Something woke me at around 2:30 AM; I think it was fear. His side of the bed was empty and he wasn't on the couch. I called the hospital, the jail … nothing. I thought that he might have gone up to San Francisco because he hated traveling during the hot day traffic and he was supposed to pick up Dana in the city the next day anyway. I called the hotel that we frequented during my gigs there … again, nothing.

I lay there, dozing and listening. I remember (or at least I think I remember) him coming home in the dawn hours. He looked inebriated. I don't know if it was a lucid dream because, when I woke up in the morning, he wasn't there. I felt the heat of panic flood my system. We were living in a small apartment under my mother's house and I went up to ask for her help. She told me not to panic, but I started to cry anyway. She hugged me for a while and I let go of some of the fear. She then suggested that I call the golf course and see if he ever showed up.

"Yes," said the man on the phone. "He had signed up to play around 6:30 last night and, in fact, a 1989 beige Honda Civic was left overnight in the parking lot." I felt a dark, cold fear overwhelm me. I thanked him, hung up and called the police. They said that they would meet me in the parking lot at the Rancho Canada golf course. I gave Lucy to my mom and left.

The officer met me in the lot and escorted me to the lone Honda. I felt icy cold and very lonely on that balmy summer morning. The doors were unlocked. The officer opened the door cautiously and we searched the car. We found Greg's wallet with the usual amount of money; his shoes; his latest script, *Lazurus*; the trunk full of empty beer bottles; and one golf ball on the dash that had the insignia "Flying Lady." A grounds keeper came out to tell us that someone had left a cart overnight on the 13th hole and perhaps it had something to do with my husband.

We took a cart over the greens towards the center of the course. We found Greg's golf cart and golf bag abandoned on the green. Four golf clubs on the ground pointed in four directions; they looked as though he had held them in his hand and released them. There were no signs of struggle, no footprints or clues and no balls left in the bag. (If you know anything about golfers, they always have balls in their bags.) I figured that he hit his last ball right on the sweet spot and sent that sucker soaring. He dropped his clubs and then he was gone. *Where?*

The terror of losing someone to the unknown is inexplicable. The frantic search was exhausting with helicopters flying over Ventana National Forest, missing person's reports and posters. I sat in my mother's backyard every night with binoculars, searching for a light somewhere in the hills. I tried to explain to my nine-year-old daughter that her father had vanished, that it had nothing to do with her and that I didn't know if he was ever coming back. I doubled the time I nursed Lucy to try and comfort her from the vibrations she was surely feeling at one year old. I experienced a torturous thing called "acute listening," which occurs when you strain your hearing for the slightest sound of approach.

After three weeks of waiting, I had to go home to Mendocino County to see if there were any clues. I ripped our house apart and found nothing. It was paralyzing because all I could do was look, wonder and wait. I couldn't afford a private detective and Greg's family wouldn't provide for one either.

I sit here now—one day before the seven-year anniversary of his disappearance—and find myself still waiting, still longing and still wondering if that unfamiliar car in the driveway might be him. Even though we moved, I still have the same phone number … just in case.

Hope is alive. You cannot deny it or dismiss it until there is proof that someone will never come back. It is a cruel and never-ending reality in our lives, but we continue. We cry, celebrate, struggle and sometimes curse the stars above; in the end, we still love—maybe more than most because we know how quickly it can all disappear. Of course, the source of most of my poetry and many monologues are inspired by this great and tragic romance. Although it was a harrowing experience, it has taught me so much about love and letting go. I learned that right now is more important than any other time. Love is in the moment. Bless it and let it go.

I saw my father die at the end of January (six months prior to Greg's disappearance) of liver and stomach cancer. I reluctantly threw dirt on his grave, as is our tradition, to make the reality of death tangible and final, but I had no idea where my husband had gone. I had lost the most important men in my life, just like that. The panic and the need to survive caused a terrible shock to my system and it affected my work.

My first performance after Greg disappeared was at the end of August for a six-week run at the Sadie Bronfman Theater in Montreal. The Bronfman was also a gallery space. Coincidentally, my show, *Family Secrets*, was mounted at the same time that a photography exhibition entitled *Death* was being presented. *Death* was a collection of startling and utterly plain images of just that. The stark images assaulted my soul. I got on stage, lost my breath and felt like I was choking. It made going to work dreadful, but I had signed a contract to do these performances and needed the money. This condition continued to plague me for years, but I am supposed to be on the stage. It is my medium, so I continue—even in the face of what I feel is humiliating. People adore my work and are grateful to be in the audience. I must speak; "Ma" said so.

For some reason, my material has not reached the mainstream. There seems to be some sort of ceiling over my contribution right now. I'm not sure if it's the right-wing powers that be, disorganization on my part, the apathy of the masses or maybe my time is yet to come. I'd like to be influential in the shift in consciousness. I believe the system is so corrupt that dismantling and restructuring it would be a waste of time and money. If there is a shift in consciousness, then the problems will remedy themselves as people become community sustained and simplify their existence.

I see my role in communications and as an emotional teacher. I believe the missing link in this global catastrophe of oppression, war and destruction is emotion. People have abandoned the responsibility of emotion. We are all born with two tangible things: a body and emotions. It is our human nature. We have disassociated with that nature in order to dominate, merchandise and profit.

In order to sustain such a destructive nature, one must divorce from one's emotional being. If the men who do these evil deeds could feel the evil deeds they do, they would not do them anymore. I am here to awaken the power of feeling one's emotions. It will energize us and keep us healthy and clear minded, which will create right action. My job is to make people feel deeply and then find their relief in laughter and not take everything so seriously. Whatever happens, it's been a beautiful and extremely entertaining ride. We really do not know the quantity of the universe, so we should enjoy a little … actually, a lot!

I believe that everyone is born with a destiny and a great work of art inside them, which is fueled by some kind of talent. My talent is to bring laughter and drama to life and interpret it on the stage. It is a sort of medicine because, after people witness my work, they feel better. I am here to inspire people to action and to consciousness. I am a revolutionary activist. I bring radical theater and music through my production company and direct solo performances. I also teach improvisation.

Love and politics influence my work; I am entertained and baffled by both. I believe the great works are about politics and the interaction of human beings. The truth of a person's life is very political. Each of us is truly an anarchist who is able to govern ourselves if we realize that we have that power and that it is our responsibility. We have the ability to respond to our lives in a productive, healthy, respectful and successful manner if we are left to our own devices. It would be wonderful to follow the laws of nature instead of the laws of man.

Lucy's in my new show, *In Touch With Reality*. I play an upper middle-class woman with plenty of money and guilt about spending it in this time of unlimited, politically insensitive consumption. Lucy plays the child who is in love with Barbie and all things corporate. Lucy loves the spotlight, like her mother (maybe even more so).

As we marched for peace on Memorial Day in Mendocino, Lucy got tired after a while and I carried her on my shoulders. As we walked, we engaged passersby in peaceful discourse She then began quoting my show on the benefits of growing hemp. "You want carpet ... hemp. You want protein ... hemp. You want fuel, paper ... hemp. You want a good laugh ... hemp." I cracked up. Lucy is my activist companion. She comes with me to low-risk demonstrations, marches and early-morning gate blockades with loggers. She feels the way I do about the government; when she hears the name "John Ashcroft," she screams. She sobbed when she heard that George W. Bush was elected. She so wanted Ralphenator (as she calls Ralph Nader) to be our president.

Dana, I'm told, carries on politically out of earshot. She is 16 now and at the time of her life where it is difficult for her to honor what I do. She's the rebel. She threatens me with plans of becoming a Republican. I think I have made the kids truly aware of the corporate invasion into our lives. In fact, when Lucy wants some commercial candy, she asks if she can just this once have some "corporate crap."

A lot of folks have given me feedback on my impact. Some say their lives are changed by my work, whether it's the inspiration to call their mothers or estranged relatives, or a simple feeling of comfort and hope that they'd been sorely missing. I hear reports of better, more direct communication as a result of my teachings. I've also had the opportunity to direct other one-woman shows.

My vision comes from above; I guess you could call it a muse. I have the ability to see the truth in simple terms, put it into character and bring it to life. I am very affected by this world and its behavior. I can see the truth behind the lies and translate it into theater. My perspective comes from loving this Earth and the people on it so much that I would die for them. I have a tremendous will that keeps me going. I try to eat organically and put things in my body that make me feel healthy. I'm also a double Gemini, so there's plenty of me to go around!

The mother is the source of all things; she is the beginning and the end. I never saw Jacob or Abraham beget anything. I believe the return of the Great Mother and the restoration of the feminine, which I equate with emotion and creation, is the way through which we will all be redeemed.

There is a fierce quality to being a warrior mother. I try to disassociate myself with the language of war, like "We're fighting for peace." I'm a peace activist, so the word "warrior" is challenging; however, if I look closely enough, part of me is willing to stand on the front lines. The truth is that we are at war. It is the world war ... the war against the world and her people. I will go to war's door and stand in the way to try and convince others that it's more fun and productive to be at peace. Being a warrior mother feels like I am ready to die for the sake of the Earth and her future.

I see the shift of the mother in this time and believe that it is being catalyzed by issues of health and poverty. Mothers are awakening to the needs of the child over slave labor and subsistent living. Another world is possible and, inside, they know it. I believe—with the co-operation of the poor, the working class, the environmentalists and the antiglobalizational faction—that we could be triumphant.

The mother created, or gave birth, to the universe and to life but is absent from our planet's religious history. How can you have a father without a mother? It is the time of the woman. She will rise peacefully and be well organized. We need to get the message out that women are the source of power; their inherent knowledge, wisdom and talent will keep them healthy and safe in this world—not the government.

I would give up my life for my children, which puts everything into perspective. I am merely a vehicle for change, possibility and hope. I am not the center of the universe. I read a prediction in the paper the other day that, within 30 years, many major mammals will be extinct, such as tigers and rhinos. The thought that Lucy and Dana will be living through the final days of nature is a powerful reckoning. For their sake, I am committed to action. Having babies connects me with the children of the world and their suffering—a beautiful opportunity for unlimited compassion and determination.

Love and nature inspire me. The absolute arrogance and stupidity of the white men in charge inspire me. I was in Washington, DC, to do reconnaissance for a September 2002 demonstration when I witnessed a lightning storm that put George W. Bush's power to shame. I prayed for it to strike the Capitol, but it was almost more entertaining to watch the Texas Republicans leave the Senate offices—with their $1.95 per gallon hats and rude, red, cowboy shit kickers—and get drenched and blown by the Mother herself.

It was a warning of what's coming. Mother Nature and her fierce protection of the Earth through natural disasters inspire me to believe that life is cyclical and death is natural and quick, not the torture of billions of people. The proportions are biblical right now; the characters are huge, monstrous and mythic in my mind and I get to do the theater that it demands. I believe that I am doing what I was born to do. This is my destiny. I don't believe that there is anyone in the world who works harder than a mother. We are a bottomless well of achievements—especially single mothers. We are on constant duty. We fall into an exhausted sleep, sometimes before we can even turn on the vibrator.

I am a lucky mother because I am not living in a war zone—at least not yet. I think of the billions of mothers whose children suffer from war and starvation and I can't bear it. It is time for these mothers to come to the center of our consciousness. The simple truth of a mother and her children, trying to survive against all odds, will awaken us to the shift in energy towards sustainable and honorable existence as a global community living in peace.

We have a choice in this world: make it better or make it worse. Mothers have an obligation to their children and a natural desire to improve their lives. I don't think it's coincidental that, at the forefront of the antiglobalization movement, women such as Vandana Shiva of India, Njoki Njehu of South Africa and Mami Josepha of Papua New Guinea are my heroes (or "sheroes"). It is time for the mother's basic instincts to direct our course into a magnificent future.

CONTACT

mothers_milk@msn.com

SUGGESTED LINK

http://www.sherryglaser.net

BIBLIOGRAPHY

Family Secrets (star and author)

Oh My Goddess! (star and author)

Remember This! An Intimate Portrayal of War Through the Eyes of Women
    (collaboration with Thaïs Mazur)

ROBIN CARNEEN

Speaking Out for Native Americans

"What happens to one happens to all, like rings on the water, touching and retouching one another."

Robin is a published poet and a Native American radio journalist covering Native American affairs for public radio and other national news programs. She hosts a weekly Native American public affairs and music show called "NAMAPAHH." She is very involved in Native media and files stories for radio with Independent Native News and the News From Indian Country *newspaper.*

Currently, Robin resides in Bow, Washington, and is an enrolled member of the Swinomish Indian Nation based in La Conner, just down the road from her. She is coordinating an effort, on behalf of the Coast Salish Institute, to repatriate a collection of over 526 Coast Salish artifacts. A single mother of two boys, she works tirelessly to shed light on Native American issues. Robin has also been an outreach worker at a Pomo Indian reservation, helping families get back on their feet.

Outside of Indian country, it is very hard for Native Americans and First Nations people to open up and talk about the "multigenerational trauma,"[1] which oppressed our culture for several generations. Since the invasion by settlers and explorers,[2] along with religious suppression and forced conversion by missionaries[3] and other religious sects,[4] our spirits were broken. We lost hope, and our way of being was forbidden by those who did not understand us and feared what they could not understand or accept.[5] The history of our near genocide and extermination, at the hands of the U.S. government[6] and its citizens,[7] is multigenerational. Our people are oral historians, passing on the painful stories of the massacres of our people and the cultural devastation that followed, which still affects our sovereign Nations to this very day.

To numb the pain, many gave up along the way and turned to alcohol, drugs, suicide, violence and crime.[8] All these are realities and are symptomatic. Destructive elements— depression, suicide, health problems and poverty—existed that contributed to the drop in population amongst our people. Many believe that establishing us as dependents of the U.S. made us the first welfare state.[9] This was a strategic and well-thought-out move by the U.S. government: to oppress us to the point where we would either assimilate or become an endangered species, like the eagles, wolves and so many others that once shared this Mother Earth in impressive numbers.

In order to ensure control and take over ownership of our ancestral lands and resources, we were moved to reservations.[10] Isolating us provided protection for the pioneers and countless others who considered our homeland up for grabs. Some tribes—both recognized and unrecognized—left without assistance from the U.S. government, despite signed treaties[11] and many promises, which were supposed to keep us all from becoming an impoverished people.[12] We have been oppressed and invisible for seven generations but have fought hard for such rights as our Religious Freedom,[13] which was also taken away from us for many years.

According to a cousin, my grandfather was Blackfeet and Cherokee. My mother, Carneen Allen, recently discovered her Pacific Northwest coast roots, for which we had been looking our whole lives. She and I are now enrolled with the Swinomish Indian Nation,[14] which is a miracle and an honor. Considering how long we have searched for the road home, and the faith and hope onto which we had to hold, the privilege of becoming a member now gives us some kind of future and is a real connection that I can pass on to my two boys, Nick and Tyler.

My father also had some ancestral native blood, possibly Choctaw or Chickasaw. However, I am still searching for his roots, hoping to find them as my mother and grandmother did, and am slowly discovering my Swinomish heritage; I hope the door will open to this past on my father and grandfather's side. My mother and father divorced when I was two years old. They couldn't work out a child custody agreement, so I was put into a foster home for a year. My mother remarried and I grew up with my stepfather, Dave Charleston, in San Francisco. He is from the Yosemite Valley Miwok tribe,[15] currently unrecognized by the U.S. government.[16]

The confusion and curiosity grew within and outside of our family about our Native American roots. Even in the diverse city of San Francisco, I was often questioned by other children and adults about my nationality. In the public schools, we were asked to indicate our minority affiliation on school paperwork. When I was born, my mother put "white" on my birth certificate because she was afraid I would be the target of discrimination if she put "Native American." My mother directed me to mark off "American Indian" on the forms, but my stepfather never talked about it. He had assimilated into the white culture and wanted us to grow up being white kids. Whenever my mother would bring up her Indian culture, he would get very upset and tell me that I wasn't Indian, even though my mother told me that I was. The older I got, the more Native American I looked; people questioned my nationality, leading me to a lifelong quest to discover who I was and where I came from as far as my Native American heritage was concerned.

One day, my half-sister, half-brother and stepfather got a check from the government. I wanted to know why we didn't get a check because my mom, my sister and I were also Indian. That was the first time there was any acknowledgement or official confirmation within our family that any of us were Native American—in the government's eyes and according to their standards[17] of what qualified a person as Native American. Even with this identification of other members of our family being designated as being Indian, my mother, my sister and I were still told by our stepfather that we were not Native American and he didn't want us to talk about it.

When I was in college, I took anthropology and archeology classes, taking a professional interest in Native American culture. The more I discovered, both inside and outside of the classroom, the more I realized that my stepfather was wrong to deny me my culture and Native American identity. I never asked him why he was so adamant that we portrayed ourselves as white people. I ignored his insistence and immersed myself into the inter-tribal world, to which I eventually had access, that started when I was college age. I learned how to do bead work, attended pow wows and found opportunities to speak to Elders in our communities, wherever I lived. For the first time, I was discovering some hints about my roots and was encouraged to keep looking.

After working for a variety of park services for about 12 years, I was employed for five years by the Department of Social Services, doing outreach work with "at-risk" families, especially Native Americans, on and off the reservations. Because of my own experience, it was important to me to go into Native American communities and do unification and prevention work. I witnessed many families endure hard times and struggle with what most people in the U.S. seem to take for granted.[18]

Most reservations don't offer substantial health care and there is a long waiting list at health facilities and rehabilitation centers; getting to other medical resources can take weeks or months, depending on staffing and transportation. It is very hard for Native Americans to get the kind of health care they need. They can't walk into a white doctor's office and expect them to understand all their medical and spiritual needs. Until 10 years ago, medicine women and men used to come and heal people in their homes; those old ways have now died out.[19]

One day, I was on a home visit for my job and noticed that there were envelopes on the wall. When I asked the child about them, he said, "Those are letters from my dad. He is in San Quentin state prison." I felt so sad for this family! The mother was raising the kids by herself, living on welfare in affordable tribal housing. Her husband was locked up because he drank, used drugs, beat her up and eventually committed a federal offense. In that moment, I understood how this type of behavior is inherent in the generations of Native Americans as they struggle with their past and their present impoverished situation. This cycle repeats itself in disenfranchised communities, on and off Indian reservations and extends across the borders into Canada and Mexico. In some cases, it is hard to tell when traditional upbringing was replaced by dysfunctional lifestyle choices and behavior.

This particular home visit haunted me and motivated me to research how many Native Americans were in prison. The more I discovered how many there were, the sadder I felt. Native Americans are underrepresented in prison statistics. I wanted to make them visible to the world and let people know about the serious issues that exist for Native Americans in the prison system. They are forced to cut their hair in state prisons[20] under the guise of strict grooming policies. They often have no access to religious rights and have limited legal counsel because of their poverty. Many of the crimes that Native American prisoners have committed—involvement in gangs, car theft and drug dealing—are possibly linked to impoverished living conditions and feelings of a dead-end future and a dead-end life.

I wanted to expose and express the feelings of the prisoners and their family's lives, so I organized a Native American prison art show, which was a huge success. The paintings and drawings were a testimony of the prisoners' struggle and strength. Many viewers were moved to tears. It was an amazing lesson to see how a disenfranchised culture needs to be given a voice and, through this voice, how they can build a deeper understanding of themselves. It was also a lesson about how important it is to bring stories—normally behind closed doors— to the public eye, so they, too, would have a better understanding of why Native Americans end up incarcerated. We even titled the three-week prison art show "Incarcer-Nation." [21]

After the prison art show, I wanted to expand the platform for Native Americans and learn more about their culture. I decided that I had to create a format so other people could learn the truth about Native Americans. I contacted a local FM public radio station[22] and they agreed to sign me on to do a show. I wanted an image that would "feed the people," so I decided to call the radio show "Metate." "Metate" is an Indian grinding rock used for making acorn and other meal—the perfect metaphor for my show: You have to break the bitter acorn open before it becomes sweet; after working and grinding it, you have something that can nourish you. My show was a resource for helping people learn about Native American culture—past, present and future—and nourishing them with information, stories and ideas.

I have two boys, 10 and 16 years old, and am raising them as a single mother. I have worked to keep my children connected to their Native American culture. As I learned in my youth, it is important to know the history of your people. If you try and be something you're not, it causes confusion and tension. My house has Native American decor in every room including images of tribes, shields on the walls, drums and pipes. My children are very proud of their culture and we often go to an event or gathering to get that connection. Since my sons were little, we've gone to pow wows. We talk about the real history of Native Americans—not the glamorized or textbook version. All of these things are important in honoring our ancestors and a way of life that goes beyond the material or technological world.

In my opinion, the curriculum in schoolbooks, which depicts a version of what happened to Native Americans in this country, is still one sided. Also, in my opinion, the books glamorize the Gold Rush era and the California missions. Until that version is challenged, Indian children will carry the generational trauma and open wounds. Non-Indian children will be miseducated with the impression and misconception of what took place in U.S. history as far as Native Americans are concerned.[23]

The truth, in my eyes and from what I have been told by Elders and descendants of some of the California Indian tribes, is that missionaries and Spaniards kidnapped and enslaved Indians and thousands of them died due to smallpox and other atrocities associated with that time. There were also massacres, at the hands of the U.S. military and disgruntled U.S. citizens, who back then didn't think twice about killing Indians. We were in the way of progress. Until both sides of history are discussed honestly[24] in school books and publicly, the ignorance and pain will be carried on for generations.

There is a slow U-turn being made by Native Americans these days—away from pain and towards healing. They are sharing who they are with the world instead of being afraid to show themselves. Allegedly, the generations within the last 30 years didn't embrace their culture as readily, so there is a huge gap in knowing the ways of their tribes and Elders. Now, Indian people realize that they need to get their language back and learn about their spirituality, medicine plants, music, songs and prayers before everything is completely lost.

Several years ago, there was a white buffalo calf born in Wisconsin and several others have been born since,[25] which caused quite a stir in Indian Country and which allegedly has the same significance to Native Americans as the white concept of Jesus coming back.[26] Indian tribes on the Northern Plains, including Sioux and Cheyenne, hold the white buffalo sacred. The National Buffalo Association has said that, even in the 1800s when as many as 80 million buffalo roamed the plains, the odds of having an albino calf were estimated at one in 10 million. The legend states that if a white buffalo calf is born, a time of healing is coming and prayers are being heard by the Creator.

Indian people are reclaiming their heritage. I believe that there will be a major resurgence in Native American values in this country. Many Native American youth are asking for this because they don't want to grow up losing their culture. This way of having to "walk in two worlds," as we call it, is hard for them and for many of us, but we can find balance and no longer have to be forced to assimilate to the white man's ways. Part of identifying with our culture is reclaiming our culture. There is a collective realization that our land, symbols, images, totems and stories got ripped off. Many Native Americans fear that they are disrespected because this misrepresentation has been going on for generations without a challenge … until recently.

There has been a great deal of commercialism around Native American identity. For example, it appears racist to some[27] to see a sports team named the "Chiefs" or a motor home manufacturer using the name "Winnebago" for a recreational vehicle (RV). Indian people are starting to stand up and say, "We never gave you permission to use the name of our tribe or the image of our people for your RV or sports team." "Crazy Horse" malt liquor, which is an oxymoron because Crazy Horse was an alcohol- and drug-free warrior, is a prime example.[28]

I feel that people's ignorance feeds the stereotypical, old-school way of thinking about Native Americans. One of my lifelong goals is to see the word "squaw" (the white man's word for "whore") forever removed in reference to Native American women. In Oregon, recent legislation was passed to remove this highly offense word[29]; however, some people still have the mentality that nothing is wrong with that word and I still see it used in many of the school books. Older people tend to hang on to this racist and derogatory way of thinking. We have an opportunity to re-educate people and use healthy, respectful language.

Indians strongly believe that there are spirits everywhere on this planet and in all things—trees, stones, soil … everything. We see the spirits in our ceremonies and feel the ancestors when we pray. In my opinion, some of the modern-day influences (such as alcohol, drugs, too much television, violent video games and movies, and sometimes too much dependency on computers) can drown the spirit you were born with and can contribute to the suppression of your spirituality.

We have to remember that these things, which have replaced our cultural and traditional upbringing, are artificial and only serve to distract us from the Red Road and lead us away from a sober, sane and healthy existence. We are rapidly leaning towards becoming a "fast-food society" and many have lost their relationship with the Earth, the animals and the plants that have nurtured us for countless generations. This insight also applies to non-Indian societies. Addictions and the disease of alcoholism is color blind. It affects us all, no matter what our race or origin. Not only are we as human beings trying to keep our heads above the polluted waters of our making, but our Mother Earth is being buried every day under technological, corporate and nuclear waste.[30]

A great example of this is the U.S. government pouring nuclear waste into Yucca Mountain—a spiritual place for the western Shashone Indians. Yucca Mountain has been selected as the repository for a maximum of 70,000 metric tons of high-level nuclear waste, which will be sent to Yucca in 43,000 shipments comprised of highly radioactive material from U.S. commercial nuclear reactors and atomic weapons facilities spread across 31 states. Ninety percent of the waste will travel via train or truck from east of the Mississippi River, which presents a high risk of accident and, in the current climate, a major terrorist threat.[31]

A major oversight is the fact that we often forget to honor our ancestors; this could contribute as well to our spiritual undoing. We must go to that place of respect for the Earth and have respect for the spirits, or we will all drown and not be able to come back up for air. I now understand, as a Native American woman, the importance of embracing my cultural heritage. It is a powerful guide to help me connect with who I am, who my people are and where we came from. What runs through my blood moves me to do what I can to heal this planet, embracing one of the most ancient wisdoms in this country: that of the Native American people.

Many Native Americans are relearning how to walk the path of the warrior. A warrior in the Native American tradition is a protector of women, children and Elders. Historically, if a tribe's food source or living area was in jeopardy, a battle would allegedly ensue. A person, male or female, young or old, needs to deeply acknowledge the source of life to possibly be chosen as a warrior.

To become a warrior, one had to make the sacrifices necessary for the survival of our Mother Earth and for the hundreds of species with which we share the planet. Those sacrifices and ceremonies[32] are varied. They can happen at a traditional Sundance, or they can be all of us waking up and getting involved with local and global issues regarding our own communities and culture. It may take time away from our jobs or personal life, but doing nothing and hoping for the best does not work anymore.

Native people call our planet "Mother Earth" because that is how much they honor her. The first shape a baby comes through is the circle—the shape of the womb. Native people understand this and their drums, some of the lodges and sweat lodges are all round—reflecting and honoring this.[33] We need to remember that the Earth is our mother and she, too, has made great sacrifices for us.

Time is running out. We have greatly poisoned that which feeds and sustains us. We must honor her, cleanse her and heal her. This process begins with honoring and healing ourselves—walking the path of the warrior, the healer, the teacher and the caretaker. Walk the path and invite others to follow or even lead the way. We may still have a chance, a glimmer of hope and truth on our side, in order to save Mother Earth and salvage what legacies have been left for us. Don't be afraid. Go on a canoe journey, hike to a sacred site, ask teachers to teach the truth, and join and participate in activism on behalf of the Earth and all its people. What happens to one happens to all, like rings on the water, touching and retouching one another.

CONTACT

res7dwhg@verizon.net

SUGGESTED LINKS

http://groups.yahoo.com/group/tetawin38 (online Native news posts for "NAMAPAHH")

http://www.indiancountrynews.com (News From Indian Country, The Independent Native Journal)

http://www.ksvr.org (KSVR 91.7 FM community radio station in Mount Vernon, Washington, featuring "Metate" and "NAMAPAHH" radio shows)

http://www.nativevoice.org (Native Voice Communications, *Independent Native News*)

FOOTNOTES START ON PAGE 207.

TERRY
GREENBLATT

Working
for Peace

"Accept the need for change within yourself
in order to engender change in the world."

Terry has been the executive director of Bat Shalom, Israel's national women's peace organiza-
tion, for the past four and one-half years. She is currently serving as Global Fund for Women's
"Activist in Residence," and mobilizing policy maker and organizational support for the Inter-
national Women's Commission for a Just and Sustainable Peace in Palestine and Israel to be
launched in 2004 in Jerusalem.

Terry has been a women's rights and anti-occupation activist in Israel for the past 20 years
and lobbies for the enforcement of equal rights for all Israeli citizens—men and women, Jews
and Arabs. She consults and speaks nationally and internationally on women's responsibility as
agents of both social and political change.

She is cofounder of Kol Ha-Isha (The Women's Voice) Center of Jerusalem and Shani (Israeli
Women Against the Occupation) and a member of the founder's council of the Community School
for Women's Studies and Economic Development in Kufar Kare. In 2002, she was honored with a
Ms. magazine "Woman of the Year" award and a Colombe D'oro Per La Pace award by the Ital-
ian Archivio Disarmo. She is also a recipient of the 2003 Liberty Award.

Throughout my life, it has been very instructive to see how women grow each other.
Maybe it has to do with a woman's innate nature to express nurturing, mending and
caretaking. Women have allowed me to witness their uncensored, unadulterated process in
all of its weakness and imperfection. The way women "be" in the world has been a primary
guide in my work.

I was born in New York in 1952. When I was 17, I dated a man who was very active in Students for a Democratic Society and its faction, the Weathermen. This group condoned the use of violence against property, not against people, as a legitimate means of resistance to the Vietnam War. The Federal Bureau of Investigation was aware of his political activities and they visited his parents' house looking for him. As good Jewish parents, they looked at us and said, "Get out of the U.S. until things settle down." They sent us to Israel, thinking we would stay there for six months, but we ended up living on a kibbutz for nine years.

The communal lifestyle of the kibbutz challenged the values with which I was raised. This new community didn't honor the status and luxury that money could provide. Everyone contributed to the community on some level. People were compensated adequately for the work they did. No one was made to feel different or less than someone else because they were more talented, virtuous or dedicated.

My boyfriend and I were the only two Anglo-Saxons on the kibbutz, so we needed to become an integral part of the community in order to continue living there. The fact that I stayed in Israel and lived on a kibbutz was a major shock to my parents. When my boyfriend and I decided to get married, my parents came to Israel and were even more shocked when we got married next to the cow sheds, with the smell of cow manure wafting through the air. It is *not* what they had envisioned!

When I was 27 years old, I met a woman on the kibbutz and we fell in love. She and I moved to Jerusalem to open the first feminist center. She had two daughters who were three and five years old. I coparented with her and was very involved in their lives. My husband and I had reached a place where it was hard to keep growing together, so our separation was very natural; he and I are still friends.

My female companion and I started up a collective to envision and establish the first feminist center in the middle of town. All of the meetings were held in our house, so our girls witnessed the process. Fliers, posters and demonstrations were a part of their lives; they were surrounded by feminist Israeli women who were against the occupation.

In Israel, it is mandatory that both men and women serve in the army. In 1990, when our youngest daughter was still in high school, we left Israel and moved to Berkeley, California. We hoped that our daughter would assimilate into the Berkeley culture and the last thing she would want to do is join the Israeli army. As she finished her last year of school, she said that she was going back to join the army. We had to let her go. This was our first big parenting challenge and a major heartbreak.

How does a person, even when their child makes a decision that they not only disagree with but makes them absolutely crazy and miserable, stay in a balanced place of love and compassion? Our daughter's decision made me feel like a total failure. The little voice that kept me going through this challenge said, "Remember what you wanted from your own mother and what she wasn't able to give you." She is now getting married to a career officer in the Israeli army and it takes every bit of my love for her to support her choice. He is an incredibly loving, responsible and serious young man who I am growing to love; he is also a major cog in the military wheel that perpetuates the occupation.

I came back to Jerusalem from Berkeley in 1995 and directed the Feminist Center for three years. Then I served as the director of Bat Shalom, a feminist peace organization, for almost five years. The history of Bat Shalom is quite unique.

In 1989, there was a meeting in Brussels between prominent Palestinian and Israeli women, which kicked off a series of dialogues that eventually led to the establishment in 1994 of an umbrella organization called the Jerusalem Link, with two independent, non-governmental organizations (NGOs): Bat Shalom, an Israeli NGO; and a sister organization called the Jerusalem Center for Women, a Palestinian NGO. We are the only bi-national institution that is both autonomous and responsible to each other under the umbrella of the Jerusalem Link.

Community activities promote the notion of a just peace. We work together to look at what we can and should be saying in a joint Palestinian/Israeli voice—as women and as feminists. The organizations are grounded in joint political principles. The one principle on which we have not come to consensus is the Right of Return. United Nations (UN) Resolution 194 states that Palestinians have the right to come back to their homes and receive financial compensation for the time they could not live in their homes and work their land. Our perspectives on this issue are often contradictory and painful, yet we continue a political dialogue and are not killing each other.

Palestinian women have opened their doors for years, looking for women allies in Israel. I have been trying to figure out how one becomes an ally, especially in a situation where one is the occupier and the other the occupied. How does one learn to serve as a trustworthy and effective ally to someone who needs you to advocate for their survival and their dignity in situations where they cannot, especially when that position marginalizes and alienates you in your own community? Justice is a compass that has served us unflailingly as we chart these new courses. As long as we are guided by that compass, I believe that we are pointed in the right direction.

In Israel, women peace activists are talking about standing up, saying no to occupation and exercising their right to refuse. Women are saying to their sons, "I don't think you should go and serve in the army in the occupied territories and, if you do, I refuse to participate. I won't wash your uniform. I won't be the sweet mother who bakes you cookies and knits you hats. I refuse to participate because, if I do, I am contributing to the perpetuation of the occupation."

Women are showing a consistent and visible resistance to what is going on so people know that there is not a national consensus about events in the occupied territories in the name of Israel. There is also a generation of young men and women who refuse to serve in the military and are invested in the civilization of our militaristic society. Their mothers (and some fathers and even grandparents) are right behind them and next to them and sometimes pull them along.

I have often heard critique from Israelis referring to Palestinian women: "What kind of mothers would send their children off to fight in the Intifada?" One can only imagine how painful it is for a Palestinian mother to confront this again and again. Animals will do whatever they can to protect their children—any mother in the world will do this—and Palestinian mothers are no different. They grieve terribly when their children go off to fight. I have met many Palestinian mothers and, while there is much about the Israeli-Palestine conflict that is open to multiple interpretations, I know this to be true.

Our government has demonized and dehumanized the Palestinians. I know women who lock their children in the house so they can't talk to Israeli soldiers. No one who knows the intensity of a mother's love can say that they choose to send their children to be blown up or shot—not a Palestinian mother, not an Israeli mother, not a Nigerian mother—no mother chooses this.

In 2002, I was contacted by Maya Abu Dayyeh Shammas, a Palestinian woman who directs the Palestinian NGO, Women's Legal Aid and Counseling Center. Equality Now, an international women's rights organization in New York City, contacted her and said that they thought they could get an Israeli woman and a Palestinian woman from the Jerusalem Link into the UN Security Council to present our joint vision for a just and viable peace. They asked her if she would speak and if she could recommend an appropriate Israeli woman; she called me and I accepted.

After a press conference moderated by Gloria Steinem, we spent an hour with the UN Security Council, speaking and sharing our perspectives. We challenged the Security Council to implement its own Resolution 1325, which states that women *must* be represented in all peace-planning, peace-making and peace-keeping initiatives, through the establishment of an International Women's Commission (IWC). This commission would ensure the significant participation of women, including civil society women, in Israel/Palestine peace negotiations and related initiatives; secure immediate and continuous peace negotiations until a just and sustainable peace is achieved; and guarantee that women's perspectives, issues and experiences be considered in any future settlement of the conflict.

For the past two years, we have been involved in envisioning and conceptualizing an IWC as a coalition of Palestinian, Israeli and international women who are committed to promoting the alternative model of political dialogue and political culture that we have developed over the past 10 years, and who support our joint political principles, which are grounded in mutual respect for the rights and dignity of both people. During this period, we were able to garner significant support through lobbying and advocacy efforts in most European parliaments, the European Union, local and international women's organizations and on Capitol Hill. The Jerusalem Link continues to educate and mobilize local women about the initiative and about the relevancy and significance of Resolution 1325.

In June 2004, we officially launched the IWC in Jerusalem (to be followed by a protest demonstration at the Separation Wall in Abu Dis). The following month, we returned to the Security Council and informed them that, due to our situation, we decided to establish an IWC without them. In light of UN Resolution 1325, we are now asking for the recognition we require and deserve.

I have learned that there are more choices and options on the road to peace than are being considered. In Israel, women peace activists feel a lot of despair right now. It has never been worse here and it is hard to have faith. We are holding on tightly to whatever piece of sky that we can claim. If we let go, the forces moving and swelling in the other direction are so huge and powerful that it would take only one wave to wash the shoreline and there would be no sign that we had ever worked for peace. It takes every bit of our energy to hold the space for peace.

Women can be a part of resolving the conflict in our region. Women will stay longer at the negotiation table before they push back their chairs and bring out their guns. Women naturally acknowledge the importance of process, maybe because we are so intimately connected to the process of children: watching them grow, learn, mature and evolve. Women are willing to invest in process. We do our politics for ourselves, our children and their children. The women with whom I work do politics from their head, their guts and their hearts. We are fully present at the table when we are working; those who are not present are challenged by those who are, which engenders a more productive discussion and analysis.

When there is an incident in the West Bank or Gaza and a family is killed in a settlement, I have heard some Israeli peace activists say, "It's too bad, but they really shouldn't have been there in the first place." These kinds of statements are very disheartening to me … no sadness, no empathy, no horror. If holding a particular kind of politics means that I must barter away my humanity, then it is the wrong kind of politics for me. This is a hard principle to live by. It is much easier to adopt the attitude of black/white, yes/no, good/bad. Sometimes one needs to stretch their heart wide enough to include those opposing their own views. This is the only hope for peace.

I once read that everyone is for social change but nobody thinks they have any changing to do. Accept the need for change within yourself in order to engender change in the world.

CONTACT
terryg@globalfundforwomen.org

SUGGESTED LINKS
http://www.batshalom.org (Bat Shalom of the Jerusalem Link)
http://www.globalfundforwomen.org (Global Fund for Women)

KRISSY KEEFER

Political Expression Through Dance

"We live in one of the most phenomenal times
in human history. The least we can do is show up
and witness what is going on and not deny it."

Krissy is the artistic director of Dance Brigade and Dance Mission Theater in San Francisco. Over the course of her 24-year dance career, she has produced over 200 performances. Krissy has received numerous grants and awards, including a Goldie from the San Francisco Bay Guardian *(1997), an "Artists Who Make A Difference" award from the* East Bay Express *(1993), an Isadora Duncan Dance Award for Special Projects (1995) and, along with George Lucas, a* San Francisco *magazine Art Achievement award (1998).*

As a white person growing up in the American south at a time when African Americans were still segregated, I witnessed apartheid right here in the United States. I was born in 1953 in Rhode Island and grew up in Florida, South Carolina and Ohio. Both of my parents came from the north—Yankees—and were college educated. They helped me see what was happening as we lived through segregation. Everywhere we went, from the laundry mat to the library, it was "Whites Only." African Americans lived in startling poverty. My parents and I openly discussed the injustices being forced on African Americans.

I was 13 years old when my family moved to Cincinnati and the civil rights movement was at its peak. Schools were closed and the city had a curfew. I was on a committee to help bridge communication between black and white kids. Of course, the Black Power movement was all over the news.

The other part of my childhood that played a major role in shaping me was my love of dance. When I was very young, my mother would walk me, my cousins and my sisters down to the beach and we danced, sung, spun and jumped. There was a tremendous sense of joy in those moments. My mother had been a dancer in New York and started me in dance classes when I was six years old. Dance was a natural expression and I became passionate about dancing and performing. As a young child, I knew that I would become a dancer.

In the 1970s, when I graduated from high school, I left Cincinnati and moved to Eugene, Oregon, to go to college. By this time, the women's movement was in full swing. I had always been encouraged to be creative and strong and say what I really thought. I had my mother's fierce spirit and great sense of humor and strove to embody her enormous compassion. As a child, I was not allowed to have a birthday party unless we invited everyone; if someone missed a bus, we gave them a ride. These were little things but they fueled and shaped me. I was a feminist as a kid but did not know it; in Eugene, I had an understanding of myself from that perspective.

While living in Eugene at the age of 21, three women and I formed the Wallflower Order, one of the first feminist dance companies in the U.S. We were young and didn't have children, so we made the company our life. We were all on food stamps and got free rehearsal space at the university. The women's liberation movement was strong at that time and we wanted to create work that reflected the strength and passion of women. Soon, we were making pieces about race, class and the environment. Laurel Near, the sister of folk singer Holly Near, was in the company, so we had a connection to the national women's music industry circuit. Holly helped us get performance gigs and, within a year, we were touring all over the U.S. and eventually went to Europe and Nicaragua.

Wallflower Order evolved into a dance company of five women. We were all trained dancers who broke from traditional modern dance and incorporated gymnastics, Kung Fu, sign language, singing and talking into our work. As the touring schedule grew, we began to grapple with internal process issues within the company. It was run collectively and we didn't know how to deal with seniority and decision-making issues. There was a lot of stress working together and we were extremely burned out from months of touring. On top of that, we moved from Oregon to Boston and then to Berkeley, California—all within a year and one-half. After months of arguing and struggling, the group broke up. It was a very painful, public process and the community was forced to take sides.

Out of that breakup, Nina Fichter (one of the Wallflower Order dancers and a childhood friend) and I formed a new dance company, Dance Brigade. We worked incredibly hard and, because we were starting over, lacked a certain joy. We were burned out but committed to keeping a company going because it was all we knew and we were good at it. We worked or rehearsed every day, including Sundays, because that was when the dancers could rehearse. Nina worked as a waitress and I taught dance classes; all the money went into the company. We based ourselves out of Oakland and, for 10 years, produced our own and other company's work and kept touring.

One of our signature works was the *Revolutionary Nutcracker Sweetie*, an enormous collaboration of 1,000 artists over the 10 years it was performed, created to work with the community, have a home season and anchor the company financially. This alternative *Nutcracker* was referred to as a political extravaganza that satirized the current state of our government and the world. It was wildly successful with the community, but I have always felt a certain resistance from the funders because of the bold political nature of our material and the fact that we were all women. Women are usually dismissed and told that what we do is not as interesting as what men do. Dance—a woman's art form—gets hit twice; male dancers are the ones who make it.

From the beginning, audiences were devoted to the company. I think we were the first dance company in the world to be about feminism and to have lesbian content. We were a group of women dancers with diverse body types and our dances had a strong, bold style. We created the style ourselves, using ballet as a base and combining martial arts, which I had studied and then continued as a company to study with Coleen Gragen and Amazon Kung Fu. We used feminist music and poetry and Laurel Near brought in her theater background. We wanted to be part of the women's movement in the very beginning. When we relocated to Berkeley, we were part of the political left. Touring internationally with Grupo Raiz (a group of Chilean exiles from La Peña) from 1981 to 1984 was a big success. We raised money and consciousness about El Salvador and Nicaragua.

Our dances told stories and reflected contemporary issues and events. We used humor and satire as an effective tool for talking about politics. We did a piece in the early '80s about the issues of Palestine and Israel, which caused some people to change their minds about the situation. Dance Brigade became a model for blending dance, social activism and women's physicality and opened a new chapter in the history of modern dance. We did a festival called Furious Feet—using the image of a body taking a stand for justice—to showcase other artists involved in socially relevant work. We produced many groups from Contraband, Uzulu Dance Theatre, Rhodessa Jones, Ferron, Ellen Bromberg, Urban Bush Women and Mexico's Barrio Rojo.

Modern dance has always been an expression of the contemporary world, born out of revolutionary activity as dancers strove to find truth and express it through their bodies. Each time a major world event happened, a new style of modern dance was created. We have been fearless in our content and style. We danced, mixed styles, sang, told stories, had startling political content, did not shave our legs, had different body types and showed intimacy among women on stage. We were powerful and passionate and committed and talented. We were very good at what we did … and we still are!

Today, the world is full of endless stories about war, injustice, pain and suffering, and I am never at a loss for material to make dances. I strive to tell the truth in a transparent and accessible way. Telling, living and practicing the truth is one of the most defiant acts a person can commit. The media are full of distortions and lies, and people have so little access to the truth and are in such denial. They want to feel safe, so they collude with the lies for a shallow sense of safety.

Sometimes I think that modern dance is an insignificant art form; other times I think it has historically been one of the main movers and shakers in the art world. The body is a powerful tool for expressing the human predicament in all of its trials and tribulations. Audiences watching dancers have an immediate visceral response, experiencing themselves and the performers' messages in a new way.

When I was 38 years old, I had my daughter Frederika and, of course, my life changed significantly. Before becoming pregnant with Frederika, I had decided not to have children for several reasons: I came from the feminist movement and I thought you only had children if you could not think of anything better to do; I was the oldest of five children and it was chaotic; and my mother discouraged me from having children because she wanted me to have a different life than her own.

When I became a mother, I loved it! My work allowed me to bring my daughter to rehearsals, dance concerts and meetings. She has become one of the company's best critics and is very talented and knowledgeable about dance. I enrolled her in dance classes when she was young and now, at age 12, she is a wonderful dancer and dramatic performer.

In 2000, I filed a complaint with the Human Rights Commission of San Francisco against the San Francisco Ballet for excluding my daughter from their program based on their criteria regarding weight and height. San Francisco has an ordinance that prevents city institutions from receiving city dollars if they discriminate against people based on weight and height. This was the first case to test the ordinance.

The San Francisco Ballet conducts their auditions by having children walk and skip around the room. Then they determine whether a child can take classes at the school based on their body type. This audition took place at the height of the "dot com" explosion when all of the modern dance studios were closing down because they couldn't afford the high rents. The San Francisco Ballet was receiving the most money and had the most resources.

The goal of the school is to get members for their company, yet they have very few dancers in the company who come from the school. I wanted them to train my daughter because they have all the money, space, pianos and teachers, and they could be a school for many things including teaching and choreography. However, they focus on their corps de ballet and maybe get one dancer every couple of years out of the school. It's a waste of time and money.

I decided to challenge their program. The case was covered internationally and, for the first time, people dove into the ballet aesthetic and challenged the assumptions and requirements for ballet dancing. It brought up many issues: eating disorders, who gets paid to dance and what they have to do to their body to get paid, the image of women on stage and where our tax dollars are going. Ballet dancers are the only dancers in this country who really get paid and they have to starve themselves to get a job. Most of them dance for 10 years until they are 30, when they are replaced. The competition is fierce, the criteria are insane and the injuries are huge.

Eating disorders in this country are at a staggering level. Starving and overeating are reinforced by the ballet, the fashion industry and Hollywood, and plastic surgery and makeovers are the latest trend. Women's bodies, the stress on them and the stress to look perfect are huge subjects and have been a driving force in my work. I am proud of trying to provide women with a different picture of what's possible with their bodies and with their desire to take a stand.

Because of my complaint, I got a lot of "bad mother" press, especially from people who don't have kids. Many thought that I was using my daughter for my own benefit and ruining her self-esteem; others said that I was doing a disservice to the ballet community. The truth is that it did not benefit me at all. In fact, I think I upset the funding community and made myself sort of a pariah. By the time I had a mediation with the ballet president, it was clear that the Human Rights Commission was not going to pursue my case based on the First Amendment, which protects the arts.

An international discussion ensued and many people agreed with me; I am often thanked by women on the street. Sometimes children are the vehicle for social change, like the southern black children who walked to school as the whole world watched. Were they being used? No. Those children who walked across the picket lines of segregated schools were making history.

Even a small act like this one—small in comparison to other world events—makes a statement and shows others that we can take a stand when something is unfair and challenges our rights as expressive human beings. As a mother, I *had* to take a stand for my daughter and for all of the little girls who have passion for dance but who will end up being torn apart because they were 5 pounds overweight or 2 inches too tall. Typecasting like this has historically been used to segregate and disempower people. We need to work to empower young girls.

Mothers suffer the burden of poor distribution of recourses in the world and the lack of humanity that accompanies it—especially in the poorer nations where there is no food, education, clean water or health care—yet raising children is so important, so hard and so often without respect. Perhaps it is out of this pain and hard work that we hold the key to liberation of the planet and of all life. I believe there is something fundamental about the compassion that mothers bring to the world.

Women understand this love, so they can't imagine ever going after someone else's children, starting a war where so many children will die or making economic policies that starve whole towns and villages. I think if women were in charge, it would be completely different because it would become all about our children. We would ask, "Whose child is going to die?" As you love your own child, your love for the world's children increases. I think about the parentless children in Third World countries who live on the streets. Then I think about my own daughter living in that situation and I feel sick.

How are we going to get out of this mess? We are living in a world that intensely demonizes women, children and the environment at the peril of civilization. My job is to pay attention and tell the truth as I see it. I am fueled by the reality of the state of the world to do whatever I can to help bring awareness and healing. I believe that if women were to rise up in all our fury and grace, and lead this planet towards healing, we could perhaps turn the tide. There are a lot of people doing good work in the world, but I feel that the world is on fire right now—*raging fire*—and we may not be able to put it out and save ourselves.

One night, I had a phenomenal dream where I was hugging my mother. Right at our breast bones, we dissolved into golden pink light and disappeared. I was completely saturated with bliss. I woke up and was full of this feeling for a week. For me, it was dream about getting back to the source of compassion: the Great Mother.

If we can openly witness what is happening, we can liberate others and ourselves in the process. People often tell me that I am negative. They are depressed about the state of the world and they don't want to hear about reality. Half of the people I know use Prozac or alcohol. Why is that? As corny as it sounds, I believe that "the truth will set you free." I am not depressed by the reality of what is going on in today's world; I feel liberated *by the truth* to face it head on.

I feel bonded to the people of the world and this bond, which has deepened through dancing their stories and having a child, is what motivates me to take a stand and act. We live in one of the most phenomenal times in human history. The least we can do is show up and witness what is going on and not deny it. I long for a world that reflects the most genuine aspirations of humanity. I long for a world where the relationship between women and children is central to all plans and discussion.

When we raise children and try to change the world, we are in a truly liberated dance. The dance of wisdom and compassion lives in the mother, in the woman's voice, in the woman's vision and through a woman's perspective. The warrior aspect is present when a woman is demonstrating on the streets, or feeding her children healthy food in a totally toxic environment or traveling around the country trying to effect change. Stay focused and keep a vision of peace and justice. Rise up and be nurturing and ferocious at the same time.

CONTACT

kkwickedwitch@yahoo.com

SUGGESTED LINK

http://www.dancemission.com (Dance Brigade's Dance Mission Theater)

LOURDES PORTILLO

Filming Struggles for Justice

"My work comes from my personal experience of living in a world full of injustice, which has inspired in me a deep sense of compassion. This is the root of change— to embrace our compassion and act from that place."

Lourdes is a director and filmmaker and describes herself as "Mexico born and Chicana identi-fied," with many of her films focusing on the search for Latino identity. Her film, Las Madres: The Mothers of Plaza de Mayo, *a collaboration with writer Susana Muñoz, won 20 awards and was nominated for the Academy's Best Documentary award in 1985.*

In 1993, Lourdes commemorated the 500th anniversary of Christopher Columbus' "discov-ery" of America with the film, Columbus on Trial. *In 1994, she was awarded a Guggenheim fellowship for her contributions to filmmaking and a Nestor Almendros Prize for courage in filmmaking in 2002. The film* Señorita Extraviada, Missing Young Woman *was winner of a Documentary Special Jury Prize at the Sundance Film Festival in 2004.*

I have been making films for 24 years. As a filmmaker, I think it is very important to tell the small stories that never show up in popular media about people who are valiantly strug-gling. These small struggles for justice, which are so significant in our culture and so ignored, are extremely important in teaching us about the effect that we can have in our communities and in the world. When we find out about these stories, we no longer feel like victims but in-stead feel that we can take action. Many of my films are made with the hope that viewers will become inspired and take a stand. In many ways, I am a storyteller for the smaller voices—the voices that would otherwise be unheard.

In 1958, when I was 13 years old, my parents immigrated from Chihuahua, Mexico, to Los Angeles, California. My parents came to the U.S. because they felt that it would be easier to give all of us an education here. I was the oldest of five children and the only one who spoke English, so I carried the burden of protecting and translating for my family. My parents came with enough money for a down payment on a house and we lived in a mostly white suburb.

Coming from Mexico, we did not know about racism. I went to a primarily white elementary school and, when I think back to that time, I realize that unspoken racism is the most insidious form. When someone calls you a name, there is some kind of relief; however, disdain, dismissal and ridicule behind your back is horrible. My entire family went through this and it instilled a profound sense of justice and created a fire within me that still burns.

I come from northern Mexico where it is very common for women to be tough and strong. Historically, life is difficult in Chihuahua and women had to be able to do everything to stand up to men; hence, the background of my family is matriarchal. There is always a level of protocol where a woman caters somewhat to a man but doesn't mean it. She knows that she is running things, but she has to make it look like the man has some say. This has been a big influence in my life as a Hispanic woman and has given me the stamina to carve out my own path as a filmmaker.

My family and I shared the dream that so many immigrants have: someday we would move back to Mexico. It took me 30 years to realize that we weren't going back. This fueled my interest in other cultures and I learned as much as I could about the world. When I graduated from high school, I went to college and studied anthropology and international relations.

In Los Angeles, I was working with a friend on my first film—an educational piece about a blind boy. I was the assistant, but the producer came up to me and said, "I don't know why you're the only one who really knows what they're doing." Those words were enough to make me think that maybe I could become a filmmaker someday. I was captivated by how films were made, what they could say and how they affected people.

At age 24, I got married, began having children and moved to San Francisco. I eventually had three sons and worked as a full-time mother. During that time, I had a deep desire to make films and to be out in the world, but my role as a mother was all consuming. Since I had children, I couldn't go to the University of California in Los Angeles or to some other special film school and learn about feature filmmaking, so I went to the San Francisco Art Institute for a master's degree in film. It was very inspiring because it was about art. I was never taught how to make narrative or documentary films; I just fell into it.

I have made two important films to date: *Las Madres: Mothers of Plaza de Mayo* and *Señorita Extraviada, Missing Young Woman,* which won a Documentary Special Jury Prize at the Sundance Film Festival in 2004. *Las Madres* was made with a fellow student from the San Francisco Art Institute. She and I had a kinship because we were both Latin Americans in a primarily white student body. We spent a lot of time talking about politics, especially about what was going on in Argentina with the rule of the Junta. We had heard about the women of Plaza de Mayo and decided that we would make a film about them.

We tried to raise money for the film and received $2,000 from individual donors who were interested in this issue. Brazilian Airways gave us two free tickets and we flew to Buenos Aires about 100 days after the Junta had fallen. It was very dangerous to go before then because the military was in power and they had full reign—one could disappear and no one would know anything. So we went when there was supposedly a dictatorship but, in fact, the military forces were still in power.

We had previously met one of the mothers in 1982 at a Mother's Day talk in Washington, DC, for the Organization of American States. She was our connection and, when we arrived in Buenos Aires, we met the other mothers. We chose certain mothers to interview and then started filming with a $2,000 budget. It was crazy to work on such a shoestring, but we felt that this story had to be told, that everyone should know about it and that everybody should help these women.

The mothers of Plaza de Mayo were the "Mothers of the Disappeared" in Argentina during the military dictatorship in the 1970s. During that time, there were dissidents who did not agree with the philosophy of the military. The government persecuted these people—most of them university students—and they were kidnapped and ultimately disappeared. ("Disappeared" means they were killed.)

The mothers started gathering at Plaza de Mayo in front of the National Palace to demand information about their family members and call for an end to the killing. The mothers tried to devise a way to effect change and get some response about what had happened to their children. These women were very intelligent and decided that, because they lived in a culture that venerates women like the Virgin Mother, the men were going to have to stay home and cook while they came together to take a stand for justice. Men were a big part of the movement because they followed their wives' request and took care of the home.

In the beginning, only a few women came; within months, over 200 women stood together in silence in front of the National Palace, demanding the truth about the kidnappings. Consequently, an international investigation into the disappearances was launched. Ever since that first day, the women have gathered one day a week at Plaza de Mayo.

When they first began to stand, some of the women wore white diapers draped on their heads with the names of their children embroidered into them. To this day, many of the women wear a white handkerchief, looking for the answer to the disappearance of their loved ones. It was unsafe for these mothers to stand in public during the military dictatorship. The original leader of the mothers of Plaza de Mayo was kidnapped and disappeared; then a French nun who had joined the mothers disappeared. The women were, of course, frightened by this, but they felt compelled to continue gathering in the name of justice and in the name of their families. When *Las Madres* was released, it was used as a tool to organize and help the mothers. The documentary encapsulated their struggle in a one-hour story and elevated their action to a historical place. It was nominated for the Academy's Best Documentary award.

The idea for my latest film, *Señorita Extraviada, Missing Young Woman*, came from a friend who showed me articles about the brutal murders of hundreds of young girls in Ciudad Juárez, an overcrowded city of 1.5 million people. Juárez is just south of the border of El Paso, which is very close to where I was born in Mexico.

The signing of the North American Free Trade Agreement has inspired a maquiladora (factory) building boom along the border. Approximately 2,500 maquiladoras, of which over 1,800 are U.S. owned, are spread along the U.S.–Mexican border. They represent 45 percent of all Mexican exports, worth over $53 billion in 1998.[1] Maquiladoras furnish the second largest source of foreign exchange for the Mexican economy, which has created a culture where anything favoring maquiladora production is emphasized while the human cost is not addressed.

The murdered Mexican women were poor and pretty; had dark, shoulder-length hair; and some were as young as 10 years old. About 30 percent of them worked in the factories—sweatshops with blaring lights and 1,000 women in each room. They had been raped and tortured; their nipples had been bitten off and their bodies were dumped in irrigation ditches and deserts. There were stories of V-shaped marks carved into their backs, suggesting sadistic ritual murders. Some of these girls may have been killed by their own relatives; there has been no clear definition of who was killed by serial killers, a boyfriend or some unknown group. Three hundred twenty female bodies have been found and 500 girls have been declared missing—over 800 women in a 10-year period.

Even though these young women were being found every week, no one was paying any attention. I asked myself, "How could all these girls be killed every week and nothing is being done?" I felt compelled to go down to Juárez and give a voice to the families of the murdered women who daily feared for their lives. Small things scare me, such as swimming in a lake; however, traveling to Mexico and taking on the horror of what was happening there didn't bother me. I was totally motivated to investigate the reason behind these murders and decided to make a documentary film about the situation.

When I first arrived in Juárez, I found a town full of fear and consumed by a shroud of complicity between police and government officials. I was told by the governor that the killings had stopped; he actually made a declaration that they had stopped. In fact, the murders were occurring almost every day. Memorial crosses had been erected on street corners and women's groups had formed to demand a full-scale investigation, but the governments of Juárez and the State of Chihuahua were not uncovering any answers and the murders continued. On three occasions, police allegedly forced confessions to create false suspects, then declared an end to the serial killings.

I was surprised to find that, even though these murders had been going on for almost 10 years, I was one of the only people covering the story. Because there wasn't any information about why these girls were murdered, I struggled to unfold the story through my film. I followed parents as they looked for their young daughters and filmed the moment when they found out that they had been murdered. Many of them had attempted to speak out and had been threatened, arrested and even tortured.

Horrible stories began to unfold. I was told that police used someone else—dying the hair and dressing the skeletal remains in clothing—to prove that they had found a family's daughter. One young woman was two minutes late to work and was shut out of the factory. Her body was found later, murdered outside of the building. Some young women have escaped to tell stories of sexual orgies and ritual killings. They have reported that these circles are made up of men from both North and South America. I also heard that there were men taking pictures of young women while they worked inside the factories, almost as if they were selecting their victims.

In Juárez, there is a powerful circle of organized crime. I surmised that this circle could be bringing in opportunistic killers who are misogynists, murdering young girls for the thrill of it or out of anger—and getting away with it. Like most circles of organized crime, prostitution and drugs come into play. Some mothers said, "We know that a lot of money is being made on the bodies of our children."

During the 18 months that it took to make the film, over 50 young woman disappeared. It was horrifying to find out, almost daily, that another young woman was missing. I began to feel that the killer was ahead of me and all around me, even though I could not see him. Towards the end of making the film, I interviewed a girl; when I came back to see this girl, her sister had disappeared. I felt incredibly paranoid and it has taken me a full year to feel safe. This was the most wrenching film I have ever made. I am still recovering from the horror of it!

Once the film was made, I traveled around the world, trying to drum up support and open people's eyes to these events. The technique I used in *Señorita Extraviada* was to sensitize the viewer to young girls and bring about an awareness of the tragedy of their loss of life. When the film premiered in Mexico, over 2,000 people came; at the end of the screening, you could cut the air with a knife. This film is bringing out previously unavailable information. I just came back from Norway where, after the showing, several of the journalists went to Juárez and wrote an article about the murders for a major Norwegian magazine.

In the case of Juárez, where you have factories that come from the U.S. and England—specifically to use that country's labor at the lowest going rate—an infrastructure of application of the law does not exist. They globalize the economy, not the legal infrastructure, and do not offer significant protection to the workers. At these Juárez factories, there are hundreds of thousands of available girls, which perpetuates violence. Where there is poverty, life is considered expendable and totally worthless. Juárez women are being exploited in the worst way—a vicious crime against humanity!

There have been attempts to do in-depth investigations of the murders, but they never go anywhere because it's all related to organized crime. I realized that these murders were most likely connected to a larger web that included drug cartels—a giant web of complicity. The Mexican government has said there is no reason to do an investigation because the "guilty" are in jail—those who have been tortured to confess to crimes they did not commit. It is an enormous cover-up and the idea is chilling.

Since the making of *Señorita Extraviada*, significant strides have been made in getting the story of Juárez out to the international community. In August 2003, Amnesty International published a report on the brutal pattern of violence against women in Ciudad Juárez and Chihuahua,[2] and the federal authorities have taken some positive steps. However, justice for the victims and their families remains a distant hope. As well as ensuring proper investigation into all these cases, the federal authorities must guarantee that the victims' families are treated with respect in their struggle for justice and are fully included in the implementation of judicial and preventive measures. The authorities should also establish an independent mechanism to review cases where suspects have alleged torture.

On Valentine's Day (V-Day) 2004, 7,000 women gathered from all over the world and marched for justice in Juárez. Dressed in pink, these women demanded that a thorough investigation be done and the murders be stopped. These marches will take place every February 14th in Juárez until the murders cease. This is a tremendous moment in the history of women who are coming together to support each other and say *no* to violence against women!

I opened *Señorita Extraviada* with the following narration: "I came to Juárez to track down ghosts and listen to the mystery that surrounds them." It was a painful film to make because of its story. At the same time, I struggled not to make it a lurid, horrible thing. I wanted to make it beautiful so that people could really take it in and have a full experience. Now, *Señorita Extraviada* has become a banner for human rights and is being shown around the world. The medium of film speaks to the inner self—the self that is seldom addressed— reaching the inner core of the human being. When I appeal to that aspect of a human being, I have an open door to their hearts.

I think all of my sensibilities and concerns come into play when I'm creating a film. How I decide to film a girl or how the camera is going to look at a woman partly comes from my own world view as a female. When I began making films, I believed that films could change the world and many of my films have fulfilled that ideal. Film is a powerful medium because it can combine the intellectual and the extraordinarily emotional; it can contain all of the elements that we have as human beings. For a film to do this, it needs to be treated like a jewel. Every aspect must be polished so that it can affect the viewer. It is necessary to speak to the soul of a human being through the art of creating film. By doing this, I hope that my films will motivate people to act and change things because their view has been expanded and their hearts opened.

CONTACT

lportillo@mac.com

SUGGESTED LINK

http://www.lourdesportillo.com (The Films and Videos of Lourdes Portillo)

BIBLIOGRAPHY

Columbus on Trial. Videotape by Lourdes Portillo, 18 min., color, 1993.

Las Madres: The Mothers of Plaza de Mayo. Film by Susana Muñoz and Lourdes Portillo, 64 min., color, 1985.

Señorita Extraviada, Missing Young Woman. Film by Lourdes Portillo, 74 min., color, 2001.

FOOTNOTES START ON PAGE 209.

MICHELLE MANGER KEIP

Martial Arts— A Tool for Life

"It is only through respecting, protecting and developing our relatedness with all beings that human beings have a chance at a future for our children and perhaps for life itself on the planet."

Michelle is a public health nurse and has been teaching health and life skills since 1976. She and her husband David Keip recently started their own school, Wellspring Aikido Arts, which offers a variety of programs for well being, personal safety and empowerment. Michelle is developing and teaching an Aikido-inspired body-mind-spirit curriculum for children ages four to seven years called "Samurai Sprouts." She is also writing a young children's book about the life of the founder of Aikido, Morihei Ueshiba.

She is the cofounder of Core Dynamics, which specializes in somatic coaching with survivors of sexual abuse and assault. She is a certified trainer with the nonprofit Kidpower Teenpower Fullpower International, which helps people learn how to use the power they have to stay safe. For over 22 years, Michelle has been training in Aikido, the martial art of harmony, and holds an advanced degree black belt. She has studied directly with many of the pioneers of somatics, exploring body-mind-spirit integration.

When I was seven years old, I snuck into the back room of our house where I'd least likely be discovered. I stood before the mirror and hid my hair behind my hands, searching for some deeper identity in my face. I felt heavy and contracted and was looking for an opening. The limited choices for identity that my parents represented and that our family culture permitted pressed in on me.

Going into that back room and looking in the mirror, I felt the thrill of doing something taboo, secretive and even miraculous. I was taking the risk to think outside the box and was rewarded by the vision reflected back to me, promising another way of life. I was alone and yet mysteriously and magically connected to another dimension.

I imagined myself walking back to the main house with my insides pulsing like a tribal drum beat and my face wearing the neutral, flat mask of invisibility. The mirror had shown me my warrior father's face to the left and my homemaker mother's face to the right. "I will find the way in between," I promised myself. I would keep this revelation secret for a very long time.

As with all generative metaphors, the image of our three adjacent faces continues to evoke new meanings and new wonderings as I see with changing sensibility. Still, my core commitment remains to follow the path related to male and female, warrior and mother, while opening into a possibility of being that is beyond those forms.

My father was a war hero, unstoppable with his powerful, global ambition. My mother was beautiful and bright, fluttering with child-like enthusiasm and wonder. Yet, because of how I suffered from their limitations, I was ambivalent about choosing either of them as role models. My mother was resigned to her role as wife and mother and let us know that she had sacrificed her dreams of being an artist to serve us. I felt ashamed for her lack of power in the world, her submissiveness and her dependency.

Later, I came to understand how angry I was that she didn't protect me and my siblings from my father's explosive, ongoing physical and emotional violence. In my pain, I rejected being a mother and being a child and instead identified with my father's strengths. I became a "perfect" adult-child. However, growing up with my father's insatiable terrorizing alerted me to the hidden, destructive side of being a dominant warrior—hidden because that is how domestic violence survives.

When I was six years old, I took my first dance class. I was ecstatic! I knew that I had found my place in the world. My parents refused to let me take any more dance classes, explaining that I was to become a career woman, not a homemaker or an artist. I was devastated. Disobeying them or voicing my desire seemed like a life-threatening risk, so I resigned myself to this loss.

The rest of my childhood was gifted with enough mystery and diversity to keep my soul alive. I spent six years in Italy and Switzerland attending international schools, which gave me the direct experience of other cultures and values. From early childhood, I struggled with depression and loneliness. I did my best to hide these weaknesses, pushing forward to make my way in the world.

My warrior self excelled in school, yet I wandered from one subject to another. I searched for a cause to inspire my heart and support my commitment of service. I graduated from the University of California (UC) at Berkeley in 1974 with high honors and Phi Beta Kappa in a multidisciplinary major, yet I felt no satisfaction in my achievement. I did not know where to go next with my life. Travels in Morocco in 1975 awakened a vision of nursing in the Third World, and I rallied my credentials and drive to complete nursing school at UC San Francisco in 1980.

During my nurse training, two pivotal moments awoke me to my forgotten commitment of finding the middle way of warrior/mother. I was learning pelvic self-exam at a women's health clinic. The lay practitioner told me, "You're not in your body." Her words lit up a vast world of possibility from which I'd been cut off. I began receiving and learning massage, going dancing with friends and trying some karate classes. I was beginning to mother myself.

After three months of karate, I told my boyfriend of a year that I was leaving him. He burst into a rage and began thrashing at me. I responded calmly and precisely with a non-injury pressure point to his face and was able to quell him enough to run to safety. With all my father's attacks in my childhood, I had never been able to defend myself. When I was attacked this time, I'd taken centered action to stop him. What was this new capacity? I'd found another clue for re-entry into my body: The warrior within me had reawakened.

I combined my academic, professional nursing approach "to" the body with an enlivened treasure hunt of experiential learning "through" the body. I studied with many prominent teachers in the perceptual and relational arts, in spiritual and attentional practices, in the creative and healing arts and in the movement of martial arts. As I journeyed, I began to peel away the survival defenses I'd harbored in my body. Many times, I misinterpreted the pain that surfaced as a sign of wrongdoing or mistake and turned to another teaching with hopes of relief from my suffering.

The most compelling thread in my path of self-potential was that of the martial arts. My boyfriend's assault had shown me how little I knew about the effects of my child abuse, which I had denied. My breakthrough capacity to defend myself after only a short period of training showed me that transformation was possible; it gave me the courage to face my fear of violence directly. I began to search for a martial arts teacher and a form that spoke to my body and soul.

My search led me to Aikido 22 years ago. I remember my first day on the mat, rolling around and feeling reconnected with my childhood passion for dance and my body's power. The teacher, Robert Nadeau, could translate this radical martial art form of nonviolence into practices one could apply to both the challenges of everyday life and one's deepest spiritual yearnings. I trained passionately several times a week for several years.

I met David in Aikido and we married; soon after, I took my black belt promotion. In 1987, we decided to have a child. For the next 10 years, Aikido became an underground current in my life as I shifted my priorities to being a householder, making a living and raising our son, Rory.

Having a child woke me up out of the culturally induced trance that had me thinking and acting like an individual rather than a social being. Before that, I had an intellectual, idealistic understanding of the importance of working together and understanding each other, but my core experience was that I was separate from others. Having a child literally and figuratively opened me up to relatedness. My internal warrior and mother aspects began to coordinate and co-create for the sake of something greater than myself, rather than fighting and competing with others for survival.

While I cherished being a mom to our gentle, wondrous son Rory, I was uncomfortable with the change of rhythm and surrender that being with him required. Having identified so long with the values of community service and achievement, and having rejected my own mother's way of mothering, I struggled to find my own parenting values. I was both relieved and in overwhelming grief as my brief maternity leave ended and I resumed full-time work as a home care nursing administrator. Captivated by the super-mom syndrome, I decided that I was too busy to attend to my distress.

Barely one year into motherhood, I was diagnosed with cancer. While surgery did away with the malignancy, I considered it a signal. I wanted to find the root cause of this profound imbalance and make the necessary changes to prevent its recurrence. I speculated that the whole transition into motherhood had provoked it. I recognized how I had unconsciously fallen into my mother's pattern of giving up on herself and her dreams in order to fulfill the socialized expectations of her domestic role. I fretted over the task of finding time and space to tend to myself in a schedule that was already too busy. Eventually, I settled into the understanding that, if I didn't take the space to mother myself, Rory might not even have a mother to care for him before long.

The cancer wake-up call empowered the warrior and the mother to come together in me. I began to cut away with discernment the activities that kept me too busy to mother myself and the fears that warned me against carving a new life path. I studied the cancer healing work of pioneer Lawrence LeShan, who theorized that reconnecting with one's "childhood dream" could strengthen one's immune system and re-ignite the core vital force. This became a primary perspective in my healing. From therapy, I realized that I'd deeply assimilated my father's abusive messages of my worthlessness.

I was blessed with a moment of revelation during an Arnold Mindell workshop. Arny is a process specialist who was working with a couple experiencing a communication breakdown. I saw that the woman needed some coaching in taking a stand with her body as well as her words. I knew in that moment that I wanted to learn how to be that kind of coach. My husband David was already working as an instructor with Model Mugging, a self-defense program for women that involved assertiveness training and full-power fighting with a padded assailant in simulated assaults. I knew that my next step was to become an instructor of this form.

Model Mugging was a beautiful coming together of my love of movement, my desire to serve through social change and my soul's path of healing from child abuse. As a female instructor, I developed the warrior/mother balance. I cultivated a safe, accepting environment while offering directive coaching for students to embody the idea that they were, indeed, worth defending. David and I began to teach together in 1990, working with women, then men, then teens and finally with children. The early years of my work were concerned with safety, boundaries and personal power. As I felt safer in myself, my work shifted into questions of forward momentum: "What do I want with my life?" and "How can I change myself?" as well as "How can we prevent child abuse and its long-term consequences?"

In 1991, David and I moved with our three-year-old son, Rory, to Sonoma County, California, to begin our own business, Core Dynamics. We shifted from the self-defense focus of our basic training to an empowerment model. The simulated fights became an opportunity for students to embody their commitment to themselves and to whatever they needed to fight for in order to reclaim their lives.

Our work surged with popularity for several years and I tasted the seduction of being a warrior/mother hero for others. Perhaps my greatest ongoing challenge has been the issue of how to balance my personal and family life with my drive to be of service in the larger world.

With Kidpower, I bridge those soulful yearnings, knowing that each child who is empowered by the teachings walks with greater peace.

Working the business out of our home since Rory was three allowed me the flexibility of choosing my hours and having time with him during the day. Coming from an isolated nuclear family, I was strongly motivated to give Rory the experience of an extended family. We cultivated close ties with a few other families who also faced the challenges of working full time and raising children. With this caring network, we rarely hired a baby-sitter; Rory still has several homes that welcome him like a family relative. Knowing that Rory was with his friends in a caring household gave me great peace of mind while David and I worked long workshop weekend hours.

Rory was seven when David and I became Kidpower instructors. An international nonprofit organization, Kidpower Teenpower Fullpower teaches self-protection and empowerment skills to people of all ages. On a grander scale than learning essential life skills, Kidpower connects children experientially with their core capacity to interact powerfully and respectfully in the world. As human beings, our most entrenched defenses—be they aggressive, submissive or frozen—are tied up with our survival fears. In a playful, kid-friendly environment, Kidpower opens up the spectrum of available, safe choices in the context of potential and real danger, empowering children to make the most centered response in any situation.

Getting help is practiced as intrinsic to all safety strategies in Kidpower. For me, this relates to the Dalai Lama's insistence that teaching about the interdependence of all beings is fundamental to nonviolence education. When a child learns that they are not alone—with all their feelings, perceptions and experiences, especially in a fearful situation—it plants the radical seed of knowing that they belong, they matter and they have the power to be a part of creating peace on Earth.

Until he was 12, Rory helped with Kidpower classes. He came with us on numerous trips to Europe in the mid-'90s, including those in Belgium and Italy, where he practiced Kidpower in French and Italian. As Rory grew older and became more confident with the cross-cultural experience, he stayed with our European friends' families while David and I taught the adult classes. Because of the tremendously beneficial influence I felt from my childhood years overseas, giving Rory the immersion experience of other cultures has been one of my primary goals as a mother. Rory has an exceptionally strong center and internal compass; I speculate that this is the result of a combination of his nature, direct parental education and extensive Kidpower training.

My health began to deteriorate as I fell into compulsive work behaviors, leaning too heavily into my dominant warrior ways of pushing harder to do more when my body's cycle naturally called for rest and nurturing. I was unable to stop myself from overwork; however, in late 1996, I was stopped without warning. In quick succession, my parents and best friend died. Although I had culminated my nursing career as a hospice nurse, I was completely unprepared for my grief.

Like most Americans, I had learned not to grieve but instead to strive forward into the future. With the loss of my loved ones, my heart was broken open and I could no longer suppress the grief of a lifetime. My dominant warrior way was brought to the ground, completely dismembered. Once again, I was faced with the life teaching that my habitual ways of working in the world were not sustainable. I entered into a long process of restoration, which centered on the mysterious path of going through my experience and beginning with my grief, rather than resisting or manipulating my feelings. This was a reparenting of myself—a cycle of deep, core inquiry and experimentation, protected by my benevolent warrior and guided by the Divine Mother.

The loss of my loved ones helped me reorient my everyday actions from, "What should I be doing?" to the question of the heart, "What matters to me?" I slowly shifted from focusing on task and work and opened to process and relationship. "How do the concerns of others connect with my concerns? What are the possibilities for taking care of our shared concerns together?" The warrior's discernment and sense of purpose began to partner with the mother's compassion and interconnectedness. Their courtship, engagement and marriage has been an organic, sacred process. I sense that I am now bearing the new life within, conceived by their sacred coupling. Now I ask, "How can I allow that which wants to come through me?" Now I pray, "Love the world through me, Divine Creator."

Recently, I was blessed with the embodied and visual memory of being sexually assaulted at age two—blessed because so much of the suffering of my life made sense given that trauma. My heart opened and softened to myself, and deep layers of defense in my body began to thaw and let go. I was mystified because, instead of feeling grief as I usually do upon recovering a painful memory, I was bathed in ecstasy.

A few months later, while working with a shaman, I briefly returned to the moment of assault. The flood of ecstasy filled me again, only this time it came with the recognition of the Divine Mother's presence. As I was being forcibly penetrated by my perpetrator, the Divine Mother was also penetrating me far deeper, permeating me thoroughly with all the resources I would need to transform this traumatic experience. I am still in awe at the dance of creation and destruction magnified in that moment. I think of it as my initiation by fire and blood into the path of being a warrior mother.

One of the core teachings of Aikido is the dynamic called "irimi," which means "entering." It is the capacity to diffuse an attack by connecting with and entering into the center of the attack with spacious nonresistance and nonattachment to outcome. With irimi, I have found my best approach to healthy mothering: learning to connect intimately while giving space and staying clear in my own center.

While we practice with simulated attacks in the martial arts, those attacks can serve as a metaphor for any conflict, any relationship or any aspect of ourselves that has "grabbed" our attention. As a spiritual path of embodiment, Aikido offers a way to bring together the courage and aspiration of the warrior with the devotion and naturalness of the mother. The synergy of these two currents creates something greater and fresher than either could alone: *the way of peace*. Aikido has given me a process, a community and a discourse to explore the soulful question I formed at age seven, looking in the mirror and wondering about the middle way between my warrior father and my feminine mother. With Aikido, I have learned that I don't need to reject their influences, but instead bring their aspects together fruitfully.

I have found inspiration in the twofold gift of being alive and of death's inevitability. The miracle of my son's birth, and waking up each morning to find him alive in my life, inspire me. When Rory was 11 months old and I was diagnosed with cancer, his existence gave me the power to face my mortality and move forward positively with my life. In my work, I have seen many women who were uncomfortable living in their "nurturer" role, taking a stand or fighting for themselves; however, as mothers, they did whatever was necessary to care for their children.

I relate to mother as the full emptiness out of which all creation emerges and into which all creation returns. Spiritually, mother is love … the essence that connects everything. For me, the warrior mother archetype wields the interrelated powers of creation and destruction, birth and death. She is the dynamic relationship between the creator (mother) and the creation (warrior); the ever-changing balancing dance and interplay of these coupling forces. The balanced and full collaboration of the right and left hemispheres of the brain could be seen as a somatic expression of the warrior mother potentiality for human beings.

As in many areas of life on the Earth at this time, the mother paradigm is going through a major destruction and recreation phase. We see the demise of the mother, who is unavailable to tend to her children; simultaneously, we witness a drastic increase in violence among children. Without the mother to encircle the child with love, the warrior aspect is out of control. We see the destruction of the Earth—the spoiling of our most fundamental nesting place.

Although our dominant culture has taught us to be greedy, insatiable consumers, mothers naturally center themselves in relationship with others. By respecting, protecting and developing relatedness with all beings, humans have a chance at a future for their children and perhaps for life itself on this planet. Women are increasingly taking a stand, speaking the truth and mobilizing action on behalf of the now: the Earth and the children of our future.

When threatened, humans generally react with the defenses of fight, flee or freeze. Recent studies show that women have the additional biological impulse to connect with others when threatened, under the influence of female hormones. All species—all life on our planet—are drastically threatened by the "territorial warrior" gone out of control. As women and as mothers, we are called upon and are uniquely equipped to fulfill our purpose to care for our young, collectively and co-creatively, for the sake of future generations.

In taking the initiative to create our future, we can reclaim the way of the peaceful warrior. We can learn to wield the life-giving "sword that cuts together" rather than the deadly sword that rends asunder. We can remember and embody the ancient teachings that hate is not overcome by hate, but by love alone. How do we sharpen this sword of love that cuts through the mire and restores our wholeness? Stop, feel and listen, within and without, and walk with heartfelt courage on the path of peace for all beings. This is the path of the warrior mother.

CONTACT
michelle@wellspringai.com

SUGGESTED LINKS

http://www.aikiweb.com (AikiWeb: The Source for Aikido Information)

http://www.asu.org (Aikido Schools of Ueshiba)

http://www.kidpower.org (Kidpower Teenpower Fullpower International)

Epilogue

For me, each woman's story has opened up a place of hope and a new sense of faith. Before I began this book, I questioned anyone's ability to affect the world ... a world that seems to be spinning more out of control every second. I now realize that there are all kinds people who are creating the real changes that desperately need to happen. The manifestation of the warrior mother archetype is unique in each of us. There are as many different ways to take a stand as there are people on this planet.

Each woman in this book was called into action by her desire to protect and heal. Inspired by a deep, inner calling and guided by a wellspring of passion, they stand up in the face of adversity. Often criticized, threatened and unrecognized, they continue to work in spite of their personal fear and lack of support. Their choice to act does not come from a rational, calculated strategy. They don't carefully measure whether or not they are going to take on a cause. Something happens, arising out of the moment, the day or the hour; without question, they begin.

Beginnings are always a mystery. When did we take our first step? When did we first fall in love? What is it that will make us rise and take a risk to do what we feel strongly needs to be done? What resides within our own heart that is calling out? What gives us the energy to take the first step towards being a warrior ... to take a necessary action that we cannot deny is the right thing to do?

So many of us are paralyzed by the world's problems: the horror and stupidity of the war machine; the loss of our precious environment; and the rampant, global, corporate capitalism consuming rather than honoring the value of human life. The corporate media spoonfeeds us and we grow numb to the pain and suffering featured in the daily news. Bombarded with one crisis after another, the magnitude is overwhelming!

We don't need to take it all on but, ultimately, we need to stay awake to the fact that all things are connected and whatever befalls this planet affects us all. Conscious thought, small actions, large actions—these all count towards redirecting our destructive course. There is no guarantee that we will be successful, but that is not the point. When we see an injustice threatening life, we embrace the willingness to join the warrior mother spirit and be part of creating a healthier world. This is the only way things are going to change: with us making it happen.

Each of us has the potential to inspire our fellow human beings and do something that matters. The stories of the women in this book show us that you do not have to be an extraordinary person to lead a movement or effect change. Each of us is an important strand in an endless weave ... the great neural net that spreads over the globe. We possess more technical tools and have access to more information than ever before. This gives us a global highway—a network—in which we can gather what we need to support our work and make our voices heard. The powers that can catalyze a major shift lie in each of us. This paradigm propels us towards a future which, above all else, holds life sacred. One thing we all know to be true: *the Earth is precious.*

As I watch my daughter, now three years old, chasing grasshoppers through the grass and climbing our large, tan bark oaks, I realize what a privilege life is. I chose to give her life and be her mother. I must protect and nurture her as well as protect and nurture the community in which she is growing up, the air she breathes, the food she eats and the water she drinks. Ultimately, I must make it known, in any way possible, that life is the most valuable thing there is and the Earth is our only home, supporting the only known life in the universe.

I hope the stories in this book give you a new sense of energy and act as guideposts—road maps for your own journey into action. I also hope that you gain a belief that anyone, including yourself, can take the first step—no matter how small—to make a change. The total effect of these incremental changes in thought, attitude, vision and action is much greater then the sum of the parts. It becomes a wave washing away the old and creating new possibilities.

Something dwells in each of us that calls out to protect that which is sacred—our families, our community or the world. Sometimes by going inside and other times by reaching out, it is a place to which we can unequivocally say "yes." Through that place, we can begin to take action. Trusting that place within is the force that keeps us moving forward with the tenacity to march through new territories, which are sometimes full of obstacles and other times full of open gateways saying, "This way."

No matter how large or small, each action taken by an individual or group is a testimony to the power of people to make a difference in the world. As famed anthropologist Margaret Mead said, "One should never underestimate that a small group of thoughtful people could change the world. Indeed, it's the only thing that ever has."

May we all come into our senses, travel the edge of possibilities and witness the path unfolding before us. May we find ourselves free from isolation and fear and arrive at a deeper source—the heart. May we honor the call of the warrior mother and rise to join her on the path towards making a difference.

Footnotes

DIANE WILSON *(story starts on page 23)*

1. U.S. Environmental Protection Agency, Toxic Release Inventory, *Victoria Advocate*, 1989.
2. Cullick, Robert, "Texas lures firm with spotty environmental history/Formosa Plastics' emissions drew strong protests in Taiwan," *Houston Chronicle* Austin bureau staff, September 10, 1989, Section A, p. 1, Edition 2 STAR.
3. Texas Marine Mammal Stranding Network (http://www.tmmsn.org).
4. Letter from Alcoa union representative to U.S. attorney general, detailing problems with mercury exposure, part of record at Lavaca Bay Superfund citizen advisory meeting.
5. The International Campaign for Justice in Bhopal (http://www.bhopal.net).
6. Union Carbide Seadrift plant wastewater permit; National Pollutant Discharge Elimination System permit, governed by the U.S. Environmental Protection Agency, issued by the state (must be renewed every four years).
7. Sorg, Lisa, "From Bhopal to Seadrift: Union Carbide's trail of tears, Hungry for Justice," *San Antonio Current,* August 22, 2002.

MARSHA GREEN *(story starts on page 29)*

1. Richardson, W.J., C.R. Greene, Jr., C.I. Malme and D.H. Thomson. *Marine Mammals and Noise.* New York: Academic Press, 1995.
2. Chaun, Raymond, M.D., "Testimony Before a Public Hearing of the Board of Land and Natural Resources on a Conservation District Use Permit Application KA-2734," Kauai, Hawaii, February 8, 1996.
3. "Dead humpbacks near ATOC source," November 15, 1995, from Hal Whitehead and Lindy Weilgart to recipients of Marine Mammals Research and Conservation (MARMAM) list (http://whale.wheelock.edu/archives/whalenet95/0242.html).
4. National Academy of Sciences–National Research Council. *Marine Mammals and Low-Frequency Sound: Progress Since 1994.* Washington, DC: National Academies Press Publications, 2000.
5. Paul Anderson, comments submitted to the final (June 11, 1999) meeting of the Acoustic Thermometry of Ocean Climate Advisory Board at Cornell University, MARMAM archive (http://www.escribe.com/science/marmam/m1719.html).
6. "Environmental Assessment for the Acoustic Thermometry of Ocean Climate (ATOC) Marine Mammal Research Program (MMRP) Acoustic Engineering Test (AET) Advanced Research Projects Agency," University of California San Diego/Scripps Institution of Oceanography.
7. SACLANTCEN Human Diver and Marine Mammal Environmental Policy and SACLANTCEN Human Diver and Marine Mammal Risk Mitigation Rules, Part II, NATO SACLANT Undersea Research Centre (http://enterprise.spawar.navy.mil/nepa/whales/diver.cfm).
8. North Pacific Acoustic Laboratory, "Taking Marine Mammals Incidental to Operations of a Low Frequency Sound Source," Scripps Institute of Oceanography's request to NMFS for permit for an

incidental take of marine mammals while deploying NPAL, *Federal Register,* Vol. 65, No. 165, August 24, 2000.

9. Letter from Joel Reynolds and Michael Jasny (Natural Resources Defense Council) to Chief Donna Wieting (National Marine Fisheries Service), "Comments on the Proposed Rule for Taking of Marine Mammals Incidental to Navy Operations of SURTASS LFA," May 31, 2001 (http://www.nrdc.org/wildlife/marine/cjrmj0501.asp).

10. Ibid.

11. Department of the Navy, Chief of Naval Operations, "Final Overseas Environmental Impact Statement and Environmental Impact Statement for Surveillance Towed Array Sensor System Low Frequency Active Sonar (SURTASS LFA) Sonar," January 2001.

12. Personal communication from Jay Murray.

13. Personal communication from Jay Murray; Stephanie Siegel, "Marine mammal facts just drops in the bucket," July 1, 1999 (http://www.cnn.com/NATURE/9907/01/sea.noise.part2/).

14. *Natural Resources Defense Council, et al. v. Evans,* Case No. C02-3805 EDL, June 30, 2003.

15. Department of the Navy, Chief of Naval Operations, "Final Overseas Environmental Impact Statement and Environmental Impact Statement for Surveillance Towed Array Sensor System Low Frequency Active Sonar (SURTASS LFA) Sonar," January 2001.

16. Turnpenny, A.W.H., K.P. Thatcher and J.R. Nedwell, "The effects on fish and other marine mammals of high-level underwater sound," report prepared for UK Defense Research Agency (FRRI 27/94), 1994.

17. "Phase I: Responses of Blue and Fin Whales to SURTASS LFA, Southern California Bight, 5 September–21 October, 1997," Quicklook: Low Frequency Sound Scientific Research Program, February 27, 1998, pp. 30-31; Tyack, P. and C. Clark, "Phase III: Playback of low frequency sound to gray whales migrating past the central California Coast, January 1998," Quicklook, June 23, 1998, pp. 22-25.

18. Miller, P.J.O., N. Biassoni, A. Samuels and P.L. Tyack, "Whale songs lengthen in response to sonar," *Nature* 405, 903, June 2000.

19. Department of the Navy, Chief of Naval Operations, "Final Overseas Environmental Impact Statement and Environmental Impact Statement for Surveillance Towed Array Sensor System Low Frequency Active Sonar (SURTASS LFA) Sonar," January 2001.

20. "Annual Report to Congress–1997," Marine Mammal Commission, January 31, 1998.

21. *Ocean Mammal Institute et al. v. William Cohn, Secretary of Defense, et al.,* 98-00160 (HG) U.S. District Court of Hawaii, 1998.

22. Cartwright, Rachel, "A comparative study of the behavioral dynamics of humpback whales (Megaptera novaengliae) mother and calf pairs during their residence in nursery waters," dissertation submitted to Manchester Metropolitan University, Manchester, UK, 2004.

23. Clark, C. and P. Tyack, "Phase III: Responses of Humpback Whales to SURTASS LFA off the Kona Coast, Big Island Hawaii," Quicklook: Low Frequency Sound Scientific Research Program, August 31, 1998.

24. "Motherless whale gets intensive care," *Honolulu Advertiser*, April 13, 1998.

25. Clark, C. and P. Tyack, "Phase III: Responses of Humpback Whales to SURTASS LFA off the Kona Coast, Big Island Hawaii," Quicklook: Low Frequency Sound Scientific Research Program, August 31, 1998.

26. Miller, P.J.O., N. Biassoni, A. Samuels and P.L. Tyack, "Whale songs lengthen in response to sonar," *Nature* 405, 903, June 2000.

27. Department of the Navy, Chief of Naval Operations, "Final Overseas Environmental Impact Statement and Environmental Impact Statement for Surveillance Towed Array Sensor System Low Frequency Active Sonar (SURTASS LFA) Sonar," January 2001.

28. Letter from C.H. Spikes, editor in chief, EIS Team, to Henry Zimon, president, Albright College, November 1999; letter from John F. Moyer, SURTASS LFA EIS Team to Henry Zimon, president, Albright College, April 2000.

MARSHA GREEN *(continued)*

29. Letter from Joel Reynolds and Michael Jasny (National Resources Defense Council) to Chief Donna Wieting (National Marine Fisheries Service), comments on the "Proposed Rule for Taking of Marine Mammals Incidental to the Navy's Operation of SURTASS LFA," May 31, 2001 (http://www.nrdc.org/wildlife/marine/cjrmj0501.asp).

30. Department of the Navy, Chief of Naval Operations, "Final Overseas Environmental Impact Statement and Environmental Impact Statement for Surveillance Towed Array Sensor System Low Frequency Active Sonar (SURTASS LFA) Sonar," January 2001.

31. Ibid.

32. Ibid.

33. General Accounting Office, "Report to the Acting Secretary of the Navy; Undersea Surveillance; Navy Continues to Build Ships Designed for Soviet Threat," GAO/NSIAS-93-53, 1992.

34. Frantzis, A., "Does acoustic testing strand whales?," *Nature* 392:29, 1998.

35. D'Amico, A., editor, "Summary Record and Report SACLANTCEN Bioacoustics Panel," North Atlantic Treaty Organization, *El Spezia,* Italy, June 15-17, 1998.

36. Balcomb, K.C. and D.E. Claridge, "Mass Whale Mortality: US Navy exercises cause strandings," *Bahamas Journal of Science* 8(2):2-12, 2001.

37. Anonymous, "Joint Interim Report: Bahamas Marine Mammal Stranding Event of 15-16 March 2000," Donald L. Evans, Secretary U.S. Department of Commerce; Gordon R. England, Secretary of the Navy, December 2001.

38. International Whaling Commission, "Report of the Scientific Committee (Annex K)," Sorrento, Italy, 2004.

39. Jepson, P. D., et al., "Gas-bubble lesions in stranded cetaceans: Was sonar responsible for a spate of whale deaths after an Atlantic military exercise?" *Nature* 425:575, October 9, 2003.

40. McClare, Robert, "Role of Navy sonar in porpoise deaths still unclear," *Seattle-Post Intelligencer,* February 10, 2004.

41. Personal communication of Dr. David Nellis, biologist with the U.S. Virgin Island Department of Fish and Game, to Eric Hawk of NMFS (Oct. 1999), cited in letter from Joel Reynolds, J.M. Cousteau, F. M. O'Regan and Dr. N. Rose to Hon. Gordon R. England, Secretary of the Navy, "Re: Request for Review of Naval Actions Involving Mid-Frequency Active Sonar," July 14, 2004 (http://www.nrdc.org/media/docs/040714.pdf).

42. Personal communication of Eric Hawk, biologist with NMFS, to Ken Hollingshead (Feb. 12, 2002); e-mail from Ken Hollingshead of NMFS to Joe Johnson and Clay Spikes (Apr. 11, 2002), cited in letter from Joel Reynolds, J.M. Cousteau, F. M. O'Regan and Dr. N. Rose to Hon. Gordon R. England, Secretary of the Navy, "Re: Request for Review of Naval Actions Involving Mid-Frequency Active Sonar," July 14, 2004 (http://www.nrdc.org/media/docs/040714.pdf).

43. Testimony of Dr. Darlene Ketten submitted to the U.S. District Court in *NRDC v. Evans,* 279 F. Supp. 2d 1129 (N.O. Cal. 2003).

44. Simmonds, M. and L.F. Lopez-Jurado, "Whales and the Military," *Nature* 387:448, 1991.

45. "Dead Whales Land in Canaries after Naval Exercises," *Reuters News Service* (Spain), July 27, 2004.

46. Kaufman, Marc, "Whale's Plight Revives Sonar Theory," *Washington Post,* July 11, 2004.

47. Brownell, Jr., R.L., et al., "Mass Strandings of Cuvier's Beaked Whales in Japan: U.S. Naval Acoustic Link," International Whaling Commission Doc. SC/56E37.

48. "Environmentalists, Navy strike deal on controversial sonar system," *The Seattle Times,* October 13, 2003.

49. Kauffman, Marc, "Activists gird for fight on Marine Act," *Washington Post,* March 2003.

50. Taylor, B., et al., "A call for research to assess risk of acoustic impact on beaked whales populations," report to International Whaling Commission Scientific Committee, Sorrento, Italy, 2004.

51. Nieukirk, S.L., et al., "Low-frequency whale and seismic airgun sounds recorded in the mid-Atlantic Ocean," *The Journal of the Acoustical Society of America,* Vol. 115, Issue 4, 1832-1843, 2004.

52. Engel, M.H., et al., "Are Seismic Surveys Responsible for Cetacean Strandings," paper presented to IWC Scientific Committee, Sorrento, Italy (SC/56E28).

53. MacKenzie, Debora, "Seismic surveys may kill giant squid," New Scientist.com news service, September 22, 2004.

54. Engås, A., S. Løkkeborg, E. Ona and A.V. Soldal, "Effects of seismic shooting on local abundance and catch rates of cod and haddock," *Canadian Journal of Fisheries and Aquatic Science,* 53:2238-2249, 1993.

55. Turnpenny, A.W.H., K.P. Thatcher and J.R. Nedwell, "The effects on fish and other marine mammals of high-level underwater sound," report prepared for UK Defense Research Agency (FRR1 27/94), 1994.

56. Dwyer, Owen, "Death Knell," *The Guardian,* October 30, 2002.

57. United Nations Convention on the Law of the Sea, December 10, 1982, entered into force November 16, 1994 (http://www.un.org/depts/los/convention_agreements/texts/unclos/closindx.htm).

58. Ibid.

FRANCES MOORE LAPPÉ *(story starts on page 41)*

1. Mittal, Anuradha, codirector of Food First/Institute for Food and Development Policy, Oakland, California (http://www.foodfirst.org), "Enough Food for the Whole World," *Washington Post,* September 15, 2000.

2. Vasilikiotis, Christos, Ph.D., "Can Organic Farming 'Feed the World'?," University of California, Berkeley, ESPM—Division of Insect Biology.

3. Barbusiaux, C., J.Y. Le Deaut, D. Sicart and J. Testart, "Ministère Français de l'agriculture et de la pêche," July 15, 2002.

4. "Talks to open on divisive issue of gene-altered foods," *Washington Post,* January 24, 2000. "The questions are so contentious that a gathering on the issue in Cartagena, Colombia, last year ended in disarray, with the United States and its allies arrayed against most of the world."

LEUREN MORET *(story starts on page 47)*

1. WAGE: We Advocate Gender Equity (http://www.wage.org).

2. WordIQ website; enter "depleted uranium" (http://www.wordiq.com/definition/Depleted_uranium = WordIQ); Department of Defense Deployment Health Clinical Center, "Environmental Exposures: Depleted Uranium (DU), Clinical Significance" (http://www.deploymenthealth.mil/508/deployments/gulfwar/enviro_uranium1.asp).

3. Gould, Jay M. and Benjamin A. Goldman, *Deadly Deceit: Low-Level Radiation, High-Level Cover-Up.* New York: Four Walls Eight Windows, 1990.

4. Brzezinski, Zbigniew, "The Grand Chessboard: American Primacy and Its Geostrategic Imperatives," 1997.

5. Memo to General L.R. Groves (http://www.mindfully.org/Nucs/Groves-Memo-Manhattan30oct43a.htm).

6. Ibid.

7. Ibid.

8. Ibid.

9. Ibid.

10. Moret, Leuren, "Depleted Uranium: The Trojan Horse of Nuclear War," *World Affairs: The Journal of International Relations,* August 2004.

11. "US CODE, TITLE 50 > CHAPTER 40 > Sec. 2302: The term 'weapon of mass destruction' means any weapon or device that is intended, or has the capability, to cause death or serious bodily injury to a significant number of people through the release, dissemination, or impact of (A) toxic or poisonous chemicals or their precursors; (B) a disease organism; or (C) radiation or radioactivity."

LEUREN MORET *(continued)*

12. "Testimony at the June 28, 2003, Public Hearing for the International War Crimes Tribunal on Afghanistan," Chiba, Japan, June 28, 2003 (http://www.mindfully.org/Nucs/2003/Moret-DU-Japan28jun03.htm).

13. Moret, Leuren, "UC Regents lose control of nuclear weapons program," *San Francisco Bay View*, September 15, 2004 (http://www.sfbayview.com/091504/ucregents091504.shtml).

14. "Memorandum to: Brigadier General L.R. Groves, From: Drs. Conant, Compton, and Urey" dated October 30, 1943, declassified June 5, 1974 (http://www.mindfully.org/Nucs/Groves-Memo-Manhattan30oct43a.htm); "Military Research Report Summaries 1974–1999" (http://www.gulflink. osd.mil/du_ii/du_ii_tabl1.htm#TAB%20L_Research%20Report%20Summaries).

15. Leuren Moret, "Depleted uranium: Dirty bombs, dirty missiles, dirty bullets: A death sentence here and abroad," *San Francisco Bay View*, August 18, 2004 (http://www.sfbayview.com/081804/Depleteduranium081804.shtml).

16. Civiak, Robert, M.D., "More Work for the Weapons Labs, Less Security for the Nation: An Analysis of the Bush Administration's Nuclear Weapons Policy," May 28, 2002 (http://www.trivalleycares. org/NPRfulltext.pdf).

17. Reported by Dr. Jawad Al-Ali and Dr. Genan Hassan at the World Uranium Weapons Conference in Hamburg, Germany, October 16–19, 2003 (http://www.uraniumweaponsconference.de/speakers. htm).

18. Flanders, Laura, "Gulf War Syndrome: Mal de Guerre," *The Nation*, March 7, 1994 (http://www. mindfully.org/Health/Mal-de-Guerre7mar94.htm); Christopher Bollyn, "Cancer Epidemic Caused by U.S. WMD: M.D. Says Depleted Uranium Definitively Linked," *American Free Press*, August 15, 2004 (http://www.americanfreepress.net/html/cancer_epidemic_.html).

19. Reported by Dr. Jawad Al-Ali and Dr. Genan Hassan at the World Uranium Weapons Conference in Hamburg, Germany, October 16–19, 2003 (http://www.uraniumweaponsconference.de/speakers. htm).

20. Ibid.

21. Personal e-mail communication, March 28, 2002.

22. Letter from Leuren Moret to Congressman McDermott, February 21, 2003 (http://www.mindfully. org/Nucs/2003/Leuren-Moret-Gen-Groves21feb03.htm).

23. Schroder, H., A. Heimers, R. Frentzel-Beyme, A. Schott and W. Hoffman, "Chromosome Aberration Analysis in Peripheral Lymphocytes of Gulf War and Balkans War Veterans," *Radiation Protection Dosimetry*, Vol. 103, No. 3, 2003, pp. 211-219.

24. Interview on KPFA radio with Major D. Rokke, Ph.D., Berkeley, CA, September 16, 2004.

25. "Testimony at the June 28, 2003, Public Hearing for the International War Crimes Tribunal on Afghanistan," Chiba, Japan, June 28, 2003 (http://www.mindfully.org/Nucs/2003/Moret-DU-Japan28jun03.htm).

26. "AC-130 Video from Afghanistan" (http://www.hk94.com/weblog/index.php?p=62&c=1).

27. "US CODE, TITLE 50 > CHAPTER 40 > Sec. 2302: The term 'weapon of mass destruction' means any weapon or device that is intended, or has the capability, to cause death or serious bodily injury to a significant number of people through the release, dissemination, or impact of (A) toxic or poisonous chemicals or their precursors; (B) a disease organism; or (C) radiation or radioactivity."

28. Moret, Leuren, "Depleted Uranium: The Trojan Horse of Nuclear War," *World Affairs—The Journal of International Issues*, July 1, 2004 (http://www.mindfully.org/Nucs/2004/DU-Trojan-Horse1jul04. htm).

29. Traprock Peace Center (http://www.traprockpeace.org/TribTest062803.html).

30. Curtin, J. Sean, "Spanish election sets off global shock wave," *Asia Times*, March 16, 2004 (http:// www.atimes.com/atimes/Front_Page/FC16Aa03.html).

31. Kuppuswamy, C.S., "Malaysia-Elections 2004: An analysis," March 24, 2004, South Asia Analysis Group (http://www.saag.org/papers10/paper961.html).

32. "Young, Liberal and in Command," *The Economist,* April 16, 2004 (http://www.economist.com/agenda/displayStory.cfm?story_id=2606595).

LADONNA REDMOND *(story starts on page 76)*

1. Frid, Martin, food and trade policy officer, "Unapproved and Unacceptable GMO," *Association of European Consumers Special Report,* June 2001 (http://www.consumeraec.com).
2. United States Securities and Exchange Commission, Washington, D.C., Form 10-K, Annual Report Pursuant to Section 13 or 15(D) of the Securities Exchange Act of 1934 for the Fiscal Year Ended September 29, 2002, Commission File Number: 0-19797, Whole Foods Market, Inc.

ELS COOPERRIDER *(story starts on page 82)*

1. Vogt, Donna U., specialist in social sciences, and Mickey Parish, congressional science fellow, "Food Biotechnology in the United States: Science, Regulation, and Issues," Congressional Research Service Report for Congress, Domestic Social Policy Division, June 2, 1999.
2. Vorman, Julie, "Washington: StarLink Recall Climb to 300 Different Items 300 taco, chip products recalled for bio-corn link—FDA," *Reuters,* November 1, 2000.
3. "Corporate might may hamper biotech crops," *Hembree Brandon Delta Farm Press,* July 18, 2003.
4. Fletcher, Victoria, consumer correspondent, "GM 'could be another Thalidomide,'" *Evening Standard,* October 7, 2003.
5. Smith, Jeffrey M. *Seeds of Deception: Exposing Industry and Government Lies About the Safety of the Genetically Engineered Foods You're Eating.* Fairfield, IA: Yes! Books, September 1, 2003.
6. Ibid.
7. Novotny, Eva, "Report for the Chardon LL Hearing: Non-suitability of genetically engineered feed for animals," *Scientists for Global Responsibility,* May 2002.
8. *Monsanto Canada Inc. v. Schmeiser Supreme Court of Canada.*
9. Lambrecht, Bill, "Monsanto helps battle Oregon voter initiative on food labeling," *St. Louis Post-Dispatch,* September 24, 2002.
10. Benbrook, Charles, M.D. *Evidence of the Magnitude and Consequences of the Roundup Ready Soybean Yield Drag from University-Based Varietal Trials.* Sandpoint, ID: Benbrook Consulting Services, 1998.
11. ____. *Impacts of Genetically Engineered Crops on Pesticide Use in the United States: The First Eight Years.* Sandpoint, ID: Northwest Science and Environmental Policy Center, November 25, 2003.
12. "County Ordinance Prohibiting Growing of Genetically Modified Organisms," voter information pamphlet for the Presidential Primary Election County of Mendocino, Mendocino County Elections, Ukiah, California, March 2, 2004. "Section 1. Finding. The people of Mendocino County wish to protect the county's agriculture, environment, economy, and private property from genetic pollution by genetically modified organisms. Section 2. Prohibition. It shall be unlawful for any person, firm, or corporation to propagate, cultivate, raise, or grow genetically modified organisms in Mendocino County."
13. Geniella, Mike, "Ruling lets language of Mendocino County ballot measure stand for March 2 election," *The Press Democrat,* December 31, 2003.
14. Weise, Elizabeth, "Use of biotech crops and animals heads for vote in California county," *USA Today,* February 26, 2004.
15. "Anti-biotech measure approved; Mendocino's Measure H backers overcome a huge fund-raising disadvantage," *Sacramento Bee,* March 3, 2004.
16. "County voters ban GMOs," *Ukiah Daily Journal,* March 3, 2004.
17. "Anti-biotech measure approved; Mendocino's Measure H backers overcome a huge fund-raising disadvantage," *Sacramento Bee,* March 3, 2004.

NINA SIMONS *(story starts on page 93)*

1. Ausubel, Kenny. *Hoxsey: How Healing Becomes a Crime.*
2. Ibid.
3. Ibid.

HELEN CALDICOTT *(story starts on page 102)*

1. Archer, J., S.S. Birring and F.C.W. Wu, "The association between testosterone and aggression among young men: empirical findings and a meta-analysis," *Aggressive Behavior*, 24, 411-420, 1998; Sapolsky, Robert. *The Trouble with Testosterone: And Other Essays on the Biology of the Human Predicament.* New York: Scribner, 1997.
2. "Our Common Future," *The Report of the World Commission on Environment and Development Report (Abstracts)*, A/Res/42/186 of 11 December 1987 (Abstract 1) A/Res/42/187 of 11 December 1987 (Abstract 2); U.S. Census Bureau, Income Surveys Branch, *Housing & Household Economic Statistics Report*, 2001.
3. Alembakis, Rachel, "France's New Rules Put More Women in Politics," *Post Gazette*, March 11, 2001; Mahmoud, Jasmine J., "The Glorious Revolution: France's Parity Law Ushers in the Era of Female Political Participation," *Harvard Political Review*, April 1, 2001.
4. American Association of Suicidology (http://www.suicidology.org); World Health Organization, *World Health Statistics Annual 1993 and 1994, 1994 and 1995*, Centers for Disease Control, National Center for Injury Prevention and Control; National Institute for Mental Health.
5. Mercola, Joseph, "Treatment of Depression More Than Triples in the US Over the Last 10 Years," *Journal of the American Medical Association*, January 9, 2002.
6. The Heritage Foundation (http://www.heritage.org).
7. "Missile Defense: Growing Concerns and Costs," *Physicians for Social Responsibility*, May 2002.
8. Caldicott, Helen. *The New Nuclear Danger: George W. Bush's Military-Industrial Complex.* New York: The New Press, 2002.
9. "Israel May have 2-300 Nuclear Weapons," *BBC News*, August 2000; Loof, Susan, "Israel Still Making Nuclear Weapons, Researchers Say," *Associated Press*, April 2004.
10. Caldicott, Helen. *The New Nuclear Danger: George W. Bush's Military-Industrial Complex.* New York: The New Press, 2002.
11. Ibid.
12. Ibid.
13. Ibid.
14. Ibid.
15. Ibid.

TERRI SWEARINGEN *(story starts on page 115)*

1. Dockery, Douglas W., C. Arden Pope, et al., "An Association between Air Pollution and Mortality in Six U.S. Cities," *The New England Journal of Medicine* (http://content.nejm.org/cgi/content/full/329/24/1753), Vol. 329:1753-1759, No. 24, December 9, 1993; Goldman, Benjamin. *The Truth About Where You Live.* New York: Random House, 1991; Common Dreams Progressive Newswire (http://www.commondreams.org/news2000/0223-03.htm), "New Study Reveals Surprising Data on Air Quality: Air Pollution in the Midwest is Worse Than in the Northeast," press release from Ohio Environmental Council, February 23, 2000; The Great Smokies.net (http://www.thegreatsmokies.net/id26.htm); Environmental Defense SCORECARD (http://www.scorecard.org/env-releases/hap/); "Clear The Air: National Campaign Against Dirty Power" (http://cta.policy.net/dirtypower/map.html).
2. Resource Conservation and Recovery Act, historical discussion/preamble and stated purpose of the federal hazardous waste law, *United States Code* at 42 USC, Chapter 82 and at § 270.40; transfer of permits [53 FR 37935, Sept. 28, 1988].

3. "Business Leaders To Stand Trial Over Iraq Arms Deliveries," *Agence France Presse*, July 14, 1995; "Swiss Go On Trial For Iraq Supergun Role," *United Press International*, January 15, 1996; "Three Found Guilty in Iraq 'Super gun' Trial," *Reuters*, February 1, 1996; "Swiss Fined For Role In Iraq Supergun," *United Press International*, February 1, 1996; "Ex-employees of Von Roll Guilty In Federal Court," *Saturday Review*, February 3, 1996.

4. "Detained Von Roll manager freed; René Lüthy, a top manager at the Swiss materials technology group, Von Roll, has been released from a German prison after one month in detention," *SwissInfo*, August 9, 2002; "Von Roll chief executive arrested; René Lüthy, chief executive at the Swiss materials technology group, Von Roll, is being held in a German prison for suspected involvement in a bribery scandal," *SwissInfo*, July 29, 2002; "Embattled Von Roll manager resigns; René Lüthy, a senior executive at the Von Roll Group, has stepped down just three weeks after being released from prison on bail," *SwissInfo*, September 3, 2002; "Ein hässlicher Verdacht: Hat Von Roll Schmiergelder an Deutschlands «Müllpaten» Hans Reimer gezahlt? Die Firma windet sich," *Sonntags Zeitung*; 2002-03-24; Seite 75. Wirtschaft (English translation © 2003 from the original German "Ein hässlicher Verdacht" by Kathy DiCenzo, edited by Karin Ascot: "An Ugly Suspicion: Did Von Roll pay bribes to Hans Reimer, Germany's 'garbage godfather'? The company squirms"); "Von Roll Used As 'Conduit' For Abb Bribes, Sonntagszeitung Says," Bloomberg L.P., *Bloomberg News*, April 14, 2002. John Miller in the Zurich newsroom (41-1) 224 4128 or jmiller16@bloomberg.net (editor); "Criminal proceedings against Von Roll Chief Executive Lüthy under suspicion of bribery," *SonntagsZeitung*; 2002-05-12, p. 7; "Thema: Nieu Beweise imMullskandal; Schweitz Connection in deutschen Mullskandal" (English translation: "Flashback: New Proofs in the Garbage Scandal; Switzerland Connection in the German Garbage Scandal"), *SonntagsZeitung*; 2003-05-11, p. 29; "Switzerland: CEO of Swiss firm Von Roll in German jail," *Reuters English News Service*, July 28, 2002; "Von Roll puts up bail for Lüthy, Swiss authorities to investigate bribery and laundering," *Neue Zürcher Zeitung AG*, 9 August 2002, 15:03, NZZ Online (*Neue Zürcher Zeitung AG*) (http://www.nzz.ch/2002/08/09/wi/page-newzzD4O1NM1F-12.html).

5. Flütsch, Von Andreas, "Ex-Von-Roll-Manager als Schmiergehilfe verurteilt: René Lüthy kassierte in Bonn ein Jahr Haft auf Bewährung," *SonntagsZeitung.ch*, March 9, 2003; "Schmiergeldaffären wegen Müllverbrennungsanlagen—Weiteres Rechtshilfeersuchen" (English translation from web: "Bribe affairs because of incineration plants—further letters rogatory"), *Neue Zürcher Zeitung AG*, 9 August 2003, Von Sda (Schmiergeldaffären-w) (http://www.nzz.ch); Flütsch, Von Andreas, "Ex-Von-Roll-Manager als Schmiergehilfe verurteilt; René Lüthy kassierte in Bonn ein Jahr Haft auf Bewährung" (English translation: "Ex-Von Roll Manager convicted as bribery accomplice; René Lüthy sentenced to one-year probation in Bonn"), *SonntagZeitung.ch*, March 9, 2003.

6. Needleman, Herb, M.D. and Philip Landrigan, M.D. *Raising Children Toxic Free: How to Keep Your Child Safe From Lead, Asbestos, Pesticides and other Environmental Hazards*. New York: Farrar Straus & Giroux, 1994.

7. U.S. Environmental Protection Agency Engineer Gary Victorine (312-886-1479). All official public notifications from Von Roll/WTI and/or the EPA regarding public hearings or informational meetings concerning permit changes carries the following notice: "A copy of the [permit, modification request, other documents, etc.] is available for review and photocopying at the Carnegie Public Library, 219 E. Fourth Street, East Liverpool, Ohio"; official e-mail communication from U.S. EPA Engineer Gary Victorine, August 5, 2004. "Regarding the issue of repository: Whenever VonRoll requests a permit modification, the regs require that they inform the public of where the request can be viewed, and VonRoll has historically been using the Carnegie Library."

8. Official Ohio EPA communication from Susan Willeke to Terri Swearingen, May 29, 1998, showing that the average amount of waste burned yearly at WTI is roughly 60,000 tons; official e-mail communication from U.S. EPA Engineer Gary Victorine, August 5, 2004.

9. Pursuant to 3734.05 (D) (6) (g) (i) Ohio Code, a development may only be approved if the active areas within a new hazardous waste facility are not located within 2,000 feet of any residence, school, hospital, jail or prison or within the flood plain.

TERRI SWEARINGEN *(continued)*

10. Von Roll Resource Conservation and Recovery Act permit, Attachment IX. CFR 261 is the definitive document that one needs in order to get the explanation of what chemicals are included in each of these codes.

11. U.S. Environmental Protection Agency, *Human Health Risk Assessment* on WTI, May 1997; U.S. EPA, Environmental Effects, Transport and Fate Committee, Science Advisory Board report on the incineration of liquid hazardous waste, April 1985; Costner, Pat and Joe Thornton, "Playing With Fire: Hazardous Waste Incineration," A Greenpeace Report, Second Edition, a compilation of the latest scientific findings on incineration, including those of the U.S. EPA (http://www.greenpeaceusa.org), 1990; Tangri, Neil, "Waste Incineration: A Dying Technology," Essential Action for Global Anti-Incinerator Alliance/Global Alliance for Incinerator Alternatives, a compilation of the most current scientific findings and studies on incineration, July 2003 (http://www.no-burn.org).

12. Brown, T.C., "Protesters Halt Permit Hearing for Incinerator," *The Plain Dealer,* September 26, 1991, front page.

13. Fitzmaurice, Evan, "The Nation's Pulse: The Clinton-Gore Incinerator," *The American Spectator,* June 1994, pp. 44-45.

14. Davis, L.J., "Where Are You Al? Our 'Earth In The Balance' Vice President Is Unable—Or Unwilling—To Stop Even As Dangerous A Project As The Ohio Incinerator," *Mother Jones,* November/December 1993.

15. U.S. EPA official communication document, January 22, 1993, "Note to: Carol Browner, Administrator, From: Richard Guimond, Acting Assistant Administrator, Office of Solid Waste and Emergency Response, Subject: WTI Incinerator Issues, Excerpt: [A] preliminary assessment done by ORD does show that risks from beef and milk consumption can be 1,000 times higher than risks from inhalation near the WTI facility."; U.S. EPA official communication document, February 8, 1993, "Memorandum, Subject: WTI Screening Level Analysis, From: William H. Farland, PhD, Director, Office of Health and Environmental Assessment, To: Brian Grant, Attorney, Office of General Counsel and Greer Goldman, Trial Attorney, Department of Justice."

16. U.S. EPA official communication document, January 22, 1993, "Note to: Carol Browner, Administrator, From: Richard Guimond, Acting Assistant Administrator, Office of Solid Waste and Emergency Response, Subject: WTI Incinerator Issues, Excerpt: [A] preliminary assessment done by ORD does show that risks from beef and milk consumption can be 1,000 times higher than risks from inhalation near the WTI facility."; Thornton, Joseph, Ph.D., "The EPA is suppressing findings of serious dioxin threat at WTI and other incinerators," March 1993; Thornton, Joseph, Ph.D., "Secret EPA Risk Assessment on WTI Released in Court; Severe Dioxin Risks Found From Contaminated Beef," March 1993.

17. Official communication from WTI Environmental Engineer Deb Rushin to U.S. EPA Region 5 Administrator Val Adamkus, April 26, 1993, providing preliminary information to the EPA regarding trial burn results; official Ohio EPA communication from Environmental Supervisor Paul Anderson to an East Liverpool, Ohio citizen, Alonzo Spencer, June 7, 1993, "Total air emissions for mercury were 9.2 lbs. on March 10, 1993 and 19.4 lbs. on March 11."; "WTI's Dioxin Emissions Found Excessive By EPA," *The Plain Dealer,* June 24, 1993; "WTI Flunks Part of Test; Incinerator Emitted Four Times More Mercury Than Allowed," *The Plain Dealer,* May 7, 1993; U.S. EPA press release, July 8, 1993, "EPA Grants WTI Temporary Authorization To Upgrade Dioxin Removal Equipment."

18. Federal Election Commission document, January 28, 1993.

19. Schneider, Keith, "Administration to Freeze Growth of Hazardous Waste Incinerators," *The New York Times,* May 18, 1993, front page; Noah, Timothy, "EPA Unveils Plans to Curb Incinerators of Hazardous Waste by Blocking Growth," *The Wall Street Journal,* May 19, 1993; Kanamine, Linda and Paul Hoversten, "EPA Cracks Down On Incinerators With Moratorium," *USA Today,* Stateline, May 19, 1993; Bureau of National Affairs, "Hazardous Waste: EPA Issues New Strategy, Freeze on

Hazardous Waste Incineration," May 19, 1993; Schneider, Keith, "National News: For Crusader Against Waste Incinerator, a Bittersweet Victory," *The New York Times*, May 19, 1993.

20. *Dave Hager, et al., Plaintiffs v. Waste Technologies Industries, et al., Defendants.* Case No. 97 CV 34, Judge Douglas Jenkins, March 20, 1997; Giambroni, Tom, "WTI Fires Back; Company files $34 million lawsuit against foes, lawyers," *Morning Journal* (Columbiana County, Ohio), March 21, 1997.

RHONDA ANDERSON *(story starts on page 132)*

1. Lee, Amy, "Recycling plant's test results in soon; State, feds probe Continental after illness complaints," *The Detroit News*, August 30, 2002.
2. Ibid.
3. U.S. Environmental Protection Agency, National Priorities List Fact Sheets for Indiana: "Continental Steel Corporation, EPA Region 5, Howard County, Kokomo, 4th Congressional District," EPA ID# IND001213503 (Last Update: January 2003) (http://www.epa.gov/superfund/sites).
4. U.S. Department of Labor, "Facts on Working Women," *20 Facts on Women Workers*, Women's Bureau No. 93-2, June 1993.
5. "Issues for Michigan's Children," State Surgeon General and Michigan Legislature addressing lead poisoning in children, December 1, 2003.
6. Lewis, Shawn D., "Fewer Mich. teens give birth, but more drop out; Kids Count report: Moms under 20 down a third since 1990," *The Detroit News*, November 21, 2002.
7. Marcus, Steven, M.D., executive director, "Toxicity, Lead," New Jersey Poison Information and Education System, professor, Preventive Medicine and Community Health, University of Medicine and Dentistry of New Jersey, June 4, 2001.

ANNA MARIE STENBERG *(story starts on page 141)*

1. North Coast Unified Air Quality Management District (http://www.ncuaqmd.org).
2. *Secretary of Labor, Complainant v. Georgia-Pacific Corporation, Respondent.* Local 3-469, International Woodworkers of America, Authorized Employee Representative. Oshrc Docket No. 89-2713 (http://www.oshrc.gov/decisions/html_1991/89-2713.html).
3. Ibid.
4. Ibid.
5. Ibid.
6. Superior Court of the State of California, Mendocino County Case #64726.
7. Bloom, Carol, Sunil K. Sharma and E. Ann Neel, Ph.D. *The Current Plight of the Kosovo Roma.* Sebastopol, CA: Voice of Roma, 2002.

ROBIN CARNEEN *(story starts on page 165)*

1. KI Movies (http://www.kumeyaay.info/movies); "The Healing Has Begun: An Operational Update from the Aboriginal Healing Foundation," May 2002 (http://www.ahf.ca/english-pdf/healing_has_begun.pdf); Witko, Tawa M., Psy.D., "Providing Culturally Competent Services to American Indians" (http://www.apa.org/divisions/div31/CoOpArticles/California/ProvidingCulturally CompetentServices.pdf).
2. "Westward Movement, American," contributed by Elliott West, B.A., M.A., Ph.D. (http://encarta. msn.com/text_761589809___12/Westward_Movement_American.html).
3. "Alaska Native/Native American Bibliography," compiled by Paul Ongtooguk (http://www.alaskool. org/native_ed/bibliography.htm).
4. Doak, Michael, "Native American Spirituality," Spring Term, 1997, University of Virginia (http:// religiousmovements.lib.virginia.edu/nrms/naspirit.html).
5. Students On Site, a Unit of the Arts of Citizenship Program, University of Michigan, "Native Americans: Early Contact" (http://www.artsofcitizenship.umich.edu/sos/topics/native/early.html).

ROBIN CARNEEN *(continued)*

6. "Bloody Island," story of Lucy "Ni'ka" Moore (http://www.geocities.com/bloodyisland2000); "Manifest Destiny" (http://www.jtharvey.com/arch/american.htm).

7. Kowinski, William S., "In 1860 six murderers nearly wiped out the Wiyot Indian tribe—in 2004 its members have found ways to heal," *San Francisco Chronicle*, February 28, 2004 (http://www.sfgate. com/cgi-bin/article.cgi?f=/c/a/2004/02/28/DDG5Q59D8J1.DTL); Wiyot Tribe (http://www.wiyot. com).

8. "Alcoholism & Native Americans: A Social Problem" (http://www.tc.unl.edu/mjwaite/mwaite-res. html); Mothers Against Drunk Driving (MADD), "Victim Services & Information" (http://www. madd.org/victims/0%2C1056%2C1795%2C00.html).

9. "Indian Service Runs Big Scale," Lewiston, ID, March 22 (year unknown) (http://content.wsulibs. wsu.edu/clipping/image/6529.jpg); "Native Americans: Tribal Sovereignty, Devolution and Welfare Reform," Devolution Initiative, W.K. Kellogg Foundation technical paper (http://www.wkkf.org/ Pubs/Devolution/Pub823.pdf).

10. U.S. Census Bureau, "American Indian Reservations" map (http://www.census.gov/dmd/www/pdf/ 512indre.pdf).

11. Dakota-Lakota-Nakota Human Rights Advocacy Coalition (http://www.dlncoalition.org/dln_ nation/treaties.htm#treaties).

12. Forman, Eric, "Review of Current Literature: Economic Development On American Indian Reservations," March 31, 1998 (http://www.planning.unc.edu/courses/261/forman/litrev.htm); Smith, Darrel, "Indian Reservations: America's Model of Destruction, A Brief Exposé of America's Devastating Indian Policies," June 1997 (http://www.citizensalliance.org/links/pages/articles/ Expose_Part_1.html).

13. Stereotype Discussion Board (http://stereotype.drumhop.com/web.html); Legal Information Institute, U.S. Code Collection (http://www4.law.cornell.edu/uscode/42/1996.html).

14. Swinomish Indian Tribal Community (http://www.swinomish.org).

15. "The Miwok Indians of Yosemite," prepared by Students of Woodland School (http://mariposa. yosemite.net/woodland/miwok.htm).

16. "Non-Federally Recognized Indian Tribes," Governor's Office of Indian Affairs, Olympia, Washington (http://www.goia.wa.gov/directory/pdf/05TRIBES_UNR.pdf).

17. "Native American Culture" (http://www.ewebtribe.com/NACulture/articles/whosindian.htm).

18. Christian Alliance–Indian Child Welfare (http://www.christian-alliance-for-indian-child-welfare. org/6928.html); *Wabanaki Legal News,* a newsletter of Pine Tree Legal Assistance, Fall 1996 (http:// www.ptla.org/wabanaki/icwa.htm).

19. U.S. Department of Health and Human Services Office on Women's Health, The National Women's Health Information Center (http://www.4woman.gov/minority/naalcohol.cfm), "Health Problems in American Indian/Alaska Native Women: Alcoholism"; U.S. Department of Health and Human Services, National Alcohol & Drug Addiction, Family & Community Resources Recovery Month 2003 (http://www.recoverymonth.gov/2003/familyresources.aspx); Wyatt, Jean, "The Roots of North American Medicine," *Indian Life Magazine,* Vol. 15, No. 3, 1994 (http://www.yvwiiusdinvnohii.net/ articles/medroots.html); Blinkhorn, Lois, "Native American Healers: Health, *The Milwaukee Journal,* October 24, 1994 (http://www.luminet.net/~wenonah/new/harmony.htm).

20. Native American Prisoner Network (http://members.tripod.com/~foltz.k/napnhome.html).

21. Point Arena CITYART opening announcement (http://www.cityart.ws/PrevIncarcerNation.htm).

22. KZYX&Z Listener Supported Community Radio for Mendocino County & Beyond (http://www. kzyx.org).

23. "Native Americans," Carol Hurst's children's literature site (http://www.carolhurst.com/subjects/ nativeamericans.html).

24. Oyate (http://www.oyate.org).

25. Double Buffalo Ranch (http://www.doubleebuffaloranch.com).

26. North Dakota Buffalo Association (http://www.ndbuffalo.org).

27. *Native American Times* (http://www.nativetimes.com/index.asp?action=frontpage&txt_Section=NE WS&frontpagecategory=12&categoryname=Civil+Rights).

28. "Message from the Estate of T'sunka Witko: One Brewing Company settles lawsuit with the family of Crazy Horse and Rosebud Sioux Tribe" (http://www.ableza.org/CHorse.html).

29. Stereotype Discussion Board (http://stereotype.drumhop.com/web.html).

30. Satchell, Michael, "Trashing the Reservations," *U.S. News & World Report,* January 11, 1993 (http://www.keepmedia.com/pubs/USNewsWorldReport/1993/01/11/34439?extID=10032&oliID=213).

31. U.S. Department of Energy, Office of Civilian Radioactive Waste Management, Yucca Mountain Project, YMP/DOE-0602, North Las Vegas, NV, December 2002.

32. Cankú Lúta (Red Road, Inc.) (http://www.canku-luta.org/oldnews/exploitation.html).

33. "Lakota: The Circle," CyberSoup's The Wild West (http://www.thewildwest.org/native_american/religion/Circle.html).

LOURDES PORTILLO *(story starts on page 183)*

1. The University of Michigan (http://www-personal.umich.edu/~kenlo/econdev/links.html).

2. "Mexico: Increased international scrutiny for violence against women in Ciudad Juárez and Chihuahua," *Amnesty International* press release, AI Index: AMR 41/045/2003, News Service No. 239, October 17, 2003.

Author's Biography

THAÏS MAZUR, M.S., is a mother, artist, activist, mountaineer and avid sailor. She has traveled around the world, adventuring and working as a radio, newspaper and investigative journalist. Thaïs became renowned for her in-depth reporting, including a four-part story on aborigines and uranium mining, which she produced while living in Australia, and her ground-breaking broadcast of the Three Mile Island nuclear accident in Middletown, Pennsylvania, on March 28, 1979. She has been granted numerous awards for her work as a choreographer and is the artistic director of the acclaimed Women In Black dance project. Thaïs lives on the northern coast of California, surrounded by a century-old botanical garden.

Photography Credits

COVER
Woman and child: Photograph by Joan Emm
Hands: Photograph by Thaïs Mazur

WOMEN
Diane Wilson: Photograph by David Wilson
Marsha Green: No photo credit
Frances Moore Lappé: Photograph by Sarah Putnam
Leuren Moret: Photograph by Robin Reynolds
Sarah James: Photograph by Pamela A. Miller
Sarita Chawla: Photograph by Ken Murphy
Jodie Evans: Photograph by Guy Webster
Ladonna Redmond: Photograph by Food and Society Fellowship
Els Cooperrider: Photograph by Evan Johnson
Susan Alexjander: Photograph by Paul Straub
Nina Simons: Photograph by Scott Hess
Helen Caldicott: Photograph by Amazing Grace
Pam Province: Photograph by Whitey
Terri Swearingen: No photo credit
Satsuki Ina: Photograph by Roy Wilcox
Rhonda Anderson: No photo credit
Anna Marie Stenberg: Photograph by Elizabeth A. Crahan
Patti Boucher: Photograph by April Jorden-Faulkner
Sherry Glaser: Photograph by Linda Sue Scott
Robin Carneen: Photograph by Ramon Morillo
Terry Greenblatt: Photographer unknown
Krissy Keefer: Photograph by Coleen Gragen
Lourdes Portillo: Photograph by Lori Eanes
Michelle Manger Keip: Photograph by Rory Keip
Thaïs Mazur: Photograph by David Russell

Notes

Notes

Notes

Notes

Notes

Notes

Notes

Notes

Notes

Notes

Notes

Notes